I0123821

Soeharto's New Order and its Legacy

Essays in honour of Harold Crouch

Edited by Edward Aspinall and Greg Fealy

Soeharto's New Order and its Legacy

Essays in honour of Harold Crouch

Edited by Edward Aspinall and Greg Fealy

ASIAN STUDIES SERIES MONOGRAPH 2

ANU
THE AUSTRALIAN NATIONAL UNIVERSITY

E PRESS

ANU

E PRESS

Published by ANU E Press
The Australian National University
Canberra ACT 0200, Australia
Email: anuepress@anu.edu.au
This title is also available online at: http://epress.anu.edu.au/soeharto_citation.html

National Library of Australia
Cataloguing-in-Publication entry

Title:	Soeharto's new order and its legacy : essays in honour of Harold Crouch / edited by Edward Aspinall and Greg Fealy.
ISBN:	9781921666469 (pbk.) 9781921666476 (pdf)
Notes:	Includes bibliographical references.
	Subjects: Soeharto, 1921-2008
	Festschriften--Australia.
	Indonesia--Politics and government--1966-1998.
	Indonesia--Economic conditions--1945-1966.

Other Authors/Contributors:
Aspinall, Edward.
Fealy, Greg, 1957-
Crouch, Harold, 1940-

Dewey Number: 959.8037

All rights reserved. No part of this publication may be reproduced, stored in a retrieval system or transmitted in any form or by any means, electronic, mechanical, photocopying or otherwise, without the prior permission of the publisher.

Cover design and layout by ANU E Press

Cover image: Photo taken by Edward Aspinall at the Indonesian Democratic Party of Struggle (PDI-P) Congress, Bali, April 2010.

Printed by Griffin Press

This edition © 2010 ANU E Press

Contents

The New Order and its Antecedents

The Legacy

Acknowledgments

Many people contributed to this book and to the conference in honour of Harold Crouch that preceded it. In expressing our thanks to all those who helped to make both book and conference a success, we are thus also acknowledging the esteem and affection with which Harold Crouch is regarded by a wide circle of Indonesia specialists.

In organising the conference, which was held at The Australian National University in November 2005, we received invaluable assistance from the University's Department of Political and Social Change and particularly its head, Professor Ben Kerkvliet, as well as the Research School of Pacific and Asian Studies. Beverley Fraser at the Department of Political and Social Change, as well as many other individuals, helped to organise the conference. We especially thank those colleagues and friends of Harold Crouch who presented papers at the conference, many of whom travelled long distances at their own expense to attend, and most of whom subsequently revised their papers for inclusion in this book. We thank them for their responsiveness and patience during a lengthy editorial and publication process. Several individuals who presented papers at the conference, notably, Andrew MacIntyre, David Bourchier, Simon Philpott and Richard Robison, were not able to contribute book chapters, but we appreciate their participation.

Our greatest thanks are reserved for Allison Ley, a member of staff of the Department of Political and Social Change, and herself a long-time colleague of Harold Crouch. She has done an outstanding job copy-editing the book and coordinating its preparation. We have relied heavily on Allison during the publication process and her good judgement, sense of humour and patience have made working with her a pleasure. Most importantly, without her professionalism and persistence we would not have been able to produce this book and we are very grateful to her for all her hard work.

Finally, we would like to express our sincere appreciation to Craig Reynolds and editorial staff at the ANU E-Press for their invaluable support and assistance, and also to the two anonymous reviewers for their very helpful comments on the draft manuscript.

Edward Aspinall and Greg Fealy

Preface: Honouring Harold Crouch

JAMIE MACKIE, EDWARD ASPINALL AND GREG FEALY

It is fitting that a book on the New Order regime and its legacy be dedicated to Harold Crouch. Professor Crouch has been one of the pre-eminent scholars of Indonesian politics during the New Order period, and he wrote the definitive book on that regime's rise to power. His work did a great deal—perhaps more than that of any other scholar—to allow generations of students and scholars of Indonesian politics to understand the origins of the New Order, and the structures and patterns of political behaviour which sustained it. In the post-Soeharto period, Crouch has continued to be a leading analyst of Indonesian politics, and has recently published a masterful book on the successes and failures of political reform.

Born in Melbourne in 1940, Crouch took an undergraduate degree in political science at the University of Melbourne beginning in 1958 when it was headed by Professor MacMahon Ball, the foremost pioneer of Australia's relations with the newly independent countries of Asia. In the early 1960s, he went to India to study at the University of Bombay for a Masters degree on Indian trade unions, at a time when few if any other Australians had gone to an Asian university for a higher degree. (This research was subsequently published in 1966.) Crouch then switched his geographical focus to Indonesia, enrolling for his PhD under Australia's then pre-eminent scholar of Indonesian politics, Herbert Feith at Monash University. In 1968, he took a teaching job in the political science department at the University of Indonesia (which Feith had previously held for a year), and he taught there from 1968 to 1971. During this period he began amassing the vast amount of material on the Indonesian army, and on Indonesian politics more generally, which would later form the basis of his PhD dissertation. His dissertation was completed in 1975 and a revised version was published by Cornell University in 1978 as *The Army and Politics in Indonesia*. At around the same time he also wrote a highly influential article on patrimonialism published in 1979 in *World Politics*. These works became milestones in the study of the New Order, and were widely admired as much for the evident care and judiciousness which had gone into crafting them, as for the insights they afforded into the foundation, inner workings and bases of the New Order regime.

Over subsequent years, although Crouch never abandoned his interest in and writing on Indonesia, he also broadened his focus to incorporate other countries of Southeast Asia. Following his marriage to the Malaysian historian, Khasnor Johan in 1973, in 1976 he took up a position as Senior Lecturer at the National University of Malaysia, a position which he held, with some side-trips, until 1991, when he took up a Senior Research Fellowship at the Australian National University in Canberra. In the intervening years he wrote *Domestic Political Structures and Regional Economic Cooperation in Southeast Asia* (1984) which though brief still stands out as one of the most successful attempts to write comparatively about the politics of the region. His period in Malaysia also formed the basis of his highly regarded overview of Malaysian politics, *Government and Society in Malaysia* (1996). During the 1990s his interest in Indonesian politics was reignited by the gathering political storms of the late Soeharto period (see for example Crouch 1992 and 1994). After Soeharto resigned, Crouch became the founding director of the International Crisis Group office in Jakarta in 2000–2001, when he started its fine tradition of producing first-class papers on important, topical subjects (see ICG 2000 for an example of such writing). It was in this period that he began to develop a line of inquiry and accumulate material for his recently published book, *Political Reform in Indonesia after Soeharto* (2010).

The preceding sketch illustrates that Harold Crouch's career has included long periods living and working in the countries he writes about. His deep immersion in the societies of the region has contributed to two trademark features of his own scholarship: first, his painstaking care for factual accuracy, based on the accumulation and careful checking of great amounts of material drawn from written sources, interviews and fieldwork, and, secondly, the great circumspection, even-handedness and fairness with which he presents this material. His deep knowledge of historical context, his often personal intimacy with the political actors who form the main subjects of his work, and his first-hand knowledge of the ideas, interests and calculations which govern their behaviour—as well as an abiding sense of fairness—all provide his work with a rare understanding of and sensitivity to the motivations of Indonesian and other political actors. It also has imparted an aversion to the quick and easy moral judgments which so often mars scholarship on Indonesia. In his address to the conference at which most of the chapters in this book were first presented, Jamie Mackie ascribed Crouch's reputation to these very characteristics, noting that 'the key to Harold's eminence has been his mixture of scrupulous honesty and accuracy, balance, fairness and real knowledge of Indonesia and of whatever he is talking about to do with it.'

Harold Crouch's combination of scholarly commitment and personal integrity have made him a role model and guide for a large number of scholars of Indonesian (and Southeast Asian) politics, not least the large number of higher degree research students he supervised. This group included many Australians and Indonesians, but also Americans, Japanese, Malaysians, Germans and others. Among the students of Indonesian politics he supervised whose dissertations have been published in recent years are Donald Porter (2002); Jun Honna (2003); Edward Aspinall (2005); Marcus Mietzner (2008a); and Chris Wilson (2008). In speeches at the conference which began the work of this book, several of his former students praised his generosity of spirit, relaxed character, tolerance for divergent opinions and scholarly rigour, and the care he had shown toward them. One of these former students, noted that what he had valued most from Crouch was not only his intellectual input, as considerable as that was, but that he 'taught me how to live', by inculcating in him values of intellectual curiosity, modesty and honesty, rather than ambition for approval or advancement. It was a striking testimony to a man who has long been widely respected as a scholar, a searcher after the truth and also far more than that. It is this spirit that this book is dedicated in his honour, as a modest tribute to Harold Crouch and his influence in the field of Indonesian political studies.

Glossary

abangan	Nominal or less strict Muslims, usually in reference to Javanese Muslims
adat	customary or traditional law
aliran	a socio-cultural stream
AMS	Angkatan Muda Siliwangi (Siliwangi Young Generation, West Javanese 'Youth' Association)
APINDO	Asosiasi Pengusaha Indonesia (Indonesian Association of Businesspeople, employer association responsible for labour affairs)
asas tunggal	'sole foundation' doctrine whereby parties and other organisations were required to adopt Pancasila as their single ideology
bahaya ex-tapol	danger of ex-political prisoners
BAKIN	Badan Koordinasi Intelijen Negara (Indonesian Intelligence Agency)
Banser	NU militia organisation
Bappenas	Badan Perencanaan Pembangunan Nasional (National Development Planning Body)
BIGS	Bandung Institute of Governance Studies
BMI	Banteng Muda Indonesia (Indonesia Young Bulls, PDI-P affiliated militia)
bupati	regent, district government head
CPM	Corps Polisi Militer (Military Police Corps)
cukong	Chinese entrepreneur
dakwah	Islamic religious outreach, proselytisation
Darul Islam	Abode of Islam
DDII	Dewan Dakwah Islamiyah Indonesia (The Indonesian Islamic Propagation Council)
DPR	Dewan Perwakilan Rakyat (People's Representative Council), Indonesia's parliament
DPRD	Dewan Perwakilan Rakyat Daerah (Regional People's Representative Council), provincial and district parliament
dukun	traditional healer, shaman

FKPPI	Forum Komunikasi Putra-Putri Purnawirawan ABRI (Communications Forum for Sons and Daughters of Military Retirees)
FDI	Foreign Direct Investment
GAM	Gerakan Aceh Merdeka (Free Aceh Movement)
GDP	Gross Domestic Product
GPI	Gerakan Pemuda Indonesia (Indonesian Youth Movement)
GIBASS	Gabungan Inisiatif Barisan Anak Sunda Siliwangi (The Combined Initiative of the Ranks of the Siliwangi Sundanese Youth)
golongan karya	functional group
Golkar	Golongan Karya (state political party under the New Order, and one of the major post-New Order parties)
gotong-royong	mutual help
Guided Democracy	semi-authoritarian regime led by President Sukarno, 1959–66; the ideology of that period
haluan negara	national will
ICMI	Ikatan Cendekiawan Muslimin se-Indonesia (All-Indonesia Association of Indonesian Muslim Intellectuals)
IMF	International Monetary Fund
IFI	International Financial Organisation
IKABRA	Ikatan Anak Buah Madura (Association of the Madurese Community)
IKMI	Ikatan Keluarga Madura Indonesia (Indonesian Association of the Madurese Family)
jihad	holy war
Jemaah Islamiah	Islamic community; covert jihadist Islamic organisation
kabupaten	regency, district
kebatinan	mysticism
KADIN	Kamar Dagang dan Industri (Indonesia Chamber of Commerce and Industry)
kepala dinas	heads of government offices at provincial or district level
kiai	Islamic teachers
kiai khos	charismatic Islamic leaders
Kodam	Komando Daerah Militer (Regional Army Command)

Komar	Komunitas Marhaenisme (PDI-P Paramilitary Wing)
Koramil	Komando Rayon Militer (Subdistrict Military Command)
Korem	Komando Resort Militer (Resort Military Command)
KNPI	Komite Nasional Pemuda Indonesia (National Indonesian Youth Committee)
KPK	Komisi Pemberantasan Korupsi (Corruption Eradication Commission)
KPU	Komisi Pemilihan Umum (National Elections Commission)
KPUD	Komisi Pemilihan Umum Daerah (Local Electoral Commission)
KSPI	Konfederasi Serikat Buruh Indonesia (Confederation of the Indonesian Workers Union)
Masyumi	Majelis Syuro Muslimin Indonesia (Large Muslim party, banned by Sukarno in 1960)
MNEs	Multinational Enterprises
MPR	Majelis Permusyawaratan Rakyat (People's Consultative Assembly, Indonesia's supreme decision-making body)
mufakat	consensus
Muhammadiyah	modernist Muslim organisation
Muspida	Musyawarah Pimpinan Daerah (Regional Leadership Assembly)
Muspida ++	Musyawarah Pimpinan Daerah (Regional Leadership Assembly, expanded version)
musyawarah	consultation
Nasakom	Nationalism, Religion and Communism
NU	Nahdlatul Ulama (traditionalist Islamic organisation, the largest Muslim organisation in Indonesia)
NIE	Newly Industrialising Economy
OPEC	Organisation of Petroleum Exporting Countries
ormas	societal organisations
P4	Pedoman Penghayatan dan Pengamalan Pancasila (Directive for the Realisation and Implementation of Pancasila)
Pancasila	The five guiding principles of the Indonesian state: belief in one supreme God; just and civilised humanity; national unity; democracy led by wisdom and prudence through consultation and representation; social justice
PAD	Pendapatan Alokasi Daerah (locally acquired revenue)

PAN	Partai Amanat Nasional (National Mandate Party)
Pangestu	Central Java-based spiritual association
pansus	special parliamentary committee
Parmusi	Partai Muslimin Indonesia (Party of Indonesian Muslims, the 'successor' party to Masyumi)
pasukan	corps
persatuan	unity
PBB	Partai Bulan Bintang (Crescent and Star Party, an Islamist party)
PD	Partai Demokrat (Democratic party)
PDI	Partai Demokrasi Indonesia (Indonesian Democratic Party)
PDI-P	Partai Demokrasi Indonesia—Perjuangan (Indonesia Democratic Party of Struggle, party led by Megawati Sukarnoputri)
PDS	Partai Damai Sejahtera (Party of Peace and Prosperity, a Christian Party)
PDU	Perserikatan Daulatul Ummah (Muslim Sovereignty Alliance)
pengajian	religious study sessions
PII	Pemuda Islam Indonesia (Indonesian Islamic Youth)
PK	Partai Keadilan (Justice Party, an Islamist party)
PKI	Partai Komunis Indonesia (Indonesian Communist Party)
pesantren	Islamic boarding school
PKB	Partai Kebangkitan Bangsa (National Awakening Party)
PKS	Partai Keadilan Sejahtera (Prosperous and Justice Party, formerly PK)
PNI	Partai Nasional Indonesia (Indonesian National Party)
poros tengah	central axis
PP	Pemuda Pancasila (Pancasila Youth, a New Order youth organisation frequently involved in criminal activity)
PSII	Partai Serikat Islam Indonesia (United Islam Indonesia Party)
priyayi	Javanese traditional elite
PPP	Partai Persatuan Pembangunan (United Development Party, an Islamic party)
preman	local hoodlums, extortionists, gangsters
RVA	real value added

raja lokal	local king
Ramadan	the Muslim fasting month
reformasi	reform
reformasi total	total reform
samadi	meditation
SAKERNAS	Survei Tenaga Kerja Nasional (National Labour Force Survey)
sekretaris daerah	regional executive secretary
SMERU	Social Monitoring and Early Response Unit (Independent Institute for Research and Policy Studies)
syariah	Islamic law
SIUPP	Surat Izin Usaha Penerbitan Pers (press publication licence)
SPSI	Serikat Pekerja Seluruh Indonesia (government-backed workers' union)
SOE	state-owned Enterprise
SBSI	Serikat Buruh Sejahtera Indonesia (the Indonesia Prosperity Labour Union)
TCF	textiles, clothing and footwear industries
TNI	Tentara Nasional Indonesia (the Indonesian Military)
ulama	Islamic scholar(s)
umroh	minor pilgrimage
usroh	Islamic cadre recruitment program

Contributors

Dewi Fortuna Anwar is a leading academic, researcher and political analyst. During the administration of President Habibie of Indonesia, she served as assistant to the Vice President for Global Affairs and Assistant Minister/State Secretary for Foreign Affairs.

Edward Aspinall is head of the Department of Political and Social Change, School of International, Political and Strategic Studies, College of Asia and the Pacific, The Australian National University.

William Case is a professor in the Department of Asian and International Studies, University of Hong Kong.

Robert Cribb is a professor in the School of Culture, History and Language, College of Asia and the Pacific, The Australian National University.

Greg Fealy is a fellow and senior lecturer in the Department of Political and Social Change, School of International, Political and Strategic Studies and the Faculty of Asian Studies, College of Asia and the Pacific, The Australian National University.

Hal Hill is the H.W. Arndt Professor of Southeast Asian Economies in the Crawford School of Economics and Governance, College of Asia and the Pacific, The Australian National University.

Jun Honna teaches at the Faculty of International Relations, Ritsumeikan University, Kyoto, Japan. He is the author of *Military Politics and Democratization in Indonesia* (2003).

David Jenkins is a former foreign editor of the Sydney Morning Herald.

Sidney Jones is a senior advisor, Asia Program at the International Crisis Group, Jakarta.

Jamie Mackie is emeritus professor and visiting fellow in the Indonesia Project, Crawford School of Economics and Governance, College of Asia and the Pacific, The Australian National University.

Chris Manning is associate professor in The Arndt-Corden Division of Economics, Crawford School of Economics and Governance, College of Asia and the Pacific, The Australian National University.

Marcus Mietzner is a lecturer in Indonesian Studies, School of Culture, History and Language, College of Asia and the Pacific, The Australian National University.

Dionisius Narjoko is a senior researcher, Centre for Strategic and International Studies, Jakarta.

Ken Ward is a former senior Indonesia analyst with the Office of National Assessments.

Introduction: Soeharto's New Order and its Legacy

EDWARD ASPINALL AND GREG FEALY

On 21 May 1998, one of the most effective and enduring of the world's Cold War military-based authoritarian regimes came to an end. On that morning, Indonesia's President Soeharto read a simple statement announcing his resignation and handing over power to his deputy, B. J. Habibie. He did so against a dramatic backdrop: the Asian financial crisis had brought catastrophe, student protesters occupied the national parliament, the smoke was still rising from parts of Jakarta's skyline after days of rioting a week earlier, the previous evening fourteen of his cabinet ministers had told Soeharto they were no longer willing to serve under him, and the chief of the Armed Forces had declared that his troops were in danger of losing control of the streets.

Political tensions had been mounting in Indonesia for more than a decade, prompting many attempts to prognosticate on what would come next (see especially Bourchier and Legge 1994). However, few people had predicted that Soeharto's regime would collapse in such a dramatic way. Even on the eve of Soeharto's resignation, many seasoned observers of Indonesian politics believed that the president would, at least, be able to engineer a political succession to his liking or that the most likely heir to his power would be the military, which conventional wisdom held to be the single-most powerful institution in Indonesia. Few expected full-blown democratisation. The pessimism regarding Indonesia's democratic potential was due not simply to the mesmerising effect of the longevity of Soeharto's regime, but also to its many apparent successes in remaking Indonesia's social, political and economic structures, to say nothing of its leader's reputation as a master politician.

In fact, no less surprising than the manner of Soeharto's resignation was what came next. Habibie took over the presidency amid much questioning of commitment to reform and ability to hold on to power. His many critics noted that he had been Soeharto's 'golden-haired boy', enjoying privileged access to the palace and loyally serving his mentor for some two decades. Moreover, Habibie was a *wunderkind* technocrat with little knowledge of social and political issues.

In his first televised speech as president, the diminutive Habibie sat at a large desk with his name plate displayed prominently in front of him and looked, both figuratively and literally, dwarfed by the challenges of his office. But in the months that followed, President Habibie announced far-reaching reforms which effectively dismantled most of the New Order's foundations. Liberalisation of the press, repeal of repressive political laws, and democratic elections all followed in short order. The military announced it was withdrawing from formal politics and the police were separated from the Armed Forces and given primary responsibility for domestic law and order. Dozens of new political parties, and literally thousands of NGOs, labour unions, farmers' associations and other civil society organisations sprang into existence. Radical new decentralisation laws were passed devolving extensive political and economic authority to Indonesia's several hundred districts. Anti-corruption bodies were formed and military human rights abuses investigated (though successful prosecutions were few).

Habibie's presidency ended in October 1999, but his three successors Abdurrahman Wahid (1999–2001), Megawati Soekarnoputri (2001–2004), and Susilo Bambang Yudhoyono (2004–present) continued the reform process, albeit in a less vigorous and sweeping manner than Habibie. The constitution has been thoroughly revised, a Constitutional Court established, the first direct presidential elections were held in 2004 and direct elections for provincial and district heads began in 2005, hundreds of politicians and public officials have been jailed for corruption (including at least seven former ministers), a measure of civilian control has been established over the military and progress has been made in cleaning up Indonesia's notoriously corrupt judicial and prosecutorial systems. With these reforms Indonesia can now claim to be the most democratic nation in Southeast Asia. Not only have its elections been largely free of violence and manipulation, but public support for democracy remained above 80 per cent, according to well-regarded opinion surveys.

Twelve years later, it is clear that Soeharto's resignation in 1998 marked a dramatic discontinuity in Indonesia's modern political history that was as momentous as (and far less bloody than) that which saw Soeharto's rise to power in 1965–66. The Indonesian political system has changed, seemingly irrevocably. It is today a flourishing democracy with a vibrant civil society and political life. Yet, the legacy of the Soeharto period remains strong and pervasive.

This continuing influence of the Soeharto years was highlighted in a dramatic way in the first months of 2008, almost precisely ten years after Soeharto's resignation, as the former strongman fell seriously ill and eventually died in Jakarta. Dealing with the venality and human rights abuses of former authoritarian regimes and their rulers is a major challenge for many new democracies. It is symbolically loaded because it can underline the desire of the new rulers to break definitively with the ideas and practices of the past; but it can be difficult to achieve this goal if powerful political and economic forces seek to protect their interests or legacy, or a significant body of public opinion looks back at the authoritarian rule with nostalgia or fondness. Only in a few cases, therefore, have former dictators been charged and convicted (Roh Tae-woo and Chun Doo-hwan of South Korea were two such exceptions).

In Indonesia, although President Soeharto had been forced to resign in ignominy he was also able to live out his final decade in more or less quiet obscurity. There were attempts to charge him with corruption, but he was able to avoid criminal prosecution on the grounds of ill-health. His lawyers even won a multi-million dollar libel case against *Time* magazine over a cover story alleging he had spirited billions of dollars to foreign bank accounts (though this was later overturned on appeal). When the former president was on his death bed in early 2008, a parade of senior Indonesian political figures passed by his bedside and praised his contribution to the nation. President Susilo Bambang Yudhoyono visited him in hospital and at his funeral seemed genuinely saddened, telling those assembled that 'We have lost one of the nation's best sons, a loyal fighter, true soldier and honourable statesman… We say thanks for his great contribution and meritorious service to the nation during his life and forgive all his faults'.[1] While some public intellectuals and political activists wrote critically about the former President and recalled the many unresolved problems he had bequeathed to the nation, overall the public mood—especially as captured in the media was laudatory and nostalgic.

The manner of the former strongman's passing, and the public controversy which surrounded it, put on display the highly ambiguous views which many Indonesians, both in officialdom as well as the general community—hold about Soeharto. It also revived scholarly debate about the deeper influence of his regime on contemporary Indonesia. For if the political transformation experienced by Indonesia since 1998 has been dramatic, the elements of continuity are just as visible. For all the new political institutions which have been established, there are also obvious signs that many underlying styles and structures persist. Pervasive corruption, 'money politics', pockets of repression, thuggish intimidation of opponents and elite dominance are just some of the most obvious phenomena which make some analysts and Indonesian political actors talk of the 'persistence of the New Order' or the 'failure of *reformasi*'.[2] The new political system is not a revitalised version of the New Order; but nor is it a complete antithesis.

It is against this backdrop that this book seeks to achieve three aims. First, it will reflect on the place that the New Order regime occupies in Indonesia's modern

---

1 'Royal farewell to Soeharto', *The Jakarta Post*, 29 January 2008.
2 See for example, 'Sri Sultan Anggap Reformasi Telah Gagal', *Tempo Interaktif*, 21 May 2008.

history. The New Order was in power for more than half of the sixty-three years since Indonesia gained independence in 1945. It still looms massively in Indonesia's post-colonial history. The passing of a decade since its demise gives us the necessary distance and perspective to begin rethinking the nature of the regime and its place in the longer time scale of modern Indonesian history.

Second, the book seeks to analyse the legacy of that period for Indonesia's new democracy. Several of the contributors examine the ways in which Indonesia's *reformasi* period has repudiated the practices and structures of the New Order era, but also the ways in which it continues them.

Third, in doing these things, the editors and contributors also seek to pay tribute to Harold Crouch, one of the chief scholarly analysts of the origins, nature, demise and aftermath of the New Order regime, who retired as professor of political science at the Australian National University in 2005. Earlier versions of the chapters in this volume were first presented at a conference in November 2005 marking his retirement. In writing for this book, Professor Crouch's colleagues and students wish to honour his contribution to the field of Indonesian political studies.

The New Order and its place in history

Youthful supporters of the army first coined the term the 'New Order' in 1966. By the 1990s, the term had become an anachronistic reminder of the regime's age, its inflexibility and its inability to adapt. But it did serve as a reminder of the scope of the ambitions which had accompanied the regime's birth. In the late 1960s the New Order regime emerged from a coalition of political and social forces which opposed President Soekarno, the Communist Party (Partai Komunis Indonesia, PKI) and the country's leftward drift during the previous decade. At the core of this coalition was the army leadership, but many intellectuals, businesspeople and anti-communist political groups also supported it. Seeing their first goal as being the elimination of the Communist party and its supporters (a goal achieved by the massacre of approximately 500,000 persons and detention of another 600,000 in 1965–66), Soeharto and his supporters then set about stabilising the economic situation and undermining other potential political challengers. It was only by the end of the 1960s and the start of the 1970s that a new political format began to settle into place (Feith 1968; Crouch 1979).

The army was the backbone of the regime, especially early on. Although military officers became less important in the regime's upper echelons in its later years, the army remained crucial for repressing and forestalling dissent right to the end. Most of the working apparatus of the regime, however, was provided by Indonesia's vast and ramshackle civilian bureaucracy which carried out the regime's developmentalist policies and held even the smallest villages in its stultifying grip. Layers of civilian politicians and intellectuals provided expert advice or links to broader social constituencies.

The New Order was a 'repressive-developmentalist' (Feith 1980) regime which built its modernising mission on an underpinning of backward-looking conservatism. Its political and economic mission was summed up by the numerous slogans, neologisms and acronyms it spawned: *dwifungsi* (the 'dual— i.e., military and political—functions' of the military), 'floating mass' (the passive role assigned to the rural population when it came to politics), *'monoloyalitas'* (the unswerving political loyalty that all state officials were required to give to the regime's Golkar party), 'accelerated modernisation', 'take-off' and the like. There is no doubt that the regime did bring about remarkable economic transformation: three decades of economic growth averaging more than 5 per cent, reduction in absolute poverty, the marked improvement in infrastructure, and health and medical services, and the coming into being of new urban middle class groups. Yet at the same time, the 'Pancasila ideology' propagated by the regime was a straight-jacketing and profoundly conservative doctrine. It tried to freeze Indonesian society in the stasis of a mythic vision of the Indonesian past, which stressed consensus, harmony and tradition, but also obedience and passivity. This vision strove to obliterate the conceptual division between state and society, and to teach individuals and groups that their interests must always be subordinated to the greater ones of the state and nation. This ideological climate naturalised and legitimised the repressive political arrangements upon which the regime was founded; it also stifled initiative and creativity, providing an environment in which corruption flourished and conformism reigned.

During the decades it was in power, there were many debates among political scientists about the New Order. Most of these debates centred on two inter-related questions: firstly, the character of the regime and its relations with wider society and, secondly, the reasons for its success and durability. In the former endeavour, most observers agreed in seeing the New Order as representing the victory and dominance of a relatively narrow part of Indonesia society, consisting of the state and its officials, over the varied social and political forces which made up Indonesian society. Scholars used a wide variety of terms to describe this concept: the 'beamtenstaat' (McVey 1982); the 'state *qua* state' (Anderson 1983); the 'bureaucratic polity' (Jackson 1978); 'bureaucratic authoritarian regime' (King 1982); and so on. There were debates about the degree to which state officials were independent from wider social forces, especially from a growing capitalist class which was emerging from within the regime's top leadership (Robison 1986), and how far they were responsive to wider business and elite groups when making policy (MacIntyre 1990). But there was broad agreement that the regime was fundamentally exclusionary in its relations with the majority of the population and that a major goal of its political structures and practices was to maintain the bulk of the population in a state of political passivity.

On the second question, virtually all credible analysts agreed that political repression was a crucial part of the regime's staying power: after all, the reliance on coercion to suppress challenges was obvious for all to see, not only in 1965–66, but also in such episodes as the 'Malari affair' of January 1974, the crackdown on students and other opponents in 1978 and the Tanjung Priok incident of 1984 in which more than 100 Muslim protesters were shot by the military. Others looked to the patrimonial distribution of rewards to supporters and potential opponents of the regime (Crouch 1979); the leadership role played by Soeharto himself (Liddle 1985); or the performance legitimacy provided by the technocrats and the economic growth they oversaw (e.g. Bresnan 1993). Still others looked to the ideas promoted by the regime, especially its 'Pancasila ideology', and debated their origins and effects (e.g. Morfit 1981; Bourchier 1997; Ramage 1995).

There was thus a sustained and deep research effort while the New Order was in power to understand the nature of this regime. It was not always easy for researchers to carry out this work: it was often difficult to gain access to remote geographical regions, or to informants or data related to politically sensitive topics. Foreign researchers faced the ever-present threat of being banned from Indonesia; domestic analysts could find their careers stymied, or suffer even worse retribution. Even so, the New Order era research effort has left a rich legacy for analysts of contemporary Indonesia and for historians. But it was also an effort which was marked, and constrained, by the preoccupations of the time. Arguably, also, analysts were especially bewitched by the apparent solidity and effectiveness of the New Order regime and were thus not only unprepared for its sudden demise, but perhaps also failed to recognise, or at least emphasise, some of its weaknesses and contradictions.[3] And, of course, analysts writing when the New Order was its height were also less able than we are today to try to locate the regime in the broader sweep of Indonesian history, and to assess its lasting significance and legacy.

Yet since the end of the New Order, we have seen few truly revisionist accounts of the regime, nor accounts which try to put that period in historical perspective or to reflect on its place in Indonesian history. To be sure, there have been many post-1998 studies on the New Order period, on topics as varied as the

---

3 For critical reflections along these lines see especially Klinken 2001. But see also Emmerson nd. who argued that Western analysts were unreasonably (and almost invariably mistakenly) anticipating the end of the regime during the New Order years.

life of Soeharto (Elson 2001); Islamic politics (Hefner 2000); opposition to the regime (Aspinall 2005); its interpretation of history (McGregor 2007); and the 'coup' of 1965 (Roosa 2006). These books all make important contributions to the historiography of the New Order period. But most of them were based on research projects which began during the New Order itself, or in its immediate aftermath, arguably without the lengthy critical distance which begets deep reflection, and almost certainly only beginning the task of reassessing the place of the New Order in Indonesia's political life.

In the early 1960s, a famous debate took place between Herbert Feith and Harry Benda, two of the most prominent members of a new generation of Western experts on Indonesia. Benda criticised Herbert Feith's book, *The Decline of Constitutional Democracy in Indonesia*, which had traced the political conflicts that led to the collapse of democratic government at the end of the 1950s, for asking the 'wrong question'. It was not appropriate, Benda argued, to ask 'what went wrong' with Indonesian democracy, because this mistakenly assumed that the democratic system which Indonesia adopted on achieving independence was suited to the country and would naturally sink deep roots there. It was more appropriate, Benda argued, to expect that Indonesia would find 'a way back to its own moorings' (Benda 1982:18), by which he meant its pre-colonial history of autocractic and feudalistic rule. Their exchange was analysed by subsequent generations of Indonesian studies students and attained canonical status in the Indonesian studies literature when included as the opening of the volume, *Debating Indonesian Politics: Thirteen Contributions to a Debate* (Anderson and McVey 1982).

Viewed from the vantage point of the present, it now appears that Feith's question was right all along, and that 'in the *longue duree* the historical exception may be the authoritarian New Order' (Klinken 2009:142). Certainly, academic tides have not flowed in favour of Benda's views. Few scholars now would trust his metaphor of culture or historical tradition as an anchor point, untouched by the present and always ready to pull it back into the past. On the contrary, as many analysts of the New Order have argued, the image of an authoritarian grand Javanese tradition was itself to a large extent a political construct, propagated and sustained by the bureaucratic class which benefited from the image of societal passivity and benign ruler-ship it encouraged (e.g. Pemberton 1994, Bourchier 1997). More obviously, the tides of political history also eventually turned against Benda. Certainly, the alacrity with which Indonesians have taken to the new democratic system since 1998 suggest that Indonesia's political 'moorings'—to the extent that the term has any cogency—may turn out to be democratic ones.

Indeed, there are many obvious parallels between the messy and rickety democracy of Indonesia in the 1950s and the current political order. Nobody yet has carried out a sustained historical comparison between the 1950s and the current era of democratic government, but the picture that Feith described in his 1962 book bears many similarities with the present. These include the basic complexion of at least some of the *aliran*—or political 'streams'—which constitute the main forces in Indonesian political life, and even the geographical bases of their strength in electoral competition which to a large degree is unchanged since the 1950s (King 2003). The fractured and multi-polar nature of the party system is another point of comparison (Mietzner 2008b), as are the dynamics of patronage and coalition-building among elites at the local level (Klinken 2009). What is missing today is the growing political polarisation of the 1950s, as well as the open search for alternatives to democratic rule: both phenomena which were embodied in the rise of an ambitious new power in the military, and in the equally rapid growth of the PKI. In short, Indonesian democracy today lacks precisely those attributes which led to its decline in the 1950s.

Tracing the roots of Indonesia's present conditions in the democratic politics of the 1950s, is not the aim of this book. These simple and by no means original observations, however, point to a task which will become more pressing for historians and political scientists of Indonesia as time goes by: that of rethinking the place and significance of the New Order regime in Indonesia's modern history. The chapters in the first part of this book represent a modest contribution to this effort. Whether the New Order period will ultimately be viewed as an authoritarian interlude between two more democratic, and ultimately more significant, periods in Indonesia's history is a question that will only be answered with the passage of more time, and the answer will depend greatly on the successes and failures of Indonesia's new democratic order. For the last twelve years, the dominant trend in Indonesia has been to view the New Order not as a failed experiment with authoritarianism, but as a looming presence, whose influence pervades and shapes all levels of post-Soeharto politics and continually threatens to drag Indonesia back into the past.

The legacy of the New Order

A second main purpose of the current book is therefore to consider the ways in which the New Order period has left its mark on today's Indonesia. In this regard, the main contradictions of Indonesia's democratisation are well-known even to casual observers: the combination of dramatic democratic transformation of the formal political system, with continuation of many of the corrupt, predatory and sometimes repressive practices which characterised authoritarian rule, especially at the local level. Such a combination is, of course, not uncommon in countries which have undergone democratic transitions in the developing and post-communist eras, and attempts by scholars of Indonesia to understand Indonesia's transformation thus mirror and draw upon a wider literature.

At the level of democratic reform, Indonesia has transformed dramatically. The New Order regime retained some of the outward appearances of democratic rule, such as regional and national legislative assemblies and regular elections (regimes which dispense with such procedures altogether are indeed rare in a modern world). Yet 'Pancasila democracy' was designed in such a way that it never threatened the core of the regime. Only three political parties were allowed after 1973, and there was much intervention within the two 'opposition' parties—PDI and PPP—to ensure that they would never threaten the regime's dominance; a majority of members of the legislative body which elected Soeharto every five years were his own appointees anyway. If all else failed, a formidable security apparatus had extensive power to take action against critics and opponents of the government, often with a blatant disregard for legality.

In these regards, Indonesia has now been dramatically transfigured. Basic political freedoms in areas like the rights of organisation, assembly and expression have been greatly expanded. Freedom House in 2006 for the first time declared Indonesia to be 'free'. The last national elections in 2009 were contested by 38 political parties representing a range of interests and each vigorously contesting for its share of power. There has been a boom in civil society organisation with a proliferation of new labour unions, farmers, ethnic or regional groups, and a plethora of NGOs coming into being. Far-reaching decentralisation has led to a dramatic flowering of democratic competition at the local level (Aspinall and Fealy 2003; Nordholt and Klinken 2007). The army has formally disengaged from politics. It is now hard, for example, to imagine Indonesia undergoing that classic symptom of authoritarian backsliding experienced by Thailand in late 2006: the coup d'etat.

On the other hand, as also noted in many analyses, the *reformasi* movement has failed to achieve many of the goals its most radical exponents set down in 1998–99. The military may have abandoned the formal political realm, but the institution is in some respects a law unto itself, raising a majority of its own funds from a range of legal and illegal economic activities with little oversight and control from the executive government and legislature, and with soldiers routinely engaging in corrupt and illegal economic activities, and, on occasions, violating the rights of citizens with impunity. The press is now free, but journalists are subject to various forms of harassment and intimidation by private actors; others are bribed to ensure that their reporting favours the powerful (Hadiz and Heryanto 2005). Corruption is all-pervasive and 'money politics' exerts strong, but not always absolute, influence over electoral outcomes in many regions. Meanwhile, many of the individuals and groups that dominated Indonesia during the Soeharto regime have reinvented themselves and still figure prominently in economic and political affairs.

With such a mixed record to choose from, it is not surprising that scholarly analysis has been sharply divided. Of all commentators, Vedi Hadiz and Richard Robison have been perhaps the most emphatic in pointing to the failings of democratisation and the elements of continuity with the New Order regime, describing the new power structure as a 'reorganization' of oligarchic power (Robison and Hadiz 2004). As Hadiz (2003:593) puts it

> the institutions of Indonesia's new democracy have been captured by predatory interests precisely because these were not swept away by the tide of reform. In fact, old forces have been able to reinvent themselves through new alliances and vehicles...

Others, especially those who emphasise institutional design, take a far more sanguine view of the achievements of democratisation. For example, Douglas Ramage (2007:135), the Country Representative of the Asia Foundation in Jakarta, has described Indonesia as a 'stable country with a democratic and decentralised form of government... and continuing on a path of democratic consolidation...' (see also MacIntyre and Ramage 2008). Most political scientists writing on Indonesia, drawing on the wider literature on democratic transitions and consolidation, have tried to steer a middle course and have made various attempts to characterise post-Soeharto governments as a 'hybrid regime' (Aspinall 2003); patrimonial democracy (Webber 2006); or a patronage democracy (Klinken 2009).

This volume

Rather than being a typical festschrift consisting of tribute pieces on unconnected topics, the editors and Harold Crouch wished to produce a volume which was thematically coherent. We therefore chose as our concern a topic which has long been at the centre of Harold Crouch's own research: the New Order regime. We asked contributors either to re-examine the New Order period or to reflect upon its legacy for Indonesia's contemporary politics and society. The editors and contributors do not claim that this book is a comprehensive attempt to do these things. In designing the overall shape of the volume the editors tried to strike a balance between thematic unity and the varied interests of the contributors who were brought together by their admiration for, and debts to, Harold Crouch.

The book is divided into two sections. In section one, contributors begin the task of re-examining the New Order. The first two contributions bring to light aspects of Soeharto's career that have not yet been subject to close scholarly analysis, indicating the degree to which the life of the long-serving autocrat remains a fertile topic for scholarly research, despite the many endeavours already made in this regard. The section begins with an essay by David Jenkins, representing a small part of a larger research project by Jenkins on the biography of Soeharto. The chapter focuses on the early fundraising activities of Soeharto, activities which have previously been poorly understood but which throw much light on Soeharto's later behaviour as president, and on the character of the regime he founded. Jenkins' discovery of an early pattern of 'stand-over tactics, extortion and straight-out theft', not only help us to understand Soeharto's subsequent career, but they help us to locate him, from an early stage in his career, in the twinned histories of military predation and '*preman*ism' (gangsterism), which have become important topics of scholarly inquiry in the post-Soeharto period.

In the second chapter, Ken Ward keeps the analytical focus on Soeharto, but does so by way of a close analysis of the former president's philosophy of power and his attitudes to Javanese 'tradition', as expressed in a revealing speech Soeharto made when he was at the height of his power in 1982. This important speech, one of the few made by the president in what he thought was a private setting to be captured verbatim, has never before been subjected to close textual analysis. In it, Ward reveals 'a high-water mark of his advocacy of a view of Indonesia inspired by Javanese concepts', capturing the inner logic of a period of official politics when the New Order regime saw political Islam as one of its prime enemies, a period that contrasts dramatically with the contemporary era of an increasingly Islamic public sphere in Indonesia. Yet, this early period has important legacies, too, for contemporary Islamic politics. In the next chapter, Sidney Jones examines some of those legacies by tracing the origins of the terrorist group *Jemaah Islamiyah* to the radicalisation engendered by the New Order regime's repression of political Islam in the 1970s and 1980s. In this chapter, Jones confronts the analytical puzzle that Indonesia's violent jihadist movement arose most powerfully in the post-Soeharto democratic period, whereas in most Islamic countries such movements emerge to challenge authoritarian regimes. Close analysis of the New Order period, however, makes Indonesia appear closer to the norm than first sight would have it. Jones uncovers trial documents from 1982 in which the grand-father of contemporary Indonesian jihadism, Abdullah Sungkar, condemns the autocratic practices of Soeharto's regime, helping us to locate his movement's origins in the 'complete frustration of an Islamist politician, decisively and permanently excluded from the system.'

The economists Hal Hill and Dionisius Narjoko examine the New Order's economic record, especially the connection between industrialisation and the opening the economy to global markets. In contrast to the generally negative assessments of the political scientists and historians in the volume, they see the New Order experience in a more positive light, as one where 'an open trade and investment regime and efficient supply-side investments were beneficial for Indonesia'. Next, Robert Cribb presents a reflective and iconoclastic essay on the New Order's historical origins and its place in the wider sweep of Indonesian history. Rather than seeing the New Order, with its bureaucratic approach to politics, as a continuation of the earlier period of Dutch colonial rule, as was previously argued by several scholars when the New Order was at its height, he points to critical discontinuities, including in the New Order's stress on conformity and meritocracy, both values that were anathema to the Dutch colonial order. Finally, Professor Jamie Mackie revisits the theme of patrimonialism, which was one of the key concepts Harold Crouch used to explain the dynamics of the New Order regime. Seeing not only patronage, but also the distribution of 'quasi-traditional fiefdoms to favoured subordinates' as central to the concept of patrimonialism, Mackie finds its analytical utility to have stood the test of time. It is a fitting tribute to both Professor Mackie and to Harold Crouch that this chapter be positioned as the keystone of the volume.

Each of the chapters in the first part of the volume, albeit in very different ways, suggest that the New Order period is far from being a closed book for historical inquiry. Instead, it continues to offer both opportunities for original empirical research, as in the chapters of Jenkins, Ward and Hill and Narjoko, and for reconsideration and reconceptualisation in the light of new theoretical insights and contemporary concerns, as in those by Jones, Cribb and Mackie. Moreover, rather than pointing to a new consensus, these chapters suggest that assessments of the New Order are likely to be as varying, and contentious, as they were when the regime was in power.

In section two, the contributors look at different aspects of Indonesia in the period since the demise of the New Order. The first two chapters focus upon the first post-Soeharto governments: Dewi Fortuna Anwar analyses the brief, but highly eventful, tenure of the Soeharto's successor, President B. J. Habibie. One of the enduring puzzles of the Indonesian democratisation is how it came that Soeharto's hand-picked successor should introduce the most far-reaching reforms of post-Soeharto era. Anwar, writing not only as a scholar but also as an insider in the Habibie government locates the answer not only in the strength of the protest movements unleased by the fall of Soeharto—the conventional answer—but also in the personal style of Habibie the man. Edward Aspinall looks to the failings of reform in the following two administrations, those of Abdurrahman Wahid and Megawati Soekarnoputri, tracing these failings to the political socialisation their leaders had experienced as 'semi-opponents' of the New Order. The legacy of Soeharto era authoritarianism thus appears not only in the political institutions bequeathed by it, but also in the political styles of those leaders conventionally seen as ushering in the country's transition to a new democratic order.

The final four chapters each address directly the core question of scholarship on post-Soeharto politics: to what extent is Indonesia progressing toward democracy or, conversely, to what extent are its politics being captured by the conservative forces nurtured by the New Order regime itself. Jun Honna discusses one of the political forces which had been a central focus of Crouch's earlier work: the Indonesian military, especially looking for signs of its continuing political influence at the local level. Focusing on the 1999–2004 period, his study is exemplary of the 'elite capture' school, and he finds considerable evidence of a continuing political role for the military, though he holds open the possibility of diminution in the subsequent period. Chris Manning provides a detailed study of the politics of labour reform in the post-Soeharto period, analyzing the effects on economic policy making and economic outcomes. To a large degree his concern is with the effects of labour policy on employment and poverty, but his analysis of the dramatically increased political clout of organised labour in the post-Soeharto period points to a degree of fluidity and openness in the new political order that, at least, seem to question narratives of continued and unchallenged elite dominance.

Marcus Mietzner provides a close study of the result of another milestone of post-Soeharto reform: the introduction of direct elections for heads of government at the local level. In a subtle analysis, he acknowledges that most candidates for government office at the local level originate from the established political elite, but he also points to a new willingness by voters to judge incumbents on the basis of their performance. Even if his analysis does not point to a displacement of the old New Order elite, it is suggestive of a degree of circulation within the elite, because 'the introduction of direct local elections has empowered voters to determine the outcome of inter-elite competition for political office.' Finally, William Case concludes the volume with a piece which pays fitting tribute to Harold Crouch's long-standing interests in comparative Southeast Asian politics, by contrasting Indonesia's democratisation with the experiences of other countries in the region. He argues that Indonesia's low quality democracy fits into a broader regional pattern in which democratisation is both facilitated and undermined by 'the weakness of social forces and the resilience of elites.' In this perspective, the continuing legacy of the New Order is less a sign of that regime's uniquely resilient influence, as part of a broader regional pattern whereby 'Elites have found that democracy helps to cement their dominance'.

As Indonesia's New Order fades into historical memory we hope that this volume will be not only a tribute Professor Harold Crouch, but also an early contribution to what will inevitably be a longer term academic debate about the nature and legacy of the Soeharto regime.

The New Order and its Antecedents

1 One Reasonably Capable Man: Soeharto's Early Fundraising

DAVID JENKINS

In the post-independence history of Indonesia, Soeharto played a hugely important role. Yet the man, as has often been observed, was frustratingly enigmatic, closed and difficult to read with any confidence. That, I believe, makes it even more important than is usual in such cases for anyone writing about Soeharto to examine closely his formative years in Central Java and his first twenty years in the army, looking for any clues that may tell us more about his character and personality.

Much of what we know about Soeharto's early years has come from Soeharto himself or from his associates, or from *The Smiling General*, a 1969 authorised biography by O. G. Roeder. A great deal of this material is suspect, slanted, hagiographic or downright mendacious. It was only in the 1970s and 1980s that we began to get what lawyers would call 'further and better particulars' about Indonesia's second President, and learn more about the dark underside of the New Order. Academics and journalists made a major contribution to our understanding. Interestingly, it was not until 2001, when Bob Elson published *Suharto: A Political Biography*, that we got the first serious, full-length treatment of the former President's life.

Twelve years after Soeharto stepped down there is an urgency to the task of looking into his past, given that documentary sources can tell us only so much and given that so many of his contemporaries and subordinates, let alone his former superiors, have died or are now growing quite old. I have been talking to these men on and off for forty years, having set off down this path when Jamie Mackie suggested during a visit to Jakarta in 1970 that I begin a clippings file on each of the six most interesting generals around Soeharto, in addition to the one I had on the President himself. Before long, I found myself with clippings files on dozens of senior officers. In the early 1990s, after an involuntary 10-year absence from Indonesia, I resumed my research, interviewing a large number of retired officers, many of whom had known Soeharto well.

These interviews, supplemented by extensive archival research, provide, I believe, a fuller and more rounded picture of Soeharto in the years before he came to power. They also confirm that some of the strengths and weaknesses that Soeharto brought to the Indonesian presidency were well developed—and well-known to his colleagues—at the time he came to office. In October 1965, Soeharto may have been little known outside the army. But to his military colleagues and to his former superiors he was anything but a mystery. Many officers had known him well for two decades or more.

In a forthcoming book I hope to take a broad look at Soeharto during those early years. In the pages that follow I will consider one aspect of that past—Soeharto's interest and growing expertise in raising off-budget funding, ostensibly for the welfare of his troops, and his willingness to tolerate, when not actively encouraging, the commercialisation of office. As a young military officer, Soeharto indulged in practices which could not stand the light of day but which were condoned, even encouraged, by the high command during the revolution and the early years of independence. In time, he turned fundraising into an art form. It will be argued in this chapter that Soeharto's fundraising in the 1940s and 1950s not only tells us a good deal about his personality and his attitude to rules and conventions but also foreshadows the freewheeling commercial practices that were to be such a feature of his New Order government. As President, Soeharto continued to adopt a cavalier attitude to the ethical issues of fundraising and to the commercialisation of office, thereby undermining the viability of the Indonesian state.

The following section will look briefly at Soeharto's fundraising practices at two early stages of his career: first, when he was a regimental commander in Yogyakarta during the late 1940s; and second, when he was commander of the Central Java Diponegoro Division in the late 1950s.

Soeharto's fundraising during the revolution

Throughout his time in the military, Soeharto was obliged to operate in an environment in which commanders could not expect the central government to meet more than a small part of their financial needs. To cover the shortfall, officers were allowed to requisition state-owned property; from time to time, some of them seized private property as well. They were also allowed to engage in business transactions occasionally, to raise the funds to support their military operations. During his time as a regimental commander in Yogyakarta in the late 1940s, Soeharto began to take a keen interest in business. He rented out army trucks to private businessmen. He bought—or simply seized—sugar from the large sugar mills and had it transported to market, to be sold to Chinese middlemen. Before long, fellow army officers began to suspect that Soeharto was pocketing some of the profits from these undertakings.

In the second half of 1949, Soeharto and one of his army colleagues set up a vehicle repair shop and a bus and trucking company, ostensibly to create employment for 'demobilised' guerrilla fighters. At the time, the two men had one truck, one bus and two sedans, all of which had been requisitioned for army purposes. They also had a complete set of workshop tools, a priceless asset in the Republican capital, where everything was in short supply after years of Japanese occupation, revolutionary instability and a tightly enforced Dutch blockade. The business was a private venture between the two men. They divided the profits between themselves. They never gave any thought to turning the money over to the army.

Many of Soeharto's military colleagues in Central Java disapproved of his fundraising, believing that he went much further than he needed to. They expressed concern that not all the money was accounted for. The Sultan of Yogyakarta was also concerned. He saw how Soeharto operated during the revolution, and strongly disapproved. He was to refer to these concerns when, at the end of 1965 or early 1966, four or five Javanese politicians and student leaders called on him at his office in Jakarta. During the meeting, the visitors pushed the idea that Soeharto would make a better President than General A. H. Nasution, a former army chief of staff who had the drawback in their eyes of being an Outer Islander. The Sultan received the suggestion coolly. There are three different versions of what he replied when his visitors said they wanted Soeharto as President.

According to the first, he said, 'What! That thief!' According to another, he asked if Soeharto was 'still in the habit of stealing?' According to a third, he invited his visitors to think very carefully about any such move, albeit using a suitably polite form of words. 'Are you sure,' he is said to have asked, 'that you want Soeharto as President? Because my experience was that when we were all working hard to push the Dutch out, he took all these things for himself.'

In the course of writing about Soeharto, I have had to chase down many stories like this and try to assess where the truth lies. In this case, it became apparent that the two more colourful versions of this encounter were based, with varying degrees of elaboration and invention, on comments made by one of the men who attended the meeting with the Sultan that day. The third—and most moderate—version proved to be the accurate one.

Soeharto's fundraising in Central Java

Soeharto spent nearly three-and-a-half years (1956–59) as the commander of the Central Java military region. But his posting, although successful in many ways, putting him on track for further advancement up the military ladder, was to end abruptly in dismissal and humiliation. This dramatic turn-around in Soeharto's fortunes arose from his need to raise much-needed funds for his command. In Indonesia in the 1950s, the high command still took the view that a certain amount of fundraising was acceptable and indeed commendable. In Soeharto's case, a quest for money turned into a fundraising free-for-all in which subordinate officers ran loose in the province, exceeding all the then current notions of propriety and restraint.

In Semarang, Soeharto engaged in what is often described as unconventional or irregular fundraising. This is a misnomer. Soeharto's 1957–59 fundraising campaign seems at times to have had more in common with stand-over tactics, extortion and straight-out theft. Under Soeharto, the Diponegoro Division's financial officers left no stone unturned when it came to raising money. They squeezed and cajoled ethnic Chinese businessmen. They imposed illegal levies on the copra trade. They seized the assets of foreign-owned businesses. They set up a lucrative smuggling operation, bartering sugar for rice. They sought 'assistance' from the manufacturers of kretek cigarettes. They controlled, 'unofficially', the distribution of kerosene in Central Java. There was, it is true, a tradition of fundraising in the Central Java command, as there was in every other military region. But as Michael Malley has noted in an impressive study of this period, the declaration of martial law and the subsequent nationalisation of all Dutch businesses 'greatly broadened the scope for military fundraising activities.' Soeharto took full advantage of that. Not long after becoming military commander in Central Java, he established two foundations, ostensibly for charitable purposes. These bodies were soon being used for other, less noble purposes, clearly with Soeharto's full encouragement.

As divisional commander, Soeharto 'needed someone with established business connections and proven business experience on whom he could rely to raise the extra-budgetary funds' required by the command. Major Soedjono Hoemardhani, the number two man in the division's Financial and Economic Planning Staff (Finek), was tailor-made for the job. An old hand in army finance, with a wide range of business contacts in Semarang, he had a nimble mind, adaptable ethics and a voracious appetite for new business opportunities. He knew how to set up companies and he knew which trees to shake to harvest the rich commercial pickings of Central Java's only major north coast port. He was a money raiser par excellence.

In some ways, Soedjono's gifts as a fundraiser ministered to all that was best in Soeharto, giving him an opportunity to look after the welfare of his men and their families, a responsibility he took far more seriously than did many other officers. They also gave him a chance to do good works for the community at large, especially farmers. In other ways, Soedjono's gifts ministered to all that was suspect and base in Soeharto's nature. During this time Soeharto seems to have been prepared to raise funds by any means, fair or foul, going well beyond what was considered normal or acceptable. Worse, according to former colleagues he began helping himself to some of the money thus raised. Why did Soeharto engage in behaviour which not only breached the norms of many Diponegoro officers but affronted his superiors in Jakarta? There were four reasons. He was deeply and genuinely concerned about the welfare of his men. He had staff officers who were unusually adept at raising funds. He thought he could get away with it. And he was insatiably greedy, not only at a professional level but also at a personal level, determined, some of his army and civilian colleagues later came to believe, to compensate for the acute material deprivation of his childhood.

By this time, army-backed smuggling had become routine in the Outer Islands; it was also emerging as a problem in Jakarta, thanks to the entrepreneurial instincts of two senior officers on the Nasution's general staff. However, the army commanders in East and West Java had not gone down this path, and there were many in the Diponegoro who were dismayed by Soeharto's actions. As commander in Central Java, Soeharto was striking out boldly—and dangerously—on his own.

Soeharto's strengths and weaknesses as a regional military commander were noted by Lieutenant Colonel G. V. Rouse, the then British military attaché in Jakarta. In October 1958, Rouse went to Semarang to attend a celebration marking the first eight years of the Diponegoro Division. It was a grandiose affair, spread over two days and attended by President Sukarno and by General Gatot Subroto, the Deputy Army Chief of Staff. Rouse judged it a great success. 'The whole performance had been carefully planned well in advance,' he wrote in his monthly report to the War Office in London

> and was carried out under the supervision of the Divisional Commander, Colonel Soeharto…. The celebration was a monument of what Indonesia can do if there is one object, the attainment of which is directed by one reasonably capable man. It was excellent and made the ill-planned, unpractical and muddled shambles which took place on October 5 in Jakarta to celebrate Armed Forces Day look the disaster it was.

In his next monthly dispatch to the War Office, Colonel Rouse was a good deal less effusive about Colonel Soeharto, about whom he had begun to receive disquieting reports. In Central Java, he now informed his superiors in London, the British-owned United Molasses Company had been experiencing 'great trouble' with the Military War Administration. This body had 'arbitrarily instructed the company' that the army would now be responsible for the sale and distribution of molasses within the country, even though all relevant storage facilities and transport vehicles belonged to the company. The company was being asked to lend these facilities to the army as a measure of its 'co-operation'. The War Administration had also decreed that no molasses was to be shipped from the port of Tegal without an army permit, which had until recently been withheld.

> After considerable investigation it appears that Col. Soeharto, Commander of T&T IV ('Diponegoro Division') and Head War Administrator of Central Java, is responsible for these troubles, hoping to divert to himself the Company's very considerable profits but, in fact, disrupting the whole organization and thereby losing a large amount of foreign exchange, which the country so badly needs.

In these successive and highly prescient dispatches, Rouse had identified two cardinal points about Soeharto. The first was his exceptional gift for organisation and leadership, attributes that would help him transform a bankrupt and almost broken-back state into one of the fastest growing Asian 'tiger' economies of the late twentieth century, before the great crash of 1997–98. The second was his almost equally exceptional greed, which was to become more and more pronounced with the passing of the years, helping to ensure that Indonesia would go on suffering long after he was finally driven from power.

As it happens, Soeharto's fundraising was of concern not only to the United Molasses Company. It was creating deep disquiet within the Central Java Military Territory, where a somewhat conservative ethos prevailed. As early as 1956, the Semarang night markets, organised by Major Munadi, one of Soeharto's more entrepreneurial subordinates, were being closely watched by the local Military Police chief, Lieutenant Colonel Soenarjo Tirtonegoro, who believed they were being used as a cover for illegal gambling. 'It was unheard of at that time' a senior Military Police officer recalled.

> So we, the MPs, were after these people. Sometimes Munadi held a *pasar malam* [night market] to raise funds…. And always under the sharp eyes of the MPs!…. Because it was unheard of at that time. No army man was doing things like that.

Central Java had always been puritanical, this officer noted, 'and suddenly they had a panglima who was not puritanical.' This had led to disquiet. 'Internally, the division was complaining. But the way the Javanese complain is silently—just whispering this, whispering that. And this MP man was against all this.'

Soenarjo, a strict disciplinarian, respected throughout the Military Police Corps (Corps Polisi Militer, CPM), took it upon himself to investigate further the allegations of financial impropriety. Before long, he included the names of Munadi and another Soeharto subordinate on a Military Police 'alert list', circulated to MP officers throughout Java and advising them of people who were of interest in ongoing investigations. He also raised the matter with the Diponegoro Chief of Staff, Lieutenant Colonel Pranoto Reksosamudro, a man noted for his probity and rectitude. Pranoto had known Soeharto for sixteen years and had once been close to him. But he was himself dismayed by Soeharto's actions and his subsequent report to headquarters was to play an important part in Soeharto's dismissal as Diponoegoro commander.

In smuggling goods to and from Singapore and working so assiduously to raise funds by other means, Soeharto had been sailing dangerously close to the wind. Nasution had promised shortly after the proclamation of martial law in March 1957 that the military authorities would take strong measures against corruption, and in November that year, following complaints that he was turning a blind eye to corruption within the army, he set up a committee to investigate the sources of income of senior army officers, particularly territorial and district commanders. In August 1959 he renewed that drive, declaring that he was ready to take 'drastic measures' to root out corruption in the army.

Soeharto was an obvious target. However it was Gatot, rather than Nasution, who delivered the coup de grace. When Soenarjo contacted Gatot about the situation in Central Java, the Deputy Army Chief of Staff sent the Inspector General of the Army, Brigadier-General Sungkono, to investigate the activities of the two foundations set up by Soeharto. Sungkono's findings were damning, pointing as they did to a widespread and systematic abuse of power. Indignant at this behaviour and without bothering to consult Nasution, Gatot flew to Semarang. Here, on 14 October 1959, he dismissed Soeharto, appointing Pranoto in his place. As it turned out, Soeharto's career was not irreparably damaged, but he never forgot this humiliation and he eventually had his revenge. In 1966, shortly after he came to power, Pranoto and Soenarjo were arrested and jailed. Various reasons were given for the arrests but friends of the two men were convinced they had been made to pay for their actions in 1959. Significantly, Soeharto did not change his ways. When, in the early 1960s, he was appointed Commander of Kostrad, the Army Strategic Reserve, he not only set up a foundation for the welfare of his men and their families but a private bank as well. (In the years after 1965, Soeharto and his associates maintained that he had behaved with complete propriety in Central Java but had been smeared by leftist officers who feared his strong anti-Communist stance.) It is not clear what, if anything, Soeharto knew of the CPM investigations into illegal fundraising at the time. However, in January 1959, about nine months before his dismissal, he piously informed a class of graduating soldiers that they had joined the colours 'not for earning their bread, but to give sacrifices to the Indonesian state and nation.'

In later years, when Soeharto was President, some analysts argued that the corruption that bedevilled New Order Indonesia had to be seen in its proper cultural context. Soeharto, they suggested, always a little too conveniently, was simply acting in the manner of a traditional Javanese prince; behaviour which might dismay outsiders was not particularly shocking in the Javanese framework. The resentment and silent opposition which Soeharto's actions generated among so many of his more honest fellow officers in Central Java in the late 1950s suggests that this argument is not at all compelling.

The case against Soeharto was never formally closed. In 1962, when he was the commander of a force that was preparing for major military operations against the Dutch in West New Guinea, his file was re-opened. This time, the examination of Soeharto's actions in Semarang involved not one but three of the nation's most senior Military Police officers, with a fourth keeping an informal, but watchful, eye on developments from the sidelines. Significantly, all four CPM officers were from Central Java, where the military police had long been interested in Soeharto's activities. After much deliberation, two officers reported to Nasution that they intended to formally investigate Soeharto. Nasution gave the go-ahead but several days later his deputy, Gatot, asked the officers to drop the matter. Priority was to be given to the West New Guinea campaign; the corruption case was to be shelved. Not for the first—or last—time in his career, Soeharto had had a lucky escape. By the time the West Irian dispute had been resolved in 1963, the danger of prosecution had passed. As Susan McKemmish has pointed out, during 1962–64, 'there was a radical change in the moral climate in elite circles as inflation made corruption more widespread.' Corruption, like treason, can be a question of dates.

Had Soeharto not pushed his fundraising so far beyond the limits of acceptability, had he not presided over what quickly became in many ways an organised crime ring, his term as military commander in Central Java would have been judged a success by his superiors. When it came to his core responsibilities as Commander, Soeharto had done all that Nasution could have asked of him. He had maintained order in a time of rising political tension. He had supported the Chief of Staff's hard line against the rebel colonels in the Outer Islands. Greed, however, had proved to be his Achilles heel.

Soeharto had shown that he was all too ready to abuse the power that was given to him. In no time at all, he had become the most innovative of Indonesia's corrupt colonels. Some of his Outer Island colleagues would have made far more money by smuggling rubber and copra—we have no way of knowing how well they each did—but none had managed to conjure money out of thin air as Soeharto and his minions had done. This was not just a crime but a folly, the more so in that it had been attempted in a province where many people, army officers and civilians alike, subscribed to a value system that put considerable store on honesty and propriety.

In 1966, seven years after Soeharto had been stripped of power for his abuse of office in Semarang, Indonesians were to find themselves living under a man who, perhaps more than anyone else in the army, appeared to believe there were few, if any, limits to what the army could do to finance itself and who was prepared to allow officers to plunder the nation's wealth for their own benefit. When it came to unbridled corruption and greed, Semarang was a foretaste of all that was to come.

Colonel Rouse, the British military attaché, had been on to Soeharto in 1958. Surprisingly, some Americans who might have been expected to follow such matters with equal interest, seem to have noticed nothing amiss. On 8 November 1965, five weeks after the coup and seven years after Colonel Rouse had begun putting Soeharto under the microscope, the CIA's Office of Current Intelligence sent the White House a secret memorandum on Soeharto. Describing him as 'the army's pivotal military and political figure', it went on to say that: 'Suharto is regarded as a strong, efficient and decisive officer. He lives modestly, is reputed to be incorruptible, and is noted for his smart appearance.'

Thinking of all this, I was reminded of the story told about the time when the elderly H. L. Mencken paid a visit to the Baltimore Sun, which had carried his columns for so many years. During the visit, Mencken's hosts took him on a tour of the building. As they passed the obituaries section, Mencken asked if he could read his own obituary. His hosts agreed. The lead in the galleys was inked up and the words printed off on a large sheet of paper. Mencken read the proof, then took out his pen and added a few words at the end. When his hosts inspected the page, they found that he had written, 'And as he got older, he got worse.' Soeharto acquired a taste for money at an early age. And as he got older and more powerful, he got worse.

2 Soeharto's Javanese Pancasila

KEN WARD

On the evening of 19 July 1982, President Soeharto received a delegation from the Golkar-affiliated National Indonesian Youth Committee (Komite Nasional Pemuda Indonesia, KNPI) at his private residence. The talk he gave was never published in Indonesia but was surreptitiously recorded on tape and then transcribed (Anon. 1982). Copies of the text were eagerly passed around in diplomatic and intelligence circles as evidence of what really made Soeharto tick. In it, he combines the role of political leader outlining to youthful supporters the concrete tasks ahead with one akin to that of the *guru* of a Javanese mystical sect explaining the meaning of life to a group of initiates.

By this time, Soeharto had established the basic framework of his authoritarian political system. Soeharto saw society as composed of a variety of groups performing different occupational functions which would all be beneficiaries of rapid economic development. The varying roles that functional groups— called *golongan karya* or *golkar*—played in the economy should not, in his eyes, give birth to ideological differences. Social conflict of any kind would threaten growth, and so was illegitimate and had to be repressed. Conflict was seen as the work of extremists. Soeharto had no inkling that growth and modernisation would themselves arouse conflict. His political system consisted of a state party (Golkar) tasked to win parliamentary elections every five years against competition from two heavily constrained political parties. Relying on support from the Indonesian Armed Forces and technocrat ministers, Soeharto reversed the economic decline of the Sukarno era. Believing that Indonesian society had to be de-politicised to bring about economic growth, he enforced a 'floating mass' policy, by which the rural masses were forbidden to engage in organised political activity except during campaigns for the largely ritualistic elections.[1] Between elections, they were under the sway of the Armed Forces and the national administrative structure, two nationwide hierarchies around

---

1 The 'floating mass' doctrine has claims to being one of Indonesia's rare, original contributions to authoritarian political thought. It was not, however, necessarily effective in de-politicising the rural *populace*, not least because it did not target religious practices that often linked the supporters of the Islamic party to their actual or potential leaders, such as Friday mosque attendance and prayer-group meetings (*pengajian*).

which Golkar honeycombed. Decades of high economic growth in Indonesia and a rapid expansion of the education system were accompanied by increasing social and economic differentiation, but Soeharto's 'functional' model of society ignored such differentiation. This outlook suited Golkar's electoral needs, as it was the natural home for those performing occupational functions, or *karya*.

Soeharto's attraction to Javanese religious beliefs became well-known from his early years in power (McDonald 1980:12). It may have begun when, as a child, he had come under the influence of a shaman (*dukun*) called Kiai Daryatmo, who was versed both in the Koran and in Javanese beliefs (meditation and mysticism, *samadi* and *kebatinan*).[2] Soeharto acquired his philosophy of life from studying with Daryatmo in the latter's prayer-house, where he helped the older man prepare traditional cures. Daryatmo is reported to have remained an influential figure in Soeharto's life for many years.[3] As president, Soeharto was surrounded by associates who were either nominal rather than devout Muslims or indeed Catholics, and who wanted to make use of mystical sects to counter Muslim political aspirations. Soeharto seemed to support this strategy in the early 1970s by endorsing *kebatinan* congresses. It appeared likely that *kebatinan* would acquire official recognition as a religion alongside the five hitherto recognised religions in the teeth of Muslim opposition. This would have reduced the number of Indonesians professing to be Muslim. In the end, however, Soeharto refrained from granting this recognition. His undertaking a minor pilgrimage (*umroh*) to Mecca in 1977 had no observable impact on his vigilance against Muslim politicians.

How much his Javanese beliefs shaped Soeharto's political outlook remains debatable. His usually controlled behaviour was certainly heavily influenced by Javanese precepts of inner calm reflected in external impassiveness. Moreover, Soeharto often indulged in practices aimed at placating supernatural forces. And his ambition to rule over a de-politicised realm was perfectly compatible with the outlook of Javanese kings, whose 'primary duties in the political sphere were to guard against disturbances and to restore order if any such disturbance should occur' (Moertono 1981:38). But he shared this outlook with his Dutch colonial predecessors, who expressed what were to become Soeharto's political goals in terms of calm and order (*rust en orde*) without themselves being in the thrall of Javanese authoritarian traditions.[4] Anderson, the western scholar who has contributed most to explaining Javanese attitudes to power, has argued that

---

2   See Soeharto, 1989, p.15. Soeharto introduces Daryatmo in his autobiography with the term muballigh, or Muslim preacher. Daryatmo came from Wonogiri in Central Java. See also Roeder, 1969, pp.119–20.

3   See Elson, 2001, p.228. Soeharto did not admit this in his autobiography. Soeharto was also believed to be influenced by the mystically inclined military officer, Sujono Humardani. See McDonald, 1980, p.131. But Soeharto denied this in his autobiography, claiming that it was he who had exerted influence over Sujono, not the other way round.

4   On the similarities between Soeharto's statecraft and that of late Dutch colonialism, see McVey, 1982, pp.84–91.

Soeharto had a 'multicolored mentality', which showed traces of revolutionary nationalism, some acquaintance with Javanese chronicles and puppet theatre, the attitudes of a petty colonial-era aristocrat and the effects of military officer training (Anderson nd). None of the major influences in Soeharto's early life prepared him to tolerate open conflict or to foster political freedom.

Soeharto depicted his government as steering a middle course between the extremes of communism and radical Islam. Although it did not reflect the vast social and ideological variety of Indonesian society, the three-party or Golkar plus two-party structure was held forcibly in place for twenty-five years. The one element Soeharto was still to add to his structure when he spoke to the KNPI in 1982 was the imposition of Pancasila as the sole legal basis for all political and social organisations.[5] But his vast program of indoctrination courses known as P4 (Pedoman Penghayatan dan Pengamalan Pancasila, Directive for the Realisation and Implementation of Pancasila) had already been underway for several years.[6] In his autobiography published in 1989, Soeharto was to report with satisfaction that by March 1983 some 1.8 million civil servants and 150,000 military personnel had already undertaken P4 courses (p.337). In all probability, most KNPI leaders present at Soeharto's residence on 19 July 1982 had already undergone some of these courses.

Pancasila's role

Soeharto's objective in addressing the KNPI representatives seemed to be to establish the ancient origins of Pancasila, the five principles first championed by Sukarno that consisted of belief in one supreme God, nationalism, humanitarianism, democracy through representative deliberation, and social justice. Soeharto told his audience that, with the 1982 parliamentary election now successfully concluded[7], the next national task was the holding of the 1983 People's Consultative Assembly session, which would approve the new Five-Year Plan and decide on the broad outlines of state policy. Soeharto hinted in passing, as he occasionally did during his last decade and a half in office, that his next five-year term would be his last, given his age (he was then 61). The possibility of his stepping-down made placing the next Five-Year Plan on a firm ideological foundation all the more important in his eyes. If he was really

---

5 Elson sees his effort to give Pancasila an ideological monopoly as one of the key stages in Indonesia's 'political corporatisation'. See Elson, 2001, p.228.

6 For an early account of P4 courses, see Morfit, 1981, pp.838–51. Morfit drew attention to the financial cost of the P4 courses, the sanctions that were applied for absenteeism and the vagueness of Pancasila's principles themselves. Morfit also suggested that the course materials imparted an entirely static and ahistorical view of the past and envisaged an unchanging future.

7 For a good account of this election, see Pemberton, 1986, pp.1–22. Golkar won 64.3 per cent of the vote in 1982, a slight improvement over its 1971 and 1977 results.

thinking of retirement at this stage, Soeharto might well have seen as urgent the task of imposing Pancasila as the sole basis for socio-political organisations, a task that would have be accomplished before his departure from office. He said that economic development would once more be Indonesia's major objective for five years, but it would be meaningless without political development. And he warned that Indonesians still did not all see political development in the same way. 'We do not yet use a single language when talking about political development.' Some people, he pointed out, thought that the freedom guaranteed in the 1945 Constitution allowed them to do whatever they wanted. This happened, Soeharto said, because Indonesians had not accepted Pancasila as the sole state ideology, the sole foundation for the state and the sole 'proper' outlook on life.

The problem was that there was, unfortunately, more than one way of accepting Pancasila. To make his point, Soeharto recounted a meeting he claimed to have had with President Sukarno in Semarang in 1956 when he was the acting Central Java military commander. He had asked Sukarno whether the Indonesian Communist Party's (Partai Komunis Indonesia, PKI) success in the parliamentary election of the previous year, in which it was placed fourth, might not endanger Pancasila. Sukarno had answered that the PKI's result proved it had popular support and now he would have to Indonesia-ise or Pancasila-ise the communists. Soeharto, for his part, had told Sukarno his policy was to 'separate' the PKI from the people's economic development, a policy he claimed then received Sukarno's blessing.[8] Without explaining what 'Pancasila-ise' might mean, Soeharto told the KNPI leaders that Sukarno had tried to Pancasila-ise the PKI through Nasakom but that this had failed.[9] In fact, he said, the PKI had exploited the legitimacy that Nasakom conferred on it to build up its strength and eventually launch a revolt. The lesson that Soeharto drew from his anecdote was that Pancasila should not be just a device or an umbrella to bring together all ideologies, such as communism, socialism, liberalism and religion (sic). If Pancasila was no more

8   Soeharto said: 'I reported that, since I did not believe that the PKI could be Pancasila-ised just like that, I was trying to distance (the PKI from) the people by carrying out development'. Sukarno replied, according to Soeharto: 'Yes, that's right. Carry on.' Soeharto continued pursuing economic development in a way that aimed at 'separating' the people from the PKI through his three decades in the presidency. If this conversation with Sukarno took place at all, it is more likely to have been in 1957, after the establishment in July of that year of the Fourth Territory Development Foundation, which was to be Soeharto's major vehicle for promoting economic development in Central Java and for raising funds for his subordinates, particularly through investment in companies involved in the distribution of primary commodities. See Elson, 2001, pp.62–63.

9   The acronym Nasakom stands for Nationalism, Religion and Communism, the formula that expressed the three main ideological currents that Sukarno tolerated and encouraged to co-operate with one another during Guided Democracy. Anderson has offered a different perspective on Nasakom, arguing that Sukarno's advocacy of Nasakom was a claim to Power deriving from his absorbing all parts of the political system within himself, while others merely remained the representatives of their respective currents or ideologies. See Anderson, 1972, p.15. Soeharto did not imitate Sukarno in this respect, since he was not prepared to admit the legitimacy of competing ideologies that he might seek to embody within himself. By 1982, Sukarno's rehabilitation was well under way with Soeharto's encouragement, and Soeharto's remarks here convey no criticism of his predecessor's approach to the PKI.

than an umbrella or receptacle (*wadah*), the adherents of those ideologies would ape the PKI and exploit their position of shelter under the Pancasila umbrella, all the while keeping their own separate ideological identities. As a result, the country would be riven by conflict. The only solution was for Pancasila to be the sole ideology or basis for Indonesian political and social organisations, replacing all other ideologies.[10]

An ancient legacy

But, for this to be achieved, Soeharto foresaw that the people would have to be convinced of Pancasila's truth. And they would be persuaded of the truth of Pancasila if they saw it as the heritage of their ancestors. Sukarno had already led the way, by asserting in 1945 and in later years that he had not invented Pancasila but had merely 'dug' it up from the 'pearls' left by the forefathers of his people. Apart from a couple of genuflections towards non-Javanese, Soeharto clearly saw those ancestors as being Javanese. Soeharto told the KNPI that their distant ancestors had bequeathed the elements that coalesced into the principles of Pancasila in ways that were too simple to be understood by over-clever scholars.[11] Modern theories such as Marxism, communism and so forth could not cast light on the ancient wisdom. Defending the early Indonesians against the onslaught of over-educated scholars, who tended to write them off as practitioners of black magic (*ilmu klenik*), Soeharto said the ancient Indonesians living before Hinduism, Buddhism, Islam and Christianity and 'ideology' reached Indonesian shores were beyond praise. Not only had they developed such useful practical concepts as mutual help (*gotong-royong*), they had also produced a science of reality (*ilmu kasunyatan*[12]), which he said contemporary Javanese already knew about but which the non-Javanese now ought to study.[13]

---

10   Few students of Indonesian politics have accepted Soeharto's view that Pancasila is at all an 'ideology', let alone one that could replace all others. King, for example, has urged that 'the Panca Sila should not be labelled an ideology (even a rudimentary one) because of its original instrumental character (a compromise establishing limits on parties), lack of logical consistency (one, supreme God vs. democracy), and lack of any future orientation'. See King, 1982, p.111, n.17. Given the non-specificity and vagueness of its principles, one can also see Pancasila as merely a slogan or a talisman. One of Pancasila's peculiarities is that it serves more readily as a weapon or instrument of the powerful than of the powerless. The oppositionist Petition of Fifty that surfaced in the early 1980s criticised Soeharto's exploitation of Pancasila but it was easily repressed.

11   This comment recalls Sukarno's hostility to western 'textbook thinking' that he condemned in the early years of Guided Democracy. There had been an intense and bitter debate in 1981 about who had 'dug up' Pancasila. It had been launched by army historian Nugroho Notosusanto, who had claimed the excavator had been the long-dead Minangkabau nationalist figure and ideologue, Muhammad Yamin. See *Sekitar Tanggal dan Penggalinya*, Jakarta: Yayasan Idayu, 1981.

12   Geertz translates this as 'highest reality'. There was a mystical sect called Kawruh Kasunyatan ('Knowledge of the Highest Reality') that was founded in Solo in 1927 and had a branch in Mojokuto. See Geertz, 1960, p.347.

13   'Yang Jawa tentu mengetahui, tetapi yang luar Jawa supaya belajar'. Soeharto's condescending comment about non-Javanese recalls his speech at the September 1957 National Conference held as Outer Islands were heading for rebellion. Still Central Java commander, Soeharto took a hard line against the Outer Island

The science of reality gave birth to the science of the origin and destination of man (*ilmu sangkan paran dumadi*[14]), and that in turn spawned the science of the perfect life (*ilmu kasampurnaning hurip*).

Soeharto then explained the meaning of these sciences. The science of reality acknowledged the reality of nature and everything in it, including man. An appreciation of nature led to the conclusion that a superior spirit had created it, and that spirit was God, the creator of the whole of Nature, including man. God gave man the necessary means for life, namely a body, a spirit and a soul. As long as these are united (*manunggal*), man is alive, but when the body and soul have separated, man is dead. God also gave man the five senses, then the power to reason, to feel and to desire (*cipta, rasa, karsa*). God also infused man with good and bad feelings or passions that are forever in conflict, such as honesty and corruption, or patience and irascibility. God also gave man the conflicting needs of being an individual and of living in society. Soeharto described these insights of the ancient Indonesians as the science of reality. According to the science of the origin and destination of man that the ancients also discovered, God determined that man would die. Where he goes at death depends on his behaviour during his life. Those who have mastered their passions will be judged to have done good in this life. The mastering of the conflicting passions was, Soeharto said, the key to a perfect life, the understanding of which was *ilmu kasampurnaning hurip*.

At this point in his talk, Soeharto acknowledged a role for religion, any religion, as religion also exhorted man to control his passions. The ancient Indonesians were for this reason tolerant of all the religions that came to Indonesia, he said, and everybody was free to choose the religion of his or her taste. But he added that one role Pancasila would not play was that of a religion. 'I have said time and again to (Muslim) religious scholars who are afraid that Pancasila will evolve into a religion, that that is not possible. Pancasila as an outlook on life, the basis of the state and as an ideology guarantees tolerance and the vitality of all religions'. While welcoming religions, Soeharto continued, earlier Indonesians had not forsaken Indonesian culture. These early beliefs in one supreme God, in self-help, and in humankind's individual and social dual nature had led to

dissidents. He said that the 54 million people on Java would feel unjustly treated if economic development was held back there to permit the regions to catch up. See Lev, 1966, p.29. Daniel Dhakidae drew the writer's attention to this speech.

14   The Jesuit scholar, Magnis-Suseno, describes *sangkan-paran* as being at the heart of Javanese mystical speculation. See Magnis-Suseno, 1997, p.118. He writes that a Javanese can only reach *sangkan-paran* if he is dedicated to this as the one aim in life and he is ready to resist the outer world's temptations, though he has to continue performing his duties in the world. *Sangkan paraning dumadi* literally means 'the origin and destination of being'. In a personal communication, George Quinn notes that 'many Javanese see life as fleeting or transitory—a short stopping off between where we came from and where we are going to. The transitoriness of life can only be understood if we are aware deep down that we come from somewhere and are going somewhere'.

the belief in the principles of unity, people's welfare and social justice that had sunk from the surface but had been rediscovered through Sukarno's articulation of Pancasila.

Soeharto's search for Pancasila's origins thus did not involve an attempt to trace each principle one by one to strands of early Indonesian thought or social practices. He was not interested, for example, in attributing self-help notions to the exigencies of co-operation in agricultural labour or the need to cope with the vagaries of nature or any other historically grounded phenomenon. Soeharto seemed content to establish the patrimony and legacy of the ancient Indonesians as being little more than a form of deism.[15]

Having spoken up to this point almost exclusively about the Javanese without actually saying so, Soeharto then offered the Javanese alphabet as further proof of the wisdom of the ancient Indonesians. This alphabet, he stressed, was developed before either the Arabic or the Latin script reached Indonesia's shores,[16] and it contained the essence of Javanese philosophy. The first five letters, ha-na-ca-ra-ka, depicted human life beginning in embryo as a naked or empty spirit, which later acquired the capacity to think, to feel and to will. The next five, da-ta-sa-wa-la, meant that man also acquired good qualities and these were equalled in power by bad qualities, as the next five letters (pa-dha-ja-ya-nya) indicated. The last five letters, ma-ga-ba-tha-nga, meant that man lived as long as his soul and body were united but then died and returned to God.[17] When he had completed his account of the meaning of the Javanese alphabet, Soeharto commented: 'That's wonderful, isn't it? Is it clear... have you understood that?'

---

15   Mulder (1992, p.10) notes that, in Javanese thinking, real knowledge is personal insight into the nature of things and their relationships that cannot be formulated objectively. 'As a result, Javanese teachings should be full of symbolism and secret wisdom that stimulate fantasy and reflection.' This seems close to Soeharto's approach towards his guests. They will have acquired no concrete knowledge of Indonesia's past through listening to him. By contrast, on occasion, Soeharto prided himself on his ability at explaining concrete phenomena, such as agricultural production.

16   Apparently at pains to emphasise the original authenticity of the ancient Javanese, Soeharto made no reference to the Indian origins of the Javanese alphabet. The Javanese Soeharto used in this section is rather obscure, and the present writer acknowledges the help of George Quinn and of Prapti McLeod in deciphering it. In a personal communication, George Quinn notes that 'what Soeharto is saying is that the initial two letters of the alphabet represent life in its primordial or embryonic form. Into this primordial 'silence' or 'emptiness' (kasunyatan) come thought (cipta), sense perception (rasa) and will (karsa) represented in the letters ca-ra-ka.' The writer has also benefited from Quinn's analysis of ha-na-ca-ra-ka in his 'Ajisaka in the 21st Century', a paper presented to the workshop, 'Script as Identity Marker in Southeast Asia', organised by the Koninklijk Instituut voor Taal- Land- en Volkenkunde and the Lembaga Ilmu Pengetahuan Indonesia, Jakarta, 29 November–1 December 2004.

17   A more common reading of the Javanese alphabet comes from a folk-tale about one Aji Saka who travelled with two companions from the land 'Above the Wind'. The companions had an argument and embarked on a fight in which both died. Aji Saka invented the alphabet with the following poem to commemorate his friends: 'There were two messengers who never refused an order; of equal strength, they both died'. The interpretation of pa-dha-ja-ya-nya is the same in both Soeharto's rendering of the alphabet and the folk-tale's. See http://www.aseanstoriesproject.org/indonesia/story 4.php. Also see Hefner, 1990, Chapter Six.

The pioneering Javanese

Soeharto summarised the kernel of the wisdom of the ancient Indonesians as being submission to Almighty God. He then listed the tenets of the Central Java-based spiritual association, Pangestu,[18] as being awareness of God, belief in God and obedience to God. Pangestu was the only spiritual movement Soeharto cited in his talk to the KNPI. He then asked how such Javanese beliefs were compatible with religion. 'Well', he said, 'religion basically teaches the same thing'. But why was religion revealed (*diturunkan*) not in Indonesia but 'over there'.

> God indeed loves humankind and it was over there (*disitulah*) that God's position was not understood, wasn't it? Therefore God had to send his Prophet with all his revelations to lead the people who lived there to the right path. (The Prophet was sent) not just for those people, however, but for all of humankind. Although the Prophet was born in the Arab world, in the Middle East, he was tasked to speak to all of humankind in order to guide them to controlling their two conflicting passions.

Soeharto's implication was that the ancient Javanese were ahead of the Arabs in understanding God and did not need a prophet to be sent among them.[19] Moreover, the teaching that the Prophet was to impart had already been discovered by the Javanese.

At this point, Soeharto was referring exclusively to Islam, indeed even transposing to Islam a principal element of Javanese belief. His words do not suggest he also had Christianity's Middle Eastern origins in mind. Hinduism and Buddhism also escaped his attention here. This passage reinforces the impression that Soeharto's remarks to the KNPI should be seen as another chapter in Hinduised Java's centuries-old debate with Islam, rather than a consistent defence of imagined ancient Javanese beliefs against all foreign religions, including Christianity. Soeharto concluded this section of his remarks by saying that all Indonesians

---

18 Pangestu was set up in 1949 after its founder, Soenarto, had received three 'revelations' over a period of seventeen years. The revelations were published in two volumes, entitled Sasangka Jati [The True Origin] and Sabda Khusus [Special Words]. Soeharto used the words *eling*, *percaya* and *mituhu* to describe the three tenets. Non-Javanese among his listeners would not necessarily have understood the first and third of these terms. These concepts are translated as *sadar*, *percaya* and *taat* in Indonesian. See Kartodirdjo, 1988. With a founder, revelations and emphasis on submission to God, it is difficult to say in what terms Soeharto would have denied Pangestu was a religion as he had denied Pancasila would become one. In his autobiography, Soeharto contented himself with a brief and dispassionate account of Javanese mystical beliefs, saying that adherents of such beliefs had to choose one of the five legal religions (later increased to six). He dropped the reference to Pangestu. See Soeharto, 1989, pp.311–13.

19 If Soeharto is claiming in this passage that the Javanese embraced monotheism before the Arabs, his would be a minority view.

were free to choose their own religion while remaining individually responsible to Almighty God. 'Those who believe in Islam, let them choose Islam, those who believe in Christianity, let them choose Christianity.'

Slipping back into the role of political leader, Soeharto went on to describe how important it had been for Indonesia's harmony to reduce the nine political parties that had contested the parliamentary election in 1971. He still seemed to harbour resentment that politicians had resisted the fusion of parties, even though the large the number of parties in existence, the more ideologies had thrived. Now, he said, he was encountering the same kind of resistance to the adoption of Pancasila as the sole ideology. Soeharto claimed the Indonesian people had tasked him to simplify the party system as early as 1966, seven years before fusion of nine into two finally took place. But at least he could draw satisfaction from the respective material/spiritual and spiritual/material orientations of the two parties, that difference being a further example of the dualism he had outlined in explaining Javanese beliefs to the KNPI leaders. As for Golkar, it stood between the two political parties as it was based exclusively on Pancasila. The Armed Forces, for their part, would guide the people from behind (*tut wuri handayani*).

Soeharto concluded his evening talk by saying that he knew the ideas he had put across would be difficult for the non-Javanese in his audience to understand. What he had outlined, nonetheless, was the legacy of the early Indonesians, whether they were Javanese or not. He gave as a non-Javanese example the practice of *tepung tawar* in Aceh, which he said the Acehnese had been unable to abandon because it was so rooted in indigenous culture.[20] The Acehnese had adapted *tepung tawar* to Islam, he explained, by reading prayers to accompany it. Here, Soeharto was placing himself unequivocally in the Javanese syncretic tradition, which the modernist Muslim movement spearheaded by Muhammadiyah had combated throughout much of the century, and in the tradition of defending customary practices (*adat*). Indeed, he was offering the adherents of traditional practices frowned on by modernist reformers the argument that those practices were valid because they were indigenous and authentic. He also suggested that maybe the early Bataks in north Sumatra had likewise left 'pearls' behind them that could inspire national sentiment. He had instructed the managers of the P4 program to look out for all such legacies. P4 indoctrination would continue

---

20   *Tepung tawar* is known as *peusijeuk* (various spellings) in Acehnese. It is a traditional practice of showering dampened leaves over participants in ceremonies such as weddings. Tepung tawar is also found in various states of Malaysia and, with a different format, is a welcoming ceremony for visitors in East Kalimantan. Whether or not it is in conformity with Islam still troubles devout Acehnese. See http://www.eramuslim. com/ust/aqd/454f0342.htm.

into the indefinite future, he promised, in order to shape the outlook of the Indonesian people so that they would unfailingly believe in the truth of the sole ideology, Pancasila.[21]

Aftermath

Although it has not been possible to determine why Soeharto used the KNPI visit in July 1982 to expound these views, it is surely beyond question that the talk should be seen as a high-water mark of his advocacy of a view of Indonesia inspired by Javanese concepts. By 1985, he achieved his long-term goal of imposing Pancasila as the sole basis for social and political organisations. But, later in the 1980s, Soeharto seemed to shift ground. Worried that he was losing control over the Armed Forces, he gave new political opportunities to devout Muslims. He sponsored the establishment of the Association of Indonesian Muslim Intellectuals (Ikatan Cendekiawan Muslimin se-Indonesia, ICMI), under the leadership of his protégé, Habibie, and he began to tolerate more overt expressions of Islamic piety in daily life.[22] He himself embarked on a major pilgrimage with his family in 1991, returning from it bearing the new first name of Mohammad.[23] Soeharto even reportedly impressed members of his entourage with accurate pronunciation of Arabic, acquired as a teenager at a Muhammadiyah school in Central Java.[24] This shift may have gained greater plausibility because his KNPI talk, against which Soeharto's new discourse might have been compared, was never published.

It is uncertain whether this latter-day Islamic piety was exclusively politically driven, or whether Soeharto felt more relaxed about Islam after Pancasila's acceptance as the sole basis for social and political organisations. Surprising as this development was in view of his KNPI talk, there was not necessarily any inconsistency in his eyes. As noted above, Soeharto's first spiritual adviser, Daryatmo, was an expert in both the Koran and Javanese religion. As he aged, Soeharto may have sought to master the same broad-ranging spiritual knowledge

21 Mulder noted years ago that the P4 program was 'remarkably Javanese', with the government playing the role of a Javanese parent vis-à-vis the populace who were still *durung* Indonesia', not yet civilised in the proper Indonesian way. See Mulder, 1992, p.121.

22 See Aspinall, 2005, pp.39–41, for other aspects of Soeharto's changed stance towards Islam.

23 It is hard to understand why Soeharto failed to see the political value of undertaking a major pilgrimage until he had been formally in office for twenty-three years unless this delay shows how intensely opposed he had been to Muslim political aspirations and had seen them as a threat.

24 Interview with Nurcholish Madjid, who was quoting Habibie, Jakarta, 21 April 1997. Habibie may not have been the best qualified associate of Soeharto's to judge. His knowledge of German is better documented than his expertise in Arabic, and he was no authority on Islamic doctrine either. Soeharto said regrettably little about his Islamic education in his autobiography.

as Daryatmo.[25] Sukarno, moreover, had had a similarly eclectic outlook. It may be easier to move from immersion in Javanist beliefs towards the expression of greater Muslim piety than to go in the reverse direction.[26]

The imposition of Pancasila as the country's sole ideological basis, by which Soeharto put so much store, was a short-lived but disastrous achievement. It was eventually abandoned in the reformist momentum of 1998–99, when the rich ideological diversity of the natural Indonesian polity re-emerged almost in its entirety. P4 courses also ceased. The Pancasila-as-sole-basis campaign was in fact a de-stabilising initiative that, reinforcing Muslim feelings of being the principal victims of Soeharto's repression, prompted an upswing in Islamic radicalism and provided a casus belli for Darul Islam and later Jemaah Islamiyah leaders and militants. Abdullah Sungkar and Abu Bakar Ba'asyir gained early notoriety as opponents of the sole basis. Nor was the sole basis struggle necessarily helpful to nationalist forces. It is arguable that the glorification of Pancasila as an indigenous, superior belief system may also have impeded secular nationalist forces from modernising their ideology. In a speech on 29 November, 2006, Indonesian Democratic Party of Struggle (Partai Demokrasi Indonesia— Perjuangan, PDI-P) chair Megawati Soekarnoputri used words that Soeharto might well have been happy to insert into his KNPI talk. She criticised the new democratic system as being unduly reliant on voting rather than consensus. She asked whether Indonesians wanted a democracy that originated in Indonesia or one that came from 'who knows where?' Why criticise (her father's) Guided Democracy only to accept the (foreign-derived) democracy that Indonesia now had? (*Gatra*, 30 November, 2006).

Soeharto died in January 2008, almost a decade after his enforced resignation. So far no signs have emerged to suggest that Indonesians will attempt a major reappraisal of his life or presidency. For any such exercise, however, his KNPI talk would repay close attention as one of the most uncompromising statements of a Javanist outlook issued by an Indonesian power holder. It thus takes its place among key authoritarian New Order documents or doctrines such as the floating-mass, 'mono-loyalty' for the bureaucracy and the dual function for the Indonesian military.

---

25   Roeslan Abdulgani, who was probably the leading Pancasila ideologue and who remained close to Soeharto until his death in 2005, was a diligent reader of the Koran who also shared Soeharto's taste for quoting Javanese maxims.

26   Adopting a more strongly Islamic persona did not prevent Soeharto from continuing to engage in Javanese religious activities. He oversaw a cleansing ceremony (ruat bumi) on being informed that the 'nail of Java', located on Mount Tidar in Central Java, had come loose. See Friend, 2003, pp.261–63.

3 New Order Repression and the Birth of Jemaah Islamiyah

SIDNEY JONES

One argument about Islamic extremism goes something like this: among Sunni Muslims, particularly over the last two decades, one can find three strands of activism: religious outreach or *dakwah* to make Muslims better Muslims or convince them to purify their practices; political activism, or non-violent efforts to achieve power by political means; and jihadism, involving the use of violence to overthrow corrupt regimes, reclaim occupied land or wage war against the enemies of Islam, including the U.S. and its allies (ICG 2005). The surest way of encouraging jihadism is to cut out the possibility of political participation for Islamist organisations. Reduced to its simplest terms, governments with majority Muslim populations risk fuelling jihadism through repression. A corollary is that the cure for violent extremism is democracy that gives a voice to radical Islamists.

Although a nice theory, it has actually not been widely tested, and at first glance, Indonesia seems the perfect refutation. After all, it was only after Soeharto fell and the political system opened up that JI began to engage in acts of violence on Indonesian soil. But if we go back to the 1970s, it gets more interesting, because it was under the Soeharto government at this time that three factors came together in a way that ultimately produced the Bali bombers.

One issue was the decision by the Indonesian intelligence agency BAKIN to help resuscitate Darul Islam (DI) at a critical juncture in the early New Order. The original DI had largely collapsed after the arrest and execution of its leader, S.M. Kartosoewirjo, in 1962. Surviving leaders of the movement had come together on their own, but BAKIN provided critical funding, in the hope that the DI network would become a Golkar asset. That was not New Order repression; it was New Order hubris that it could control and co-opt an organisation that had fought the Indonesian state for more than a decade in the 1950s and early 1960s. It was a revived DI that was later to give JI much of its organisational base inside Indonesia.

But the second factor was the suppression of Muslim political parties in a way that not only denied Indonesian Islamists any role in the government but made them the target of active repression, particularly in the lead up to the 1971 elections. It is questionable whether a man like Abdullah Sungkar, JI's founder, would have made common cause with DI if the New Order government had allowed a party like Masyumi, the largest Muslim party before its banning by Sukarno in 1960, or any party headed by Mohammad Natsir, to function freely.

The third was the direct result of the first two: the grafting on to a revived insurgency of that disenfranchised Islamist elite's attributes, including an internationalist outlook, access to funds and contacts, salafist inclinations, and intellectual power. The Indonesian Islamic Propagation Council (Dewan Dakwah Islamiyah Indonesia, DDII), founded by Natsir in 1967, had all those characteristics, and the fusion of DI and DDII proved potent. Banning independent Muslim parties also meant the removal of any meaningful political role for the youth organisations that shared their goals, such as the Indonesian Youth Movement (Gerakan Pemuda Islam, GPI) and Indonesian Islamic Youth (Pemuda Islam Indonesia, PII)—hence the attraction of a militant, clandestine movement that the fused DI-Sungkar alliance became.

By itself, DI could not have produced JI. It was a parochial, ideologically unsophisticated guerrilla movement with no significant international connections. Without the New Order restrictions on political expression that propelled a highly educated, modernist Muslim urban elite into its arms, DI would have remained an ongoing but very localised problem. So here are two imponderables. If Indonesia's democratic transition had begun in the 1980s instead of the 1990s, would we still have JI? And if we still have JI seven years after Soeharto's downfall, does that mean that the thesis that political liberalisation helps curb terrorism is wishful thinking, or is there a time lag that has to be factored in before the effects of liberalisation are felt?

Examining the three factors mentioned above may help provide answers.

The resuscitation of DI

One of the worst mistakes made by the Soeharto government was Ali Moertopo's decision, against the better judgment of others in BAKIN, to help revive and consolidate the DI leadership in 1971 (Conboy 2006:16–19). Moertopo and others, including Col. Pitut Suharto, thought they could use DI as a tool for bringing in the Golkar vote and promoting an anti-Communist stance at the same time. After all, here was an organisation that BAKIN thought it controlled and that had a clear constituency in Java, which was the real target of BAKIN's efforts to create the Golkar machine. It had proven anti-Communist credentials and at least one senior leader—Danu Muhammad Hasan—was on the BAKIN payroll (Pranoto 1978:32).

The political protection and the money given to DI at that stage paved the way for the re-establishment of a national base for the organisation, or at least one that extended to Java, Sumatra, and Sulawesi. It set in motion events that led to the establishment of Komando Jihad in Sumatra, the disillusionment of DI with Moertopo's promises, and the discovery of shared interests between DI and other opponents of Soeharto's rule, particularly from the ex-Masyumi camp.

Darul Islam came back to life as an organisation, one dedicated to the establishment of an Islamic state, just before the government forced existing Muslim parties to amalgamate in January 1973, thus creating the United Development Party (Partai Persatuan Pembangunan, PPP). Its revival also preceded a critical debate began in Indonesia over a proposed marriage law that would have allowed Muslim women to marry non-Muslim men and had other provisions that were anathema to the Muslim puritans in Indonesia. These issues clearly left their mark on the organisation.

But as late as 1976, with the 1977 elections on the horizon, Moertopo reportedly believed he could still use former DI members as a machine to turn out Golkar votes, and was unperturbed by the fact that DI had used the political space available to form a military organisation that engaged in a series of attacks on civilian targets from Medan to Solo, later to become known as Komando Jihad (Conboy 2006:16–19). All of BAKIN's contacts were with the generation of men who surrendered after 1962; it appeared to be oblivious to the fact that these men had taken advantage of widespread unhappiness in Muslim ranks to recruit a new generation; that the DI message had already spread beyond its original base; and that the old and new members were anything but supportive of the New Order.

One of the people drawn into DI in the mid-1970s was Timsar Zubil, then secretary of the North Sumatra branch of a Masyumi-affiliated student group, PII. In 1976, Timsar launched one of the first salvos in the Komando Jihad campaign, the bombing of a movie theatre and two churches in Medan. He was tried and sentenced to death in 1978, had his sentence commuted to life, and was released in 1999 when Habibie freed political prisoners. In an interview in 2001, he cited several factors for why DI decided in 1976 to apply 'shock therapy' to the New Order in the form of these bombings. These included the formation of the PPP and the dissolution of parties with a genuine mass Islamic base; the refusal of the Soeharto government to recognise the results of the

Parmusi[1] election in 1974 and its retention of a discredited party leadership; the controls placed on preaching activities and other Islamic gatherings; and almost as an afterthought, the spread of vice and dens of iniquity (*tempat maksiat*) (*Darul Islam* January-February 2001:28–30). The political element was clear. Parenthetically, it is also interesting that he chose a few churches to bomb—an action for which he apologised for many years later. But it suggests that the influence of DDII—an organisation with a strong anti-Christian streak—was already beginning to make itself felt on the DI organisation.

The Sungkar factor

It was Abdullah Sungkar who embodied the DI-DDII connection as much as anyone else. A member of a long-established, relatively well-to-do family of Yemeni extraction involved in the batik trade, Sungkar's relationship with DDII Solo almost certainly preceded his involvement with DI. As a student, he had been a member of GPI, one of the more radical student organisations; he would have been directly affected by the banning of Masyumi in 1960, when he was 23.

He and Ba'asyir joined forces in 1967 to set up a radio station in Solo that was shut down by the New Order in 1975 for its anti-government harangues. In March 1977, he was arrested without warrant or charge and detained in Semarang for 48 days for urging his followers not to vote in that year's elections—among other things because the Soeharto government did not allow two candidates who should have been running, in his view, Mohammed Natsir and Mohammed Roem, on the ballot.[2]

Both men had been prominent Masyumi leaders and were the natural choices to head a new party, the Partai Muslimin Indonesia (Parmusi), that Soeharto reluctantly allowed to emerge in 1968. But because Natsir and a few other Masyumi notables—not Roem—had supported a regional rebellion in West Sumatra in 1958, Soeharto refused to countenance any political revival of Masyumi as an institution or its former leaders as individuals. The condition for Parmusi's creation was that no one from Masyumi have a leadership role. Roem was nevertheless elected general chairman in late 1968. In 1970, prior to the 1971 elections, Soeharto engineered his ouster, replaced him with a pliant apparatchik, and in 1973 forced the merger of Parmusi and other Islamic parties to form the PPP (Ward 1970; Samson 1973).

---

1 Parmusi (Partai Muslimin Indonesia) was the 'successor' party to Masyumi.
2 'Ideologi Negara Pancasila Gerakan Komunisme dan Ajaran Islam didepan Sidang Pengadilan Negeri Sukoharjo: Suatu Eksepsi', 20 Februari 1982 and in Berita Acara Pemeriksaan Abu Bakar Ba'asyir and Abdullah Sungkar, No.1/Pid.Subv/1982/P.N. Skh. In his defence plea, Sungkar denies urging others not to vote but defends his own decision not to take part.

Sungkar was fiercely political, and had genuinely independent Islamic political parties been allowed under the New Order, he almost certainly would have signed up. At the trial of Sungkar and Ba'asyir in 1982, the prosecutor accused the two men of not raising the Indonesian flag raising at their school, Pesantren al-Mukmin, better known as Pondok Ngruki, as all schools were required to do. They were also accused of not inviting the village head to attend events there; of undermining Pancasila; and of holding religious study sessions (*pengajian*) where they slandered Indonesian officials and urged villagers to disobey man-made, as opposed to Islamic, law. Soeharto's intelligence apparatus had plants at these sessions who instantly reported back to the district military command.

Sungkar used his defence plea to blast the New Order for what he considered to be its sins since it came to power in 1966. The long list represents as trenchant a criticism of the New Order as many of the documents produced by the 1978 student movement, which had been crushed four years earlier (Akhmadi 1981). It included:

- Engineering the 1970 'coup' against the Parmusi leadership;
- 'Hijacking' of another Muslim party, United Islam Indonesia Party (Partai Serikat Islam Indonesia, PSII) in 1972. PSII's leader at the time was opposed to the creation of the PPP, so, according to Sungkar, Ali Moertopo engineered his removal and broadcast the manipulated election on national television. Sungkar contrasts this with the government's more subtle intervention in 1970 in the Congress of the old Sukarnoist Indonesian National Party (Partai Nasional Indonesia, PNI.)
- Manipulating political parties in general;
- Controlling mass organisations, including those representing journalists, farmers, fishermen, workers and youth. Sungkar documents how the New Order, in the name of creating professional federations, succeeded in creating monolithic 'fusions' that served as an arm of the government. Regarding the founding of the National Indonesian Youth Committee (Komite Nasional Pemuda Indonesia, KNPI), he notes that the only organisations that did not join were the two associated with the old Masyumi: Indonesian Youth Movement (Gerakan Pemuda Indonesia, GPI) and PII;
- Controlling parliament, so that only after political parties had been brought into line was an election law passed that gave the Indonesian Armed Forces 100 appointed seats;
- Manipulating the 1971 and 1977 elections and the blacklisting of 2,500 former members of the Masyumi party;
- Introducing the concept of 'mono-loyalty' for civil servants, meaning they had no choice other than to support Golkar, the New Order's political machine;

- Carrying out arrests, detentions, torture, rape and other violations against members of political parties during the 1971 campaign. (Here he cites Abraham Lincoln—except that it was actually circus founder, PT Barnum—that 'you can fool some of the people all of the time and all of the people some of the time but you can't fool all of the people all of the time.') [3]
- Failing to apply the Jakarta Charter, which would constitutionally require Muslims to carry out Islamic law;
- Cynically controlling, through the Ministry of Religion of the pilgrimage to Mecca at the same time its officials were going overseas and engage in gambling, prostitution, and adultery without any restrictions;
- Refusing to release students from school during Ramadan the Muslim fasting month;
- Holding the closing ceremonies of the 1979 Asian Games in Jakarta at a time that coincided with evening prayer and drew children to television sets instead of the mosque;
- Placing schools and mosques and all religious activities under the surveillance of the internal security apparatus, Kopkamptib;
- Treating Pancasila and government symbols like the flag as sacred and turning Indonesia into a totalitarian state;
- Encouraging animism and primitive beliefs. This was a reference to the government's 1977 decision to recognise Javanese beliefs (*aliran kepercayaan*) as being consistent with 'belief in one God', the first principle of Indonesia's state ideology, Pancasila (Bresnan 1993:194–97);
- Closing the old Masyumi newspaper *Harian Abadi* in 1974 while Catholic and Protestant newspapers like *Kompas* and *Sinar Harapan* are allowed to continue;
- Detaining Muslim preachers who criticise the government. Among several names mentioned are Syafruddin Prawiranegara and AM Fatwa, individuals involved in the 'Petition of 50', a 1980 statement critical of Soeharto;
- The dissolution of student organisations in 1978 by Daud Joesoef, then education minister; and
- Passing the 1974 marriage law, noted above.

It is difficult to imagine anyone from the circle of Kartosoewirjo's ex-fighters serving up such a detailed political rant. This does not sound like Darul Islam— it sounds more like what it was, the complete frustration of an Islamist politician decisively and permanently excluded from the system. The only thing missing is a call to revolution.

---

3 Sungkar defence plea, 1982, p.8.

That is where DI comes in. By the time he read out that statement in court, Sungkar had been a DI member for at least six years and in detention for half that time. At some stage, he must have consciously decided to use DI as a vehicle for bringing down the Soeharto government, especially since it offered a national network, an unimpeachable legacy and mystique, and a cadre of experienced guerrillas. There is no evidence that Sungkar had any immediate plans for armed rebellion—he was too smart for that, and in any case most of the DI leadership had been arrested in a crackdown between 1978 and 1982. But the Soeharto government's treatment of him and other political activists set him on a course of active opposition, using the DI structure to build an Islamic base through a cadre recruitment program pioneered by the Muslim Brotherhood's Hasan al-Banna called *usroh*.

Sungkar and Ba'asyir were sentenced to nine years but released on a technicality almost as soon as their trial concluded, and they had two years to try and build their base, mostly in Central Java and Jakarta, before the prospect of re-arrest loomed. At that point, the two men fled to Malaysia.

In Malaysia, the DI-DDII-ex-Masyumi alliance comes full circle. One of Sungkar and Ba'asyir's first visitors was Abdul Wahid Kadungga, a DDII activist, personal secretary to Natsir and, for good measure, the son-in-law of the leader of the DI rebellion in South Sulawesi, Kahar Muzakkar (Conboy 2006:42–43; ICG 2003). Kadungga had just come from meeting with Abdullah Azzam in Pakistan at a time when Saudi money was beginning to become available in large quantities to send foreign fighters to Afghanistan. The money was channelled through the Rabitat al-Alam al-Islami, the World Muslim League, and its vice-president was Natsir, Kadungga's boss.

Thus began Sungkar's program of sending Indonesians for training to Afghanistan, financed by the Rabitat, with the aim of building up the capacity of Indonesian Muslims to take on the Soeharto government militarily. The first batch of recruits, including Zulkarnaen, the man who became head of Jemaah Islamiyah's military operations, were not DI members. They were GPI members who only later joined DI.

If it had been only ex-fighters of the DI rebellion in West Java, Aceh, or South Sulawesi who had gone to Malaysia in 1985 (and there were some), would they have been able to build the base among Malaysians and Singaporeans that Sungkar and his followers succeeded in doing? Probably not—there were few in DI ranks, at least of that generation, that had the religious knowledge or political savvy of Sungkar. The men he brought with him to Malaysia were mostly from the Yogya-Solo area who honed their preaching skills at a mosque associated with Gajah Mada University, one of Indonesia's premier secular institutions, and were well-versed in the writings of al-Banna and al-Maududi.

That internationalist outlook almost certainly ended up being a factor in the ability to recruit non-Indonesians—a factor that was to have major implications for the growth of JI.

The disaffection of the 1980s and the *usroh* movement

The explosion of the *usroh* movement on Indonesian college campuses in the late 1970s and early 1980s further fused the DI and Islamist agendas. The idea, first proposed by Hasan al-Banna of the Egyptian Muslim Brotherhood, was to gather groups of ten to fifteen people—called *usroh*, ('family' in Arabic)—who were prepared to live strictly according to Islamic law. If enough *usroh* groups were formed, they could constitute the building blocks of an Islamic state. The idea took hold in 1977, when apparently independently, two groups circulated manuals on how to form *usroh* groups. One was a network of mosque-based youth in which GPI and PII were well represented, which quickly drew in university-based activists; the other was the Ngruki pesantren, which took the lead in forming *usroh* groups in Central Java.

The movement's popularity can be understood in part as the consequence of having no other vehicles for political expression at a time when there was huge ferment in the Muslim world—and the formation of these groups exploded exponentially after the Iranian revolution of 1979. If political parties had been allowed to exist, *usroh* might have led to the creation of something akin to the Muslim Brotherhood-inspired Prosperous and Justice Party (Partai Keadilan Sejahtera, PKS) twenty years earlier, without any association with DI. But Sungkar and Ba'asyir, who began forming *usroh* groups before they fled to Malaysia, understood the potential of what was effectively the creation of a cell structure for religious and political objectives, and they turned it into a recruitment mechanism for DI.

The movement reached its height between 1983 and 1985, a consequence both of the Iranian revolution, and of the anger against the Soeharto government for its declaration in 1984 that henceforth only Pancasila and not Islam or any other religion or ideology, could serve as the ideological basis for mass organisations in Indonesia.

Testimony from JI members arrested in 2003 for trying to recruit and train a new special forces unit in the aftermath of the 2002 Bali bombs attests to the importance of these groups in the mid- to late 1980s for bringing new people into the DI organisation, including many who were later sent to Afghanistan or Mindanao for training, or who ended up fighting in the conflicts in Ambon and

Poso. They tapped into grievances of Islamist organisations whose exclusion from the body politic was, if anything, even more pronounced than it had been a decade earlier.

Conclusion

At the height of the New Order, then, we have the organisation that was later to become JI taking shape. Darul Islam gave it the historical tradition, a basic structure, and the goal of creating an Islamic state in Indonesia; Sungkar and DDII gave it the puritanical inclination and the internationalist outlook. The *usroh* gave it a new kind of cell structure and a method of recruitment. That conjoining of factors was, if not caused by, at least facilitated by the lack of other independent organisations that could channel anti-government and Islamist aspirations.

So, there are two questions left: if the New Order had not destroyed political parties—or continued the destruction begun by Sukarno—would JI exist today?

The war in Afghanistan would still have occurred; Indonesians would still have gone there to train. But the non-DI people went by and large to help the Afghans—not to acquire the capacity to take on Soeharto. They returned as individuals, without any particular incentive to marshal their skills for an organisational goal, although the bond among them was such that someone with determination and charisma might well have been able to mobilise them for collective action.

Communal conflicts in places like Ambon and Poso would still have erupted and militias mobilised along religious lines would still have emerged. This would almost certainly have created local militias like the Makassar-based Laskar Jundullah, but it is highly unlikely whether such conflicts by themselves could have generated a transnational organisation.

DI would still have existed, and DI will still splinter for a long time to come. But whether men like Sungkar and the first generation of Afghan alumni would have been drawn into DI, and whether DI would have been drawn into salafi jihadism, if the New Order had been less repressive, is another question.

Sungkar and others who joined DI in the late 1970s were reacting to more than just the New Order's stifling insistence on political control. Political Islam was defined as the enemy, the extreme right, juxtaposed with Communism, the extreme left. Islamic books and newspapers were banned, activists calling for application of Islamic law arrested. The recognition of Javanese beliefs as a religion was a calculated move by Soeharto's advisers to reduce the percentage of people identifying themselves as Muslim and therefore the level of government assistance to mosques and Islamic schools (Liddle 1978). The association of 'pure Islam' with regional rebellions was still very much present in the minds of Soeharto and his military advisers more than 20 years after the Revolutionary Government of the Republic of Indonesia (Pemerintah Revolusi Republic Indonesia, PRRI) rebellion in West Sumatra—and Moertopo's courting of the West Java DI members notwithstanding. What some ex-Masyumi members were experiencing was not just a curb here and there on freedom of expression or political participation; it was systematic persecution. And it backfired more dramatically than Soeharto or Moertopo ever could have imagined.

4 Managing Industrialisation in a Globalising Economy: Lessons from the Soeharto Era

HAL HILL AND DIONISIUS NARJOKO

One of the first decisions of the Soeharto administration was to re-engage with the global economy through a series of sweeping policy liberalisations. As a result, since the late 1960s Indonesia has been a largely open economy, and it has industrialised rapidly during most of this period. These two observations—openness and rapid industrialisation—immediately raise a number of interesting and important analytical questions, for the country itself, for any evaluation of the Soeharto regime, and for development issues more generally.

For example, are these events connected and, if so, which way does the causality flow? More generally, how has increased integration into the global economy affected Indonesian industrialisation and economic development? It is a well-established proposition that more open economies generally grow more rapidly. But, equally, they are more vulnerable to sudden changes in the global economy, including especially external shocks. Moreover, answers to these questions shed light on the central question of this volume, concerning Soeharto's record and his legacy.

The 'general case' is of course an average of a highly diverse set of individual country observations. To gain deeper insights into these global-national interactions, detailed country case studies are an important supplement. Indonesia provides much illuminating material on these issues.[1] Therefore, the purpose of this chapter is to examine the record of Indonesian industrialisation since the 1960s as the country became increasing integrated within the global economy. Two particular episodes are highlighted. First, we examine the three decades of rapid industrial growth and structural change during the Soeharto period, characterised by the adoption of broadly 'orthodox' economic policies and in the context of a largely benign and supportive international economic

---

1   We draw in particular on Hill, 1997 for an analysis of the Soeharto era industrialisation, and Narjoko, 2006 for a detailed, firm-level examination of the crisis impacts. See also Bird and Hill, 2006.

environment. We then focus on the second episode, the impact of the deep economic crisis of 1997–98, and its immediate aftermath of painful restructuring and slower economic growth. We conclude by drawing some general lessons for Indonesia, and other developing economies, concerning the management of industrialisation strategies in an open economy.

At the outset, it needs to be emphasised that Soeharto presided over a remarkable industrial transformation of the country. For much of his period of rule, and certainly after the fading of the oil boom, industry was the leading sector of the economy. Its share of GDP and employment trebled and doubled respectively during this period. Real output rose approximately 18-fold. For the first time in its history, a sizeable factory sector emerged, and Indonesia became a significant industrial exporter. As we shall see below, for a complex set of economic and political reasons, post-Soeharto regimes have had difficulty matching these accomplishments.

The New Order period: rapid industrialisation, 1967–97

We highlight here four key features of industrialisation in the Soeharto era: growth, rapid structural change, the 1980s reforms and the shift to export orientation, and ownership patterns.

In the mid-1960s, Indonesia had barely commenced the process of modern industrialisation. It lagged well behind its Asian neighbours, experiencing neither the state-orchestrated heavy industrialisation of China and India, nor the export-oriented growth then getting under way in the Asian NIEs. Its modern industrial sector, such as it was, was dominated by a few large state-owned enterprises, which in most cases had been established by Dutch commercial interests before the Pacific War, and subsequently taken over by the state as part of the 1957–58 nationalisations.

First, Indonesia experienced very rapid industrialisation and structural change through to 1997, a sudden and sharp contraction in 1998, and slower growth thereafter (Table 4.1). Annual industrial growth was at least 9 per cent in all but two of the 27 years, 1970–96. Initially, catch-up and import substitution were the principal drivers. There was a decade of oil-driven growth, and the beginnings of a brief and costly heavy industry strategy. From the mid-1980s, labour-intensive exports became a significant engine of growth. This growth came to an abrupt halt with the crisis of 1997–98. The contraction in the manufacturing sector was about the same as for the economy as a whole. Thereafter, positive growth has been recorded from 1999, but at lower rates than pre-crisis.

Table 4.1: Economic Growth by Sector, 1970–2006

	1970–84	1985–97	1997–98	1999–06
Tradable	*5.1*	*5.4*	*-1.7*	*3.5*
Agriculture	3.7	2.9	-0.2	2.9
Mining and Quarrying	4.9	2.7	-0.3	0.6
Manufacturing	11.4	10.3	-3.1	4.9
Non-Tradable	*9.5*	*7.4*	*-6.6*	*5.4*
Construction	13.0	9.7	-14.5	5.5
Financial	11.1	8.1	-10.3	4.7
Transport and Communication	11.1	7.5	-4.1	9.6
Electricity, Gas and Water Supply	12.8	13.7	7.7	6.9
Trade, Hotel and Restaurant	8.0	7.5	-6.2	4.9
Services	8.0	4.6	-0.1	4.0
GDP	6.7	6.3	-4.2	4.4

Second, accompanying this growth has been rapid structural change, as the industrial sector evolved from the production of simple consumer goods and basic resource processing to a wide range of manufactures of increasing technological sophistication. As noted, the process of modern industrialisation did not commence in Indonesia until the late 1960s. From 1965 to 1997, the share of the industrial sector in GDP more than trebled (Table 4.2). Within it, non-oil manufacturing grew very rapidly, its share of GDP more than doubling from 1980 to 1997. Since the crisis, the share of industry has remained broadly stable, with a slight dip in 1998–99 when resources returned to agriculture as a crisis-survival strategy.

Table 4.2: Share of GDP by Major Economic Sectors 1970–2006 (%)

	1970	1985	1999	2006
Tradable	*72.3*	*56.7*	*53.0*	*51.1*
Agriculture	55.3	22.7	17.1	14.1
Mining and Quarrying	6.6	18.2	9.7	9.1
Manufacturing	10.4	15.8	26.1	27.8
Non-Tradable	*27.7*	*43.3*	*47.0*	*48.9*
Construction	3.1	5.3	5.8	6.1
Financial	0.0	6.4	6.9	9.2
Transport and Communication	3.6	5.3	7.1	6.7
Electricity, Gas and Water Supply	0.6	0.4	1.6	0.7
Trade, Hotel and Restaurant	20.5	14.6	15.8	16.9
Services	0.0	11.3	9.8	9.2
GDP	100.0	100.0	100.0	100.0

Within manufacturing, structural change has been equally rapid. Since 1975, when the industrial structure began to be measured on a regular and reasonably accurate basis, there has been a shift towards a more diversified industrial structure. The major labour-intensive and footloose industries grew rapidly during the export phase. Wood products expanded fast in response to the prohibition on the export of unprocessed timber, before encountering environmental constraints in the 1990s. Heavy industry grew quickly through to the mid-1980s in response to protection and major state investments. Within machinery and equipment, the auto industry grew rapidly under the impetus of prohibitive protection for most of the Soeharto period, but collapsed in 1998–99. Electronics has become increasingly important and export-oriented, but never as prominent as in neighbouring East Asian economies.

Third, Indonesia became a significant industrial exporter from the mid-1980s. In retrospect, the 1980s was a crucial period in Indonesian economic history. At the beginning of the decade, as oil prices first tapered off, and then fell sharply, the country was highly exposed to the international oil market. Oil, gas and related minerals provided about two-thirds of government revenue and almost three-quarters of merchandise exports. Indonesia could well have followed other major developing OPEC members—notably Mexico and Nigeria—into a debt crisis.[2] Instead, the decline in oil prices triggered a major reassessment of trade and industry policy. The political economy pendulum swung in favour of the technocrats and their supporters who advocated a more liberal economic agenda, including reduced protection, a more open posture towards foreign investment, and simplified export procedures (Basri and Hill 2004).

Initially, manufactured exports were concentrated in resource-based activities, especially plywood, reflecting the country's natural resource endowments and the prohibition of unprocessed commodities (Table 4.3). Its industrial export base began to widen significantly as the reforms took hold, with textiles, garments, footwear, electronics, furniture, sporting goods and toys also registering rapid growth. The share of labour-intensive products in total manufactured exports increased in the wake of the 1980s reforms, from about 45 per cent in the mid-1980s to 61 per cent by 1996. Export growth then tapered off in the post-reform period, mainly due to slower demand in Indonesia's major export destinations. Increased competition in export markets, a slackening in the reform momentum, slower productivity growth and the real rupiah appreciation around the mid-1990s were also contributing factors.

---

2   See Gelb and Associates, 1988 for a comparative assessment of the management of the 1970s oil boom in selected developing countries. Indonesia emerges as the country which most effectively recycled its windfall oil boom revenues, and which adjusted most quickly to the downturn in prices.

Table 4.3: Exports by Factor Intensity Groupings, 1980–2005 (% or $ Million)

		1980	1985	1990	1995	2000	2005
Resource Intensive		142	1,090	3,641	6,283	6,937	7,555
% Share of total manufacturing		29	55	41	28	20	19
Major Item(s)							
641	Paper and paperboard	0	21	123	731	1,745	2,030
634	Veneers, plywood, etc.	68	941	2,785	3,825	2,287	1,669
635	Wood manufactures nes	5	11	274	837	939	1,001
625	Rubber tyres, tubes, etc.	0	7	66	182	293	650
522	Inorganic chemical elements, oxides, etc	2	35	27	68	172	388
Labour Intensive		165	617	4,167	10,226	13,100	13,523
% Share of total manufacturing		34	31	47	45	38	34
Major Item(s)							
821	Furniture and parts thereof	3	7	286	864	1,528	1,862
651	Textile yarn	3	13	109	813	1,327	1,622
843	Women's outwear non-knit	24	115	471	886	1,324	1,361
851	Footwear	1	8	561	1,998	1,605	1,348
845	Outer garments knit non-elastic	2	26	389	621	896	1,129
Capital Intensive		185	301	1,378	6,803	12,561	14,147
% Share of total manufacturing		38	14	13	27	42	47
Major Items(s)							
752	Automatic data processing equip't	0	0	0	170	2,018	1,850
763	Sound recorders, phonographs	0	0	2	693	823	1,275
764	Telecom equip, parts, accessories	1	7	60	389	1,752	1,157
778	Electrical machinery nes	3	1	65	387	662	1,129
772	Switchgear etc, parts nes	1	0	0	106	471	1,128
		491	2,007	9,186	23,312	32,598	35,225
		100	100	100	100	100	100

These reforms 'worked' in the sense that there was the strong and immediate export response observed above. Indonesia grew quickly out of the early 1980s recession and, although external debt rose sharply in the mid-1980s, debt/GDP ratios remained comfortable, and began declining from the end of the decade. The reforms were also good for equity, as employment expanded significantly in the new export-oriented factories on Java. For the first time in its history, Indonesia became 'East Asian' in the sense of emerging as a major industrial exporter.

A fourth feature is the country's ownership patterns, which are unusual in some respects. There are high levels of ownership concentration, both in the sense of corporate conglomeration and seller concentration. Claessens et al (2000) have documented the former, finding that Indonesia exhibited the highest level of corporate concentration in East Asia in 1996, with the top 10 families owning 57.7 per cent of listed corporate assets.[3] In terms of plant-level industrial concentration, Bird (1999) found high levels of concentration, typical of those in relatively small, late-industrialising economies. Over the period 1975–93, concentration levels were declining steadily, though in the latter year the simple average 4-firm concentration ratio was still 54 per cent. Concentration ratios were significantly lower once allowance is made for imports.

Indonesia's industrial ownership patterns reflect the interplay of history, policy and industrial organisation factors. In the mid-1960s, no foreign capital was present, and the 'commanding heights' of the economy, such as they were, were in state hands. The state-owned enterprise (SOE) sector continued to be important throughout the Soeharto era. Indeed, there were never any significant privatisations, in any of the country's three modern economic crises, that is, in the mid-1960s, the mid-1980s, and the late 1990s. The oil boom period financed a major expansion in the SOE sector, initially in heavy industry, and later the Habibie high-tech projects. Meanwhile, foreign investment returned to the country from the late 1960s in response to the newly liberal policy regime and generous fiscal incentives. Initially, most of it went into import substituting 'tariff factories'. Then, responding to the reform signals in the first half of the 1980s, efficiency-seeking, export-oriented investments became more important.

As is the case in most countries, domestic firms are the major players in Indonesian industry. They account for more than 50 per cent of manufacturing value added in all 2-digit industries except ISIC 38 (fabricated metals, dominated by electronics) and the relatively minor ISIC 39 (miscellaneous manufacturing). They also employ most of the industrial workforce in aggregate (79 per cent),

---

3   That is, in terms of the shares of its leading conglomerates in output and capitalisation. Note, however, that the mid-1990s data were dominated by Soeharto-linked conglomerates that have since been largely dismantled, and thus the figure would be lower now.

including at least one-half in all 2-digit industries. Among domestic firms, SOEs are important in certain 'strategic' industries, such as fertilizer, steel and cement, together with some firms that were inherited from the pre-1966 nationalisations (eg, sugar processing) and never subsequently relinquished. During the recent crisis, the SOE sector in general contracted, especially in the case of the prestige projects, which were heavily dependent on direct government support. Other firms have been accidentally nationalised as part of the 1997–98 financial crisis, but the government has indicated that it intends to divest most of them.

Foreign ownership has risen steadily since the economy was opened up in the late 1960s. The share of these firms in non-oil manufacturing value added rose from about 23 per cent in 1975 to 29 per cent in 1995 (Table 4.4). The share rose higher still in the wake of the crisis, in response to policy liberalisations and the opportunity for foreign firms to buy distressed local assets. Moreover, as we will document below, foreign firms have been better able to endure the crisis. As is evident in the 2-digit ownership data, and consistent with industrial organisation theory, multi-national enterprises (MNE)s are important in ISIC 38, dominated by electronics and the automotive industry. They are also important in basic metals (principally steel and related products), the chemical industries, and a few labour-intensive activities (textiles, garments, footwear and miscellaneous manufactures) where knowledge of export markets is important.

Table 4.4: Share of Foreign Ownership in Manufacturing Value Added (%)

Sector	1980	1985	1990	1995	2000	2004
All sectors	30	22	22	29	39	36
31. Food and beverages	21	12	8	11	16	22
32. TCF	22	29	17	24	35	34
33. Wood products	12	13	10	12	9	14
34. Paper products	13	9	30	32	12	28
35. Chemicals	42	27	34	41	46	33
36. Non-metal products	55	41	21	25	38	35
37. Iron and steel	32	19	24	43	39	24
38. Machinery, autos etc	44	29	46	44	66	63
39. Other	60	41	20	62	48	30

After the New Order: deep crisis and adjustment since 1997

As we have seen, the industrial sector contracted very sharply in 1998, at about the same rate as the economy as a whole. Its recovery since then has been at about the same rate as other sectors. This is largely as would be expected: unless there are large, sector-specific events (such as an oil boom), or a very rapid loss in comparative advantage (as has occurred in agriculture in some very high-growth, resource-poor economies), economy-wide factors are the major determinant of sectoral growth rates.

But what is of particular interest, and the focus of this section, is whether (and if so why) the crisis affected industries and firms more or less uniformly. Both theory and intuition would suggest that the effects would be uneven. There were three major events at the time of the crisis: a very sharp contraction in growth rates, from about 7 per cent per annum pre-crisis to -13 per cent in 1998; a collapse in the dollar exchange rate, from about Rp2500 to below Rp10,000 (and bottoming out at Rp17,500); and the near collapse of the formal financial sector. Given that the manufacturing sector comprises a collection of highly heterogeneous enterprises in terms of key attribute—age, size, technology, ownership patterns, sales orientation, debt-structure, location, not to mention entrepreneurial propensities—it would be very surprising if all firms responded to these major events in a similar fashion. For example, a firm that was capital-intensive, highly leveraged to US dollar denominated debt, and selling primarily in the domestic market would be among the most severely affected. This was broadly the case among, for example, steel and auto producers. By contrast, labour-intensive firms with low debt and exporting most of their output would be expected to be largely unaffected by the crisis; in fact to even benefit from it owing to the highly favourable exchange-rate movements from mid-1997. Such an outcome, with a lag, could be observed among some of the country's garment exporters, for example.

More formally, if the impact of the crisis was uneven across firms, what factors—what firm and industry attributes—might be expected to have shaped firm-level responses to the crisis? We hypothesise the following:

Sales orientation of firms: Export-oriented firms are expected to perform better than domestic-oriented ones. This is principally because the former are able to take advantage of the boost to competitiveness from the sharp exchange-rate depreciation. Moreover, and importantly for Indonesia's recovery, unlike eras of generalised recession the global economy continued to be buoyant over this period.

Ownership: Foreign firms should be less affected. They have 'deeper pockets', are less connected to the failing domestic financial sector and, with their global market reach and knowledge, they are able to quickly facilitate sales redirection from domestic to export markets.

Size: The impact on firms of differing size is not clear. Large firms might be expected to be more competitive, owing to economies of scale and stronger financial resources. Yet, in the face of extreme shocks to the business environment, small firms are sometimes more flexible and nimble, they are less 'top heavy', and they may be less heavily indebted.

Industry: Firms in labour- and natural-intensive industries should be less affected compared to those in capital-intensive industries. Exchange rate movements will be expected to reinforce Indonesia's comparative advantage in these activities, particularly in the case of the high domestic value-added resource-based industries. Firms in these industries are also more likely to be export-oriented, and thus they have a 'head start' in shifting to exports. By contrast, firms in capital-intensive industries, in which Indonesia does not typically have a comparative advantage, are more likely to be domestic-market oriented, more likely to receive import protection (which was generally lowered during the crisis), and they are more likely to be heavily indebted.

To address these questions, we draw upon a data set that is unusually rich by developing country standards. This is the annual survey of large and medium firms conducted by Indonesia's Central Board of Statistics (Badan Pusat Statistik, BPS).[4] This series is designed to survey all large and medium non-oil manufacturing establishments, defined as those employing at least 20 workers. The survey is published as *Statistik Industri*, but we utilise here the unpublished, establishment-level data tapes. The survey questionnaire covers most operating aspects of these establishments. Crucially for our purposes, establishments are identified by a code, which enables them to be traced over time. We are thus able to construct a very rich panel data series, and to examine the behaviour of firms over this period of growth, crisis and recovery. These data constitute the source of information contained in Figure 1 and the tables that follow.

While the survey is comprehensive, inevitably there are some gaps in the coverage. Two in particular limit our analysis. First, as noted, the unit of observation is the establishment not the enterprise. Thus we cannot detect whether an establishment is a stand-alone operation or is part of a business group. More broadly, given the importance of business conglomerates and the business-finance nexus, especially in the late Soeharto era, firm behaviour at the time of the crisis could presumably have been influenced by membership of a conglomerate, especially one which was 'palace-connected' or linked to an affiliated bank. This is a major limit on any detailed political economy analysis of the impact of the crisis. Second, the survey provides some information on firms' debt and leverage, but the details are incomplete. For example, there are

---

4   Note that, for expositional convenience, we use the terms 'firm' and 'establishment' interchangeably, but strictly speaking in all cases we are referring to the latter concept.

no data on the currency in which the debt is denominated, the nature of the financial institution (on- or off-shore, state, private or foreign, etc) and whether the borrowings were hedged.

We measure the impact of the crisis by taking the percentage difference in the level of some performance measures for each firm between the period of crisis and immediate adjustment (that is, 1997–2000) and the pre-crisis period 1995–96. That is, the two years immediately prior to the crisis are arbitrarily but plausibly taken as our benchmark period. This period could have been shorter or longer, but two years is arguably sufficient to capture conditions prior to the crisis. Note that the data are collected on an annual basis, and therefore it is not possible to capture firm dynamics over shorter periods. For example, the crisis actually commenced in July 1997, and began to impact on real levels of economic activity by the fourth quarter of that year. But the data are not sufficiently disaggregated to detect these developments.

An investigation of firm-level adjustments should ideally employ a variety of performance indicators, including output, employment, and profitability. Trends in these indicators will likely diverge, since they are measuring different phenomena. For example, typically employment does not decline as sharply as output during a recession, as firms tend to 'hoard' labour, owing to the difficulties or reluctance to shed workers. In the following statistics we focus on just one indicator, real value added, which is arguably the most important. The analysis can also be conducted with reference to other variables.

The crisis severely affected firm demographics, as indicated by entry and exit rates (Figure 4.1). Entry rates, which had previously been buoyant, fell sharply from 1997, to less than half the pre-crisis rates, and remained subdued. Exit rates almost doubled at the peak of the crisis. Since output began to recover in 2000, the inference is that most of the initial post-crisis expansion was explained by firms that survived the crisis.

The outcomes also differed significantly across major industries, as hypothesised above (See Thee 2000 and Fukuchi 2000). Table 4.5 shows the percentage change in real value added (RVA) by industry over the two immediate pre-crisis years, 1995–96. Some industries actually survived the crisis and even expanded significantly. Examples include the labour-intensive sectors of textiles, garments, footwear (ISIC 32) and the small 'other' group (ISIC 39), and the resource-based sectors, wood and paper products (ISIC 33 and 34). By contrast, heavy industries and machine goods (ISIC 37 and 38) contracted. The effect was very severe in the former group, especially with its protected, uneconomic, state-dominated steel industry. These conclusions are formally supported by the factor intensity groupings in Table 4.6, especially for firms in labour-intensive industries. These contracted the least, and were expanding again by 1999–2000.[5]

Figure 4.1: Entry and Exit Rates in Indonesian Manufacturing in Terms of Number of Plants (EN1 and EX1) (%), 1994–2000

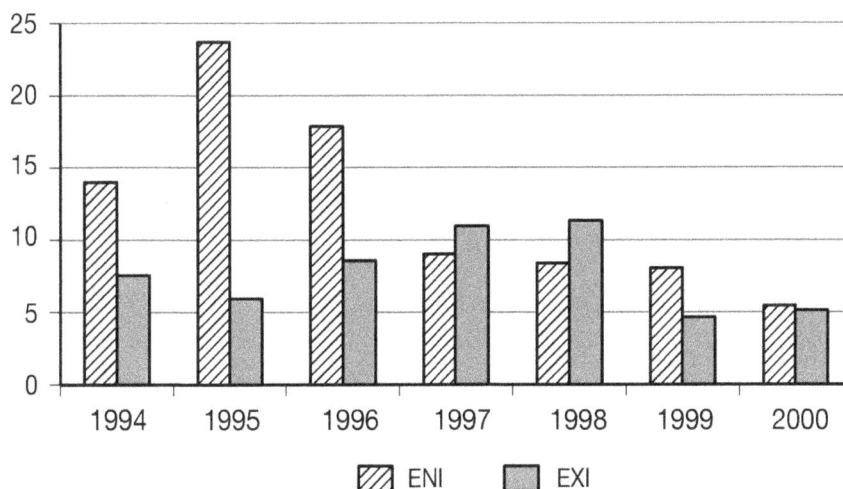

Table 4.5: Aggregate RVA Difference by Broad Industry Group (%)

ISIC	Industry	1997	1998	1999	2000
31	Food and tobacco products	14.3	16.8	15.4	19.5
32	Textile, garment and leathers	8.5	30.7	18.6	24.4
33	Wood products, including furniture	8.2	58.0	33.0	31.0
34	Paper and paper products	15.7	52.0	27.5	40.0
35	Chemical, rubber and plastics	33.2	16.3	49.2	64.2
36	Non-metallic mineral products	29.3	2.6	-1.3	29.1
37	Basic metal industries	22.6	-74.7	-69.9	-63.9
38	Machinery and equipment	4.7	-3.9	-3.6	56.2
39	Other manufacturing	39.9	86.6	44.0	52.8

Source: Authors' computation.

---

5   Note that, in interpreting the data in Table 4, it is important to bear in mind that there are not many negative numbers because they refer to the difference as compared to 1995–96, which was a high-growth period. There were of course negative *annual* growth rates during the crisis years, particularly in 1998.

This is the industry story. What about firm-level effects? Table 4.6 shows these, with firms classified according to the attributes discussed above. Here too we discuss these with reference to changes in real value added compared to the pre-crisis years.

Table 4.6: The Crisis Performance Impact by Plant Characteristics

Plant characteristic class	%ΔRVAi,t		
	1998–2000	1998	1999–2000
Sales orientation class			
Domestic oriented	-19.6	-22.2	-12.1
Low export oriented	-19.9	-22.1	-13.6
Moderately export oriented	-3.0	-4.2	1.4
Highly export oriented	8.9	11.5	5.0
Ownership class			
Foreign	8.6	4.6	20.9
Private-domestic	-16.0	-17.9	-9.7
Government	-26.6	-26.3	-23.7
Foreign ownership class			
Low	-42.5	-45.4	-19.1
Moderately low	-6.4	-14.5	18.0
Moderately high	-4.8	-7.8	3.2
High	31.9	29.6	38.5
Size class			
Small 1	-15.4	-17.4	-8.5
Small 2	-21.5	-23.2	-15.6
Medium 1	-17.5	-19.8	-11.8
Medium 2	-11.1	-13.4	-5.3
Large	1.4	1.2	2.3
Industry factor intensity class			
Resource-intensive	-18.9	-14.9	-16.2
Labour-intensive	-5.7	-9.0	1.7
Capital-intensive	-25.0	-31.7	-12.8

Source: Authors' computation.

In the case of sales orientation, the firms are classified into four groups, based on pre-crisis patterns: those which sold their output solely in the domestic market and three groups of export orientation. As predicted, sales orientation matters, significantly. For example, domestic-oriented firms contracted quite sharply, by around 20 percent, both in 1998 and through to 2000. By contrast, the highly export-oriented firms (defined as more than 50 per cent of output exported) actually grew quite strongly, by 9 per cent through to 2000. The moderately export-oriented firms (10–50 per cent of output exported) initially contracted somewhat but were growing again by 1999–2000. The low export-oriented firms (0–10 per cent of output exported) performed similarly to those selling to the domestic market. This suggests the possibility of some sort of 'threshold' effect. The story is of course more complicated than this: there are lags, differences across industries, and outcomes depend on conditions in competitor countries (several of which also experienced sharp exchange-rate depreciations). But, undeniably, the key message is that export orientation was a key to recovery.

In the case of ownership, the firms are classified into three groups: domestic (private), state and foreign, again defined from the pre-crisis period. Here too there are significant differences, and the results conform to a priori hypotheses. The deep-pocketed and well connected foreign-owned firms (technically, defined as those with any foreign ownership) continued to expand, and at a faster pace from 1999. By contrast, both the domestic groups contracted, the SOEs particularly so. The performance of the SOEs deserves special comment. These were invariably inefficient enterprises, for a variety of reasons related to their multiple objectives, social missions, top-heavy management and poor incentives systems. In good times, the government was able to effectively bankroll them either directly or via the financial sector. When these props were removed during the crisis, the SOEs were unable to adjust. Their location in capital-intensive industries, which was in most cases deliberately part of their mandate, further compounded the problems.

Since the foreign-owned group includes all firms with foreign firms, it is useful to examine whether the levels of foreign ownership matter. One might expect a positive relationship between these levels and firm performance, on the grounds that the parent company might be more committed to its affiliate— and have more control over it—the higher its stake. The data in Table 5 reveal this to be very much the case: firms with high foreign ownership (80 per cent plus in 1995–96) grew strongly throughout the period, whereas the low foreign ownership (less than 20 per cent) group contracted, in fact even more than the two domestic groups. The two intermediate groups of firms initially contracted but, unlike the domestic groups, they were expanding again in 1999–2000. Interestingly, and contrary to expectations, majority ownership does not appear to have been the critical consideration. That is, the benchmark defining whether foreign ownership matters appears to be more than just majority ownership, but in fact a very high foreign share.

Firms were also classified into five size groups, based on the size of their workforce: 20–49, 50–99, 100–199, 200–499, and 500+ workers. We argued above that there was no clear theoretical guidance for outcomes based on size. A popular literature in Indonesia at the time of the crisis asserted that small firms were more likely to have survived, but there is significant empirical evidence to the contrary. The results in Table 5 suggest that size is not a key variable, other than for the very large firms, which continued to grow, albeit slowly, after 1997. Among the other groups, the differences are not large, with the smallest and largest groups contracting somewhat less. As we will see shortly, the differing performance across size groups also reflects the effects of other factors, notably ownership and sales orientation.

The analysis thus far has been a single-variable story. Obviously though, as argued above, a variety of firm characteristics combine to produce the final outcome. Typically, these variables go hand in hand: larger firms are more likely to be foreign-owned and export-oriented, for example. Econometric analysis is required to investigate the impact of these factors. This is beyond the scope of our chapter, but drawing on Narjoko (2006), the following findings emerge. The first is the importance of export orientation, the effects of which are positive and statistically significant. As expected, the effect weakens over time, reflecting the fact that the initial sharp nominal depreciation was subsequently eroded by high inflation. Similarly, the positive relationship between foreign ownership and performance is confirmed. The results also show that the share of the foreign partner matters, and that the minimum foreign share required to ensure no firm contraction is quite high, about 40 per cent.

In addition to the impact of these attributes separately, we also examined the interactive effect of sales orientation and foreign ownership, on the presumption that the two are likely to be highly interrelated. That is, both the performance and survival of export-oriented firms may well depend on foreign ownership, as the latter may well facilitate a faster switching effect owing to these firms' knowledge of international markets and their stronger financial position. The results support this prediction. That is the effect of export orientation in lowering output contraction was higher in plants with high foreign ownership shares.

In the case of size, the regression results differ from the descriptive analysis, in that they suggest that larger firms contracted more than smaller ones. However, the results are generally weakly significant.

Conclusions

To return to our main questions, these contrasting episodes, of rapid growth over three decades followed by a very sharp contraction in 1997–98, draw attention to the highly episodal nature of Indonesian economic development. They have important implications more generally for any assessment of the Soeharto regime and for managing the industrialisation process. In particular, they highlight both the opportunities presented by opening up to the global economy but also the challenges, and by implication the importance of introducing a range of complementary policy and institutional reforms to manage this process. In aggregate, of course, Indonesia is a much richer country now compared to the mid-1960s, even after the crisis and slower growth of the past decade. But a clear lesson is that, while the country has benefitted from its more open economic policies, deep crises are economically very disruptive and socially painful. Clearly, policies need to be set in place to avoid them as far as possible. Many of these broader lessons go well beyond this chapter, and most are not industry-specific, but it will be useful by way of summary to briefly draw attention to some of the key issues.

The main positive message learnt from the New Order experience is that an open trade and investment regime and efficient supply-side investments were beneficial for Indonesia. This can be seen from Indonesia's three decades of rapid growth and the rapid improvement in living standards. A number of lessons stand out. One is that the country has grown rapidly when it has opened up its trade and investment policies. This was illustrated in the two major liberalisation episodes, in 1966–68 and 1982–86. In both cases, the economy responded swiftly and growth accelerated to 7–8 per cent. Of course, this was a 'liberalisation plus' story, in which a range of additional pre-requisites was also present: sound macroeconomic management, regime credibility, international support, and an expanding, largely open global economy.

Other elements of the commercial and social policy regime have underpinned these reforms. There were massive investments in infrastructure during the Soeharto era, particularly in the road network. By the mid-1990s, the country's physical infrastructure was at least as good as that in comparable countries (eg, China) and in most cases superior. The sharp decline in infrastructure post-crisis is now looming as a key constraint on growth. There was also a large expansion in education participation rates from the late 1960s, with almost universal primary school enrolments by 1980. In this respect, Indonesia was certainly 'East Asian' rather than 'South Asian', in that mass schooling enabled greater social mobility and participation. It also served to strengthen the country's capacity to absorb, and benefit from, greater openness to foreign capital and trade. But arguably Indonesia could have done better in tapping into global opportunities. Although education was broad-based, the technical and higher education sectors remain relatively under-developed. Moreover, the government's industrial support and extension programs have generally been weak, poorly targetted, with limited and unpredictable funding, and vulnerable to capture by vested interests. In this respect, Indonesia differs from the earlier experience of Korea and Taiwan, and more recently China. Its industrial upgrading process is therefore likely to proceed more slowly (Chu and Hill eds 2006).

While three decades of strong growth amply illustrate the benefits of openness, the deep crisis of 1997–98 is testimony to the pitfalls. The origins of the crisis are still being debated: between fundamental causes and triggers, and between domestic and international factors.[6] But there can be no doubt that the sudden change in risk assessments which prompted the capital flight, initially from Thailand and subsequently some of its neighbours, underlines the importance of managing integration into the global economy.

Three key lessons have emerged from the crisis. One is that global commercial integration in turn demands international-quality institutions and regulatory capacity where it really matters. Especially important are the key areas of financial supervision, central bank management, the finance ministry, and commercial law enforcement. Weaker capabilities in these areas are likely to result in slower growth and greater vulnerability to crises. Second, exchange-rate management is critical, since it is the major price variable through which a crisis is initially transmitted. Like most of its neighbours, Indonesia ran a fixed but adjustable regime prior to the crisis. Economic agents responded to the façade of certainty, and borrowed heavily in foreign currencies. One lesson from the crisis episode is that this strategy of attempting to fix (or heavily manage) the nominal rate in the face of large and potentially volatile short-term capital flows is highly risky. Hence the advocacy of the so-called 'corner solutions', either in the form of floating rates or hard pegs. In the wake of the crisis, Bank Indonesia has adopted a floating rate regime, albeit heavily managed, and the business community appears to have adjusted surprisingly quickly to it.

Third, there continue to be calls to manage capital mobility, especially the short-term, volatile flows. While intuitively attractive, there are obvious risks in such a strategy. It disconnects the country from global capital markets, it requires a high-quality, incorruptible central bank, and it may in any case be impracticable where international boundaries are highly porous. However, there may be a case for light-handed measures which slow short-term capital mobility, but which leave foreign direct investment (FDI) flows unaffected. Some of these measures

---

6   See Hill, 1999 for an analysis of the crisis and its immediate aftermath, and Temple, 2003 for an interpretation of Indonesia's long-term economic growth up to and through the crisis period.

could include monitoring short-term flows, limiting the ability of foreigners to borrow in the domestic currency, or imposing a surcharge on capital that exits prior to a defined period.

To connect these lessons back to our analysis of Indonesian industrialisation, these cautionary tales on the impact of globalisation in no way weaken the case for open trade and FDI policies. When properly managed, they have contributed to rapid growth. Moreover, as we have shown, the firms which were the best connected to the global economy, through trade, investment and particularly both, led the country's economic recovery.

For a volume in honour of Professor Harold Crouch, the missing element in the above story is of course the political economy of industrial policy. This has always been one of the most contested and contentious areas of economic policy making in Indonesia, reflecting the struggle between the technocrats, 'nationalists' and a variety of rent seekers. During the Soeharto era, the president effectively adjudicated on policy, guided by the dictum attributed to one of the country's most influential economists, the late Professor Moh Sadli, that 'bad times make for good policies and good times frequently the reverse'. Thus during periods of looming or actual crisis, in the mid-1960s and mid-1980s, the technocrats were allowed to be in the ascendancy, and they delivered major economic reforms that led to recovery and faster growth. During periods of buoyant economic growth, in the 1970s and the first half of the 1990s, they were less influential. In the 1970s, state-led industrialisation was again emphasised, with funding from the oil boom. In the 1990s, the technocrats were again increasingly marginalised, by both the high-tech projects of Dr Habibie and the Soeharto family conglomerates.

A new political economy dynamic has emerged in the post-Soeharto era. Once again, the technocrats held sway at the peak of the crisis, and their power began to wane as recovery got underway. But in this democratic era, there are new, less predictable policy actors. The technocrats are no longer the united group they were under Soeharto, and their modus operandi is different. The executive and bureaucracy are weaker, while the legislature, the regions, labour and civil society have more power. Political parties require funding. By all accounts, corruption is just as serious as it was under Soeharto, but it is now much less predictable. Liberalism remains politically unpalatable. It is therefore likely that the policy pendulum will continue to swing back and forth, as it has periodically since the 1960s, with consequences for Indonesia's long-term development dynamics.

What are the implications for any assessment of Soeharto and his legacy? A decade after the crisis, Indonesian industrialisation appears to have embarked on a different trajectory, one of slower growth, lower investment, weaker employment generation (see Chapter 10 by Chris Manning), and indifferent export performance (Athukorala 2006). Initially, the crisis was the main explanation for these trends, but it is clear now that they are primarily the result of the new policy regime, combined with much more severe international competition. That is, first, investors are still holding back, particularly for projects with long-time horizons, owing to uncertainties in the commercial climate.[7] Second, as noted the country's infrastructure investment lags its neighbours, and is becoming a serious constraint on growth. Third, it is now missing out on East Asian style labour-intensive growth, to the detriment of job-seekers and efforts to achieve rapid poverty reductions. Fourth, Indonesia is not a major participant in the rapidly expanding global production networks that are increasingly centred in East Asia. This in turn is primarily the result of the country's continuing ambivalence towards foreign investment, and its less efficient logistics for these highly trade-oriented operations.

It would of course be simplistic to assert that these problems have arisen only in the post-Soeharto era. All have been present to some degree since Indonesian Independence. The high point of policy reforms in the country was the 1980s, and all administrations since then have found it difficult to maintain the pace of reform. When major economic and political crises occur, economic policy making becomes that much more difficult. For most of the Soeharto era, Indonesia out-performed its fellow developing Asian giants, China and India. The challenge now is to try to keep up with them.

---

7   For example, according to the World Bank's *Doing Business* 2008 report, Indonesia ranks 123 out of 178 economies, below its more developed Southeast Asian neighbours Singapore (1), Thailand (15), Malaysia (24), as well as Vietnam (91).

5 The Historical Roots of Indonesia's New Order: Beyond the Colonial Comparison

ROBERT CRIBB

In the middle of the 1960s, Indonesian politics took an apparently profound turn. The personalised, charismatic rule of the country's first president, Sukarno, gave way to the dour, sometimes almost anonymous, administrative style of a new president, Soeharto, a general and former head of the army's strategic reserve. Indonesia's strident leftist engagement with world affairs gave way to a quiet alignment with the West. Within Indonesia, the permitted space for public politics contracted sharply: whereas shrill ideological assertion had been the motor of politics under Sukarno's Guided Democracy, the regime of Soeharto relegated explicit ideology and demonstrative politics to the margins of public life. And economic decay gave way to a sustained programme of development that raised Indonesia from the ranks of the world's poorest nations to become an incipient Asian tiger.

Soeharto called his regime the New Order, and it was indeed a sharp contrast with the 'Old Order', a term which came to encompass both the Guided Democracy of Sukarno and the seven years of parliamentary democracy which preceded it. But where, if it was indeed new, did the New Order come from? Part of the answer lies, of course, in the broader global developments of the time. Indonesia was one of several repressive developmentalist regimes (Feith 1982a) in the Third World in which authoritarian leaders employed state power and the support of the United States in the name of kick-starting what was meant to be a self-sustaining development process. In this respect, Soeharto's Indonesia resembled the South Korea of Bak Jeonghui (Park Chung Hee), the Philippines of Marcos, and the Iran of Shah Mohammad Reza Pahlavi. As the divergent fates of these cases suggest, however, global circumstances were not the only determining factors at work in the emergence or functioning of these regimes. To understand where they came from, we also need to look at history. But which history?

In the immediate aftermath of independence (1945) and the Dutch transfer of sovereignty (1949), the dominant assumption amongst scholars of Indonesia had been that Indonesia was embarked on a steep but otherwise straightforward path to modernity (and specifically to liberal democracy). Dutch colonialism, it was said, had set the archipelago on a path to modernity, creating the modern state and giving access to modern ideas, and in doing so it had sown the seeds of its own destruction as Indonesian nationalism arose to claim independence by turning the West's own values and rhetoric of freedom and justice against it. With independence secured, Indonesia's task was 'nation-building', a code term for constructing a civil and political order which resembled those of the western democracies. Already in the mid-1950s, however, the prolific and underrated Dutch-American scholar Justus van der Kroef began to reflect on the persistence of apparently traditional patterns of politics in Indonesia. In an idiosyncratic and rather philosophical article, he identified what he called a 'colonial deviation' in Indonesian history (Kroef 1956). By this coinage, he meant that the colonial era, including its immediate aftermath in the form of the Dutch-inspired liberal political order of the early 1950s, could be seen as a departure from the 'natural' pattern of Indonesian politics and that what followed in the broad decolonisation process might be something other than a simple following of the trajectory mapped our earlier by the West. Van der Kroef was writing at a time when the strains in Indonesia's parliamentary system had not yet brought it down and his insight was correspondingly speculative. By the early 1960s, however, the disappearance of the parliamentary order, apparently without significant regret among the forces then dominating the political system in the Indonesian political system, seemed to suggest that some hitherto unrecognised dynamic was at work.

The idea of a colonial and liberal democratic deviation in Indonesian history was cemented into scholarly analysis in 1962, when Harry Benda, reviewing Herbert Feith's *Decline of Constitutional Democracy*, memorably described Feith as 'presenting us highly sophisticated and persuasive answers to an intrinsically mistaken, or irrelevant, question' (Benda 1964:450). Sukarno's Guided Democracy, Benda suggested, could be seen as a return to indigenous political forms which reflected basic cultural understandings of politics that had survived the colonial era despite the gloss of westernisation. Benda's proposition resonated with a contemporaneous scholarly determination to purge Indonesian history of the idea that the Indian culture which had dominated the archipelago from the 1st century to the 14th had been a consequence of Indian imperial initiative. Citing van Leur's memorable characterisation of foreign influences as a 'thin and flaking glaze', scholars argued that Indonesians had held the initiative and had been highly selective of foreign cultural elements (Leur

1955:95). Benda's argument thus marked the first of a series of influential works arguing the centrality of the cultural dimension in Indonesian politics (Willner 1966; Dahm 1969; Anderson 1972).

Barely had this line of argument taken off when Sukarno's Guided Democracy came to a violent end in 1965–66 and Soeharto's New Order took its place. Soeharto initially appeared to be returning Indonesia to a modified version of the old liberal trajectory (one in which democracy was temporarily postponed in the name of practical development). Soeharto had been in power for barely half a decade, however, when observers began to notice intriguing resemblances between his rule and that of the colonial order which had come to an end in 1942. The first scholar to develop this argument in print was the Dutch sociologist Jacques van Doorn in a book entitled *Orde-opstand-orde* [Order, rebellion, order] (1973). Ruth McVey then explored the idea in a paper, 'The Beamtenstaat in Indonesia', written in 1977 but not published till 1982. She suggested that the ruling elites in both the late colonial order and the New Order were culturally alien from the people they ruled, the Dutch because of their obvious foreignness, the New Order elite because of its wealth and cultural assimilation to the West. As aliens, both elites lacked the rhetorical tools to recruit the loyalty of their subjects, and in consequence they both adopted a strategy of political demobilisation. She also suggested, less convincingly, that both elites were driven by a 'gnawing sense of illegitimacy' into an emphasis on superficial legal forms and on the promise of an eventual transition to democracy (McVey 1982:84,87) but in the end she implied, despite her article's title, that differences outweighed similarities.

The scholarly thesis that Soeharto was the heir of the late colonial state achieved its most developed form in an article, 'Old state, new society', published by Ben Anderson in 1983. Anderson characterised the New Order as a 'resurrection of the state and its triumph vis-à-vis society and nation' (p.487). The resurrected state was that which the Dutch East Indies Company had founded in the early 17th century and which had expanded dramatically over the subsequent centuries, encompassing most of the archipelago and penetrating with increasing force into the daily life of its inhabitants. The central characteristic of this state, as portrayed by Anderson, was its self-serving purpose: it had no responsibility to its society and the main purpose of its revenue collecting activities was to fund itself as a gigantic consumer of Indonesian wealth. These resources in turn gave it the power and the confidence to impose its will on reluctant parts of the archipelago such as Aceh. The Republic of Indonesia which declared independence in 1945 claimed to be the successor state of the Netherlands Indies in international law, but, according to Anderson, it differed from the colonial state in key respects: its leaders were not from the colonial establishment, they based their claim to power on an idea of representing the

Indonesian people and for two decades the state presided over a society out of control. The New Order, by contrast, with its managed elections and its vast sources of funds from resource rents and foreign aid, independent thus of a public tax base and consequent public responsibility, and with its brutal adventure in East Timor, replicated central features of the colonial state. In Anderson's analysis, moreover, Soeharto as an individual played a central role in this replication because his career had begun in the security apparatus of the colonial state. In Anderson's view, Soeharto consciously constructed the New Order as a new incarnation of the colonial state, asserting its power over society and its access to resources for its own officials.

Anderson's development of Van Doorn's insight has had a persistent, though indefinable, effect on the scholarly interpretation of the New Order.[1] Pheng Cheah cites Anderson when describing the New Order as 'the genealogical heir of the Dutch colonial state' (2003:255); Anwar cites him approvingly (1994:160); Nordholt's discussion of a 'genealogy of violence' in Indonesia nods respectfully in his direction (2002). Like all provocative insights, however, the equation of New Order and colonial era runs the risk of being carried beyond the level of insight into the realm of truism. It may be time, therefore, to put insight into perspective by identifying a few key areas in which the New Order and the colonial signally fail to resemble each other. In fact, in important respects, the New Order constituted the apotheosis of reaction against the colonial order.

Unity and diversity

Perhaps the single most striking difference between the New Order and the colonial era lay in the New Order's emphasis on unity, uniformity and conformity. By contrast, the colonial era was characterised by a thoroughgoing fragmentation of society, culture and politics.

It is a cliché of colonialism in most of the world that it applied a technique of divide and rule. The case that colonialism in the Indonesian archipelago divided a previously united society would be hard to make, but there is no doubt that the Dutch systematically preserved difference within their political order. This strategy of preserving difference emerged initially out of purely pragmatic calculations. The Dutch East Indies Company, and after it the Netherlands colonial regime, had as their main aims (until 1900) the extraction of profit from the Indonesian archipelago. They had no sense of an obligation to provide services to their colonial subjects and, as a matter of frugality, they aimed to leave the indigenous peoples of the archipelago as far as possible under

---

1   As of 24 February 2008, it counted 30 citations in the ISI Web of Knowledge, 34 in Google Scholar and 140 in Google Books.

their indigenous rulers. As time passed, frugal practice turned into colonial doctrine: the Dutch increasingly believed as a matter of principle that colonial peoples should be ruled according to their own cultural norms. Given that those norms existed in a vast range of forms, the colonial authorities presided over a baroquely complicated administrative system. The colonial order distinguished between directly and indirectly ruled territories, the latter numbering some 282 at the end of the colonial era and covering about half the area of the colony (though much less than half the population). Laid over this administrative order was a legal system bifurcated between government and Native law, and bifurcated again, but not along the same lines, between government and Native courts. Through the system of customary law (*adatrecht*), the Dutch recognised thousands of local practices, different from district to district, as having the force of law, especially in matters to do with land use, marriage and inheritance. Laid over the system again was an immensely complex system of racial classification. Although there was a crude classification of the population of the archipelago into three categories Europeans, Natives and Foreign Orientals (Fasseur 1994), this classification was made less salient by the existence of dozens of sub-classifications within each category. Japanese (classified as European from 1899) were not treated the same as Germans; Chinese were not treated the same as Indians or Arabs. The category of 'Native' (*Inlander*) counted in some circumstances, but in other circumstances it was less significant than the fact that one was Javanese or from, say, Banyumas.

Even if the Dutch did not consciously intend to keep the inhabitants of the archipelago disunited as a device for sustaining colonial rule, they employed the diversity argument with alacrity as soon as a nationalist challenge emerged in the early 20th century. The Leitmotiv of the Dutch defence of colonial rule in the final decades before the Second World War was an emphasis on the uneven development of Indonesians. This proposition allowed them to claim that continued colonial rule was necessary to protect the weaker elements of Indonesian society from the stronger (an argument which carried on through the war years into the strategy of creating a federal, semi-independent Indonesia with the different regions under varying degrees of colonial tutelage; this argument also ultimately underpinned in the separation of West New Guinea from Indonesia in 1949).

For Indonesian nationalists, in consequence, refuting the Dutch assertion of diversity and creating their own basis for unity was an obsession. Nationalist leaders routinely observed that the overwhelming numbers of Indonesians would give them a decisive advantage if only they could achieve true *persatuan* (unity), rather than mere association, mocked by Hatta as *persatean* (being like unrelated pieces of meat skewered on a bamboo stick) (Legge 1981:157). The Pancasila took form as an encapsulation of Sukarno's conviction that Indonesian identity was underpinned by belief in a set of noble principles, not just by shared hostility to colonialism. The Dutch strategy during the Indonesian revolution of constructing a federal state as a pliant alternative to the nationalist Republic and their separation of West New Guinea from Indonesia at the time of the transfer of sovereignty in 1949 only fed this obsession, so that two or three generations of nationalists grew up believing in national unity as a first principle and seeing secession in any assertion of local identity.

The origins of the New Order's obsession with unity (redoubled as *persatuan dan kesatuan*) lay clearly in this nationalist reaction to the diversity which underpinned the colonial regime, even if it was exacerbated by a somewhat tendentious misreading of the rebellions of the 1950s as separatist.[2] The Soeharto regime banned locally based parties, starved local languages of state support, herded local identities into a straightjacket of tropes typified by the 'Beautiful Indonesia in Miniature' (Taman Mini) theme park in which the vast cultural diversity of the archipelago was reduced to a single standard for each province, most of the standards being nudged in style towards a single hybrid Malayo-Javanese archetype. A single, coordinated education system, sustained encouragement for population movement as a way of blending the peoples of the archipelago, and the heaviest of military hands set against real and presumed secessionists, all these were implicit in the old nationalist slogan that identified an Indonesia stretching 'from Sabang to Merauke'. It was an obsession with the essential unity and uniformity of the archipelago that ran diametrically against the rich cultural profusion of the colonial era.

Meritocracy

Soeharto has been gone from power for more than ten years now, but it is still discomforting to say it: the New Order was a meritocracy, or at least it was a meritocracy if one takes a flexible enough view of merit. In this respect, too, the Soeharto regime was utterly unlike the colonial order.

The horror stories that Indonesians tell each other about Dutch colonialism focus on brutal military operations, from genocide in the Banda islands in 1621 (Hanna 1978) to the bloody conquest of Aceh between 1870 and 1900 (Veer 1980), and on economic exploitation, from the callous treatment of labourers in the construction of the Great Post Road along the island of Java in 1808 (Nas and Pratiwo 2002) to the tormenting of workers on the tobacco plantation of

---

2   The major revolts of the 1950s—the Darul Islam uprising, the Madiun affair, and the PRRI and Permesta rebellions, as well as smaller events such as the APRA and Andi Aziz affairs—were all directed as national politics, not at the breakup of Indonesia. The only revolt which aimed at secession was that of the Republic of the South Moluccas in the early 1950s.

Sumatra in the late 19th century (Breman 1989). These barbarities, however, were concentrated in a relatively small number of regions of the archipelago and took place during relatively short periods of time. What almost all Indonesians experienced under the colonial order, however, was a fundamental constriction of opportunity.

This constriction operated in several ways. Perhaps most important of all was the pervasive presence of aristocracy in the colonial administrative structure. Indigenous aristocracies played a key role in the colonial order, because the Dutch believed that they possessed traditional authority over the mass of the people and were therefore a bulwark of political stability. As we know from the research of Sutherland (1979), the aristocracies were not simply preserved but enhanced. Whereas in the pre-colonial period there had been a great deal of fluidity in aristocratic status, so that able commoners could rise into the elite and incapable descendants could disappear from it, the colonial system fossilised the social order as it was at the time of the imposition of Dutch rule. Aristocrats were not only affirmed, but were encouraged to take upon themselves the trappings of minor royalty, all for the sake of making a regal impression on the lower classes. This situation applied not just in the indirectly ruled regions but in regions that were nominally directly ruled. Recruitment to the indigenous administrative corps in Java, the Native Administration (*Inlands Bestuur*), was determined by birth, with the most senior Native post, the district head (*bupati*), restricted to members of the traditional Javanese elite (*priyayi*) aristocracy.

The entrenchment of aristocracy meant a serious restriction of social mobility through the administration. Whereas social hierarchies in most pre-colonial states in the archipelago were remarkably fluid, in the colonial era it ceased to be possible to recruit talented individuals from the lower classes into the indigenous ruling elite, because inferior origin made them ineligible. It was also impossible to recruit Indonesians into the European administrative corps (in contrast with the Indian Civil Service of British India, for instance), not only because of European racism but because the system could not countenance a Native commoner rising to a position where he would have authority over Native aristocrats.

Alongside this class-based restriction were the better known obstacles to advancement created directly by race. Although overt racial discrimination, in the form of segregated facilities, was almost unknown in the colonial Indies, lack of formal education and lack of the necessary class connections effectively excluded Indonesians from managerial positions in most private firms and in the specialist technical sections of the colonial administration where lack of aristocratic status was not an issue. The huge offence that the colonial system committed against all its Native subjects was to close off the main paths to social mobility in a society that yearned for advancement.

The nationalist movement, by contrast, was a consistent enemy of ascriptive privilege. Not everyone went as far as Tjipto Mangoenkoesoemo who called for the Javanese language to be 'killed' because its system of levels of address made it inseparable from aristocratic privilege. But most nationalists agreed that reforming access to government positions should be a central element in their agenda. At the outbreak of the national revolution in 1945, there was a series of social revolutions against aristocracies along the length of Java and Sumatra, in which discontented subjects and rival elites took advantage of the post-war power vacuum to sweep away aristocratic incumbents, sometimes simply consigning them to powerless citizenship, sometimes killing them (Lucas 1991). From a social point of view, too, the new nationalist elite was remarkable for its diverse social origins. The new president, Sukarno, had trained as an architect, his deputy, Mohammad Hatta as an economist. The army commander was a former teacher, the governor of South Sumatra had been a star in light romantic films, the head of the military academy had been a dentist. The barriers erected by the colonial system were breached and the cohort of hungry, capable nationalists flooded into governing positions.

Soeharto was part of the same generation. A village boy, possibly illegitimate, he would have had little hope for a glittering career under the Dutch. In the fluid politics of independent Indonesia, however, he made the most of his opportunities and rose to a position from which, when circumstances suddenly favoured him, he could seize power. Soeharto's presidency was a confirmation of the fact that in the new Indonesia anyone could become president. And the New Order he constructed was precisely in the image of the nationalist movement. Although he made brief use of the Sultan of Yogyakarta, Hamengku Buwono IX, as vice-president, and although he pandered to his wife's connections with the minor princely Mangkunegaran family, the people he surrounded himself with were newcomers—the ruthless, the clever, the lucky, and the opportunist. Soeharto's technique, too, of circulating subordinates through the political system, promoting some, discarding others, catapulting a select few into new and unexpected posts was correctly interpreted at the time as a cunning system of control which centred political prerogative in the hands of an inscrutable president. But it was also a highly effective system of social mobility; no one was disqualified from power by lack of social rank as had been the case in the colonial era. Disqualification came rather from lack of ability, lack of willingness to do the president's work and, in the closing years of the New Order, lack of obsequiousness. If there were times when Soeharto's court seemed to resemble a zoo, it was a convincing sign that no social standing was needed to make the grade in New Order Indonesia as long as one had the right abilities. Here, too, the New Order's preoccupations were diametrically opposed to the ascriptive obsessions of the colonial order.

Propaganda

The New Order was brutal towards those whom it saw as threats. It was callous towards those it needed to use, or whose living spaces it needed to confiscate, for the sake of development. But many Indonesians benefited from the greater social order that the New Order provided and from the pervasive programmes for economic development and social improvement. In one respect, however, the New Order touched the whole of Indonesian society in a way that was as negative as the pervasive lack of social mobility that characterised the colonial system. This respect was propaganda, which infused the New Order in a way that no-one could ignore and which poisoned public life. In the colonial era, by contrast, propaganda played almost no role at all in upholding Dutch rule.

Although the term propaganda is sometimes used to describe any kind of display which intentionally upholds or undermines a political order, the term is better treated more narrowly as referring to a set of messages designed to influence public opinion on a specific topic. The Dutch metropolitan and colonial governments had become aware of the value of propaganda in influencing global public opinion early in the 20th century. From about the beginning of the twentieth century, there was talk in the international community of redistributing colonies to emerging powers such as Germany, the United States and Japan, so that they could have a hand in the task of colonial development. Netherlands was small and weak at the time, and the Dutch metropolitan and colonial governments had been anxious that they might lose parts, or even all, of the colony. This fear prompted a small-scale publicity campaign to inform the world of what the Dutch saw as the good work they were carrying out in the Indies.

But in the direction of the Natives there was no such effort. The reason for this was that the colonial order did not rest to any significant degree on the active consent or direct mobilisation of its indigenous subjects. As we have seen, the lynchpin of colonial rule was aristocratic authority. Although this authority might require reinforcement by means of ceremony and pageant, it was hardly amenable to modern propaganda. Nor was the racial hierarchy of colonial society an attribute that lent itself to being 'sold' by propaganda means. To the extent that the Dutch were interested in the motivations of individual Indonesians, the debate which ran through Dutch colonial policy from at least the middle of the 19th century was whether Indonesians could be lured into activity by economic incentive or whether their attitude to the world was governed by a culturally determined sense of social obligation. The idea that propaganda might create a sense of commitment to the colonial order was simply not present.

In fact the Dutch did believe in propaganda, but only as a tool employed by their enemies. From the first emergence of nationalist objections to Dutch rule, the colonial authorities suspected that naïve, good-hearted Natives were being led astray by Islamic and/or Communist propaganda. Censorship of political materials and the exiling of 'agitators' was thus a key part of the colonial strategy to maintain power (Poeze 1982–1994). But the Dutch themselves never ventured into any form of serious counter-propaganda.

Serious political propaganda, rather, was introduced to Indonesia by the Japanese occupation. The Japanese military authorities were at best sceptical about power of traditional rulers to mobilise Indonesians for the war effort, and they had no time to devise systems of economic incentive. Instead they immediately established a Propaganda Section (Sendenbu) with the task of persuading Indonesians to back occupation policies and participate enthusiastically in the war effort (Kurasawa 1987). There was no precedent in Indonesian history for such a concerted effort to change public opinion. Although in some respects the Japanese simply released pent-up resentment of colonial rule that pre-dated the Occupation, the propaganda of the Japanese period had a profound awakening effect on Indonesian political consciousness. It was a lesson obvious to most nationalist leaders, and the subsequent war of independence from 1945 to 1949 was conducted not only in the battlefield and at the negotiating table but also in the form of a propaganda struggle for the hearts and minds of Indonesians.

As well as comprehending the power of propaganda to shape attitudes, the Indonesian nationalists learnt a subsidiary lesson about propaganda from the Japanese. This lesson was that, in its attention to public opinion, propaganda is a kind of bastard child of democracy. Propaganda does not mean accountability or even consultation, but it shows an underlying respect for the masses by regarding their opinions as important. The Japanese eagerness to win public support contrasted sharply with the transparent disappointment of many Dutch with their colonial subjects. The comment of an unnamed colonial official in the 1930s—'As soon as we withdraw our hands, everything sinks back into the marsh' (Furnivall 1948:229)—is reminiscent of nothing so much as the reported comment of the Russian Tsar a few decades earlier; offered the suggestion that his people might have lost confidence in him, he responded to the effect: 'Surely the question is whether I have confidence in them?'[3]

Soeharto came to power in 1965–66 after an era of intense propaganda in Indonesian public life, and his initial reaction was to sweep propaganda, and all manifestations of politics, into the dustbin of history. After the Malari riots of 1974, which appeared at the time to be a serious popular challenge to his regime, he changed direction and turned propaganda into a central element of

---

3   For an allusion to this (perhaps apocryphal) comment, see Gerhardie, 1939, p.450.

his political enterprise. By means of the P4 programme[4], he made ideological indoctrination a pervasive element in the national education system (Morfit 1981). This attention to propaganda marked Soeharto out as very different from the earlier colonial rulers, but in his use of propaganda he also differed sharply from his immediate nationalist forebears. Despite the huge effort that was put into inculcating the Pancasila into generations of school and university students, as well as public servants, military personnel and anyone else who came within reach, his aim was not to change people's minds by locking on to their emotions as the Japanese and Sukarno had sought to do, nor even to create a simulacrum of democratic consultation. Rather, his propaganda can be characterised by the term 'white noise', which was coined to describe featureless noise generated for the purpose of masking other sounds. Like white noise, the Pancasila was not meant to be noticed and acted upon (it lacked not just the intellectual but also the emotional content to become a serious guide to action). Rather it was intended to fill with nothingness the intellectual space that might otherwise have been contested by real political thinking. This empty character of the New Order's Pancasila is the explanation for the sudden disappearance after Soeharto resigned of what purported to be national ideology inculcated into the Indonesian people in millions of hours' instruction over more than two decades.

Urgency

Whereas the effort that the New Order put into propaganda was essentially directionless, its commitment to economic development was consistently sustained and purposeful. Although Indonesia is reputed to be a place of 'rubber time' (*jam karet*), where deadlines drift on the margins of life without ever being met, there was nothing casual about the New Order's commitment to the development effort. The most important positive characteristic of the Soeharto era, and the feature which lifts it above other Third World authoritarian regimes whose record was marred by brutality and corruption, was its sustained programme of development whose benefits reached far beyond the immediate interests of the ruling elite. No official document title sums up the New Order's intentions better than Ali Moertopo's *Basic thoughts on the acceleration and modernization of 25 years' development* (1973). Soeharto and those about him were aware that Indonesia was running a race. The dismal economic legacy of Sukarno meant that it started the race from the back of the field, but the New Order's managers were convinced that astute planning and implementation would enable them to move clear of the basket cases, plough past the middle of the field and follow eventually in the footsteps of Japan, South Korea and

---

4 *Pedoman Penghayatan dan Pengamalan Pancasila*, Guide to the Realisation and Implementation of Pancasila.

Taiwan. These managers were acutely aware that every delay meant prolonging Indonesia's sojourn amongst the less developed countries and prolonging hardship for the Indonesian people. They were driven by a sense of purpose and urgency.

The development strategy which Soeharto and his lieutenants implemented in fact had a significant resemblance to the so-called Ethical Policy of the Dutch colonial government in Indonesia in the early 20th century. This policy, a remarkable reversal of the exploitative policies of the 19th century and earlier, was the world's first sustained attempt to devise a set of policies to deliver economic development in the tropics. The programme was, by most standards, a failure, partly because of its experimental character, partly because funds were too limited to follow through the policy's ambitious aims, and partly because the Dutch were too quickly disappointed by the results (Cribb 1993). By the 1930s, economic development strategies had largely disappeared from the colonial political agenda, and when they reappeared in Indonesia in the late 1960s, they came from thinkers in other parts of the world. In that respect the New Order was no more the direct descendant of the Dutch colonial order than were any of the developing countries which applied the models recommended by Rostow and others.

There were two key differences, moreover, between the Dutch and the New Order in their development policies. First, the Dutch were not significantly driven by any sense of urgency. The initial impetus for the Ethical Policy was a sense of moral obligation to the Indies, a debt of honour incurred by means of exploitation during earlier centuries, which should be expunged by paying attention for the first time to the welfare of the indigenous people of the archipelago. Misgivings over the Policy, rather, were more than anything else based upon a fear that it had moved too fast, creating a discontented 'intellectual proletariat' which was ripe for seduction by subversive outside ideas. Second, the Ethical Policy was relatively short-lived. It was slower to start than the New Order's development programme and came to a more rapid end. By the 1920s, the Ethical Policy had begun to give way to that last justification of foreign rule, mentioned earlier, that only foreigners could protect the weaker sections of Indonesian society from the stronger. This justification was completely without a sense of urgency. It implied that Dutch rule would always be necessary to keep the peace. During his last years, it is true, Soeharto also showed a loss of policy vigour, but he never abandoned the development paradigm, and there was a gathering air of impatience in Indonesian politics as younger people waited for the old man to depart (see Cribb 1990:24; Crouch 1992:61–62; Schwarz 1994).

Conclusion: dualism and historical roots

The past works powerfully in the present. Institutional structures and habits of mind that were shaped in earlier periods can live on long after the forces that brought them into being have ceased to function. The persistence of the past is often a critical source of social resilience and cultural capital that sustains societies through difficult times. It can also work, however, as a straightjacket that restricts opportunities to shape the future. For this reason, most political programmes involve sustaining some elements from the past while rejecting others. Indonesia's recent history has been marked by unusually strong reactive swings against the immediate past. Supporters of the present *reformasi* era insist that it is a radical departure from the New Order, pointing to such dramatic reforms as decentralisation (with its far-reaching administrative, political and cultural consequences), democratisation, the letting go of East Timor, the removal of legal restrictions on Chinese Indonesians, and serious attempts to combat corruption. The New Order in turn painted itself as antithetical to Sukarno's 'Old' order, Sukarno sharply contrasted his Guided Democracy with the 'free-fight liberalism' of the parliamentary era, the Republic of Indonesia presented itself as the polar alternative to Dutch colonialism; even the Ethical Policy was presented as a fundamental reversal of the exploitative colonial policies of the 19th century.

This sense of repeated elemental changes of direction in Indonesian leads easily to a dualistic fallacy, as if Indonesia has simply flipped, time and again, between two basic options. Dualism is a powerful philosophical device, but it is crude history. Like other political orders in the Indonesian archipelago, the New Order was both a reaction to and a continuation of the political forms that preceded it. We can find in its complex structure elements that perpetuated forms and assumptions drawn from the Guided Democracy, from liberal nationalism, from the Japanese occupation, from the Dutch colonial era and from pre-colonial polities. At the same time it was a reaction against each of the eras that preceded it. To assert, on the basis of just a few similarities, that the New Order was in essence a resurrection of the colonial era is polemic rather than serious analysis. The colonial era contributed both institutions and assumptions to independent Indonesia, but it also provided a crucial antithetical model against which the New Order defined its vision for the archipelago.

6 Patrimonialism: The New Order and Beyond

JAMIE MACKIE

Harold Crouch's 1979 article on 'Patrimonialism and Military Rule in Indonesia' was in my view one of the most illuminating contributions to our understanding of the New Order political system published anywhere during its thirty-two year history (Crouch 1979). By drawing attention to the importance of patronage and the various forms of patron-client relationship which became so prominent under Soeharto's rule, it provided a more satisfactory macro-level explanation of some of its most puzzling features than has ever been advanced by any other political scientist. Various forms of patronage are to be found in most developing countries, of course, perhaps all, and are easily observable in nearby Malaysia, Thailand and the Philippines (especially in the Marcos years), although much less so in Singapore, for its own unique reasons.[1] But none of them is usually characterised as a patrimonial political system to the degree that Indonesia was under Soeharto. Why that is so is no great puzzle, but worth considering later for the light it throws on the singular characteristics of the Indonesian political system which have led us to describe it in terms of its patrimonialist features.

His article still stands as a persuasive and insightful analysis of the modalities of Soeharto's regime when he and it were both approaching the height of their power. Although I disagree slightly with some parts of his argument, Crouch certainly made us much more aware than we had been previously of patronage as a crucial feature of Soeharto's political system that became more and more deeply entrenched under his rule (almost intentionally so, I will suggest), becoming especially prominent after 1980 as his political authority became unchallengeable and the financial resources under his direct control increased enormously. Patronage has continued to be an important aspect of the 'money

---

1 Singapore under Lee Kuan Yew and his successors could not in the least be described as a patrimonialist regime, despite its strongly authoritarian aspects. Patronage relationships of the Soeharto type play little part, if any, in maintaining the enduring dominance of his party, the PAP (or his authority within it), or Lee's influence over the business world. The preponderance of public-sector corporations and foreign business firms over the feeble private business sector, coupled with Lee's extraordinary success in refusing to tolerate corruption among government officials (a legacy of his early Socialist inclinations and singular financial puritanism) has made Singapore's experience of business-government relations quite unique.

politics' of the post-Soeharto system of governance also, even under democracy and reform (*demokrasi dan reformasi*), but in a very different political context, as if it has become almost a pathological feature of the Indonesian political system—with damaging socio-political effects which I suspect will not easily be remedied. But patrimonialism implies something more than mere patronage, as we shall see, and while several aspects of the New Order patrimonialist system still persist, it would be going too far to categorise the post-1998 political order as such.

President Soeharto's ability to utilise patronage extensively to ensure the loyalty of his subordinates and leading members of the national elite, coupled with the formidable coercive powers at his disposal as head of the Armed Forces (in particular its intelligence apparatus) and the huge advantage of vastly greater financial resources available to him than his predecessor, President Sukarno, could ever dream of, plus the immense concentration of many strands of political, military and financial power he was able to bring together in his own hands at the apex of the political system, all had the cumulative effect that he wielded virtually unchallengeable control by the early 1980s which lasted until early 1998. It was partly because the system of government he created had some intriguing similarities with the patrimonial power of traditional rulers in the pre-colonial past that the term 'patrimonialism' initially seemed appropriate for his regime, although there were clearly some important differences.[2] But the key aspects of New Order patrimonialism had much deeper roots than just that. If we assume that the word refers primarily to the patronage aspect of Soeharto's regime, along with various other features mentioned above, it provides a better characterisation of the regime than any of the other catch-phrases commonly used to describe it, such as militarist, dictatorial, neo-colonialist, bureaucratic authoritarian and so on (see Anderson and Kahin 1982).

The word patrimonialism had not been widely used with reference to Indonesia before 1979, except rather briefly in Benedict Anderson's famous 1972 article on 'The Idea of Power in Javanese Culture', which may have drawn Crouch's attention to the concept (Anderson 1972). But Crouch's article brought it into far greater prominence. In fact, the term has since proved to be even more apposite to our analyses of the second half of Soeharto's rule, for reasons I discuss below, than it had been prior to the late 1970s when Crouch's ideas on the matter were taking shape. (That post-1979 tendency ran counter to the main thrust of his argument, however, which was that patrimonialist tendencies and a modern socio-political system were essentially incompatible.) The term also

---

2   Crouch summarised the differences between traditional patrimonial states and modern ones with patrimonial features on pp. 572–23 of 'Patrimonialism', stating that 'the environment in which patrimonial characteristics have persisted has been very different from the one in which they originally appeared. Modernisation has brought new challenges that threaten the capacity of governments to meet demands and maintain stability.'

has quite direct relevance to the post-Soeharto period, insofar as patronage is still a widespread feature of the political system that has taken shape since 1998, along with the general assumption which still persists that official positions can and will be used for purposes, inter alia, of personal or group benefit. But the patrimonialist aspect of the *demokrasi dan reformasi* years since 1998 has been submerged beneath the new and very different phenomenon of 'money politics', which is now so prevalent at both the local and the national level, as well as the far more pluralist character of the political system. Yet some vestiges of the mentalité associated with traditional patrimonialism still persist and are unlikely to fade into obscurity for many years.

In reviewing Crouch's argument about patrimonialism and its applicability to Indonesian politics, this chapter takes the view that while he accurately identified the key political dynamics of the New Order system as they were emerging in the late 1970s, he overestimated the degree to which the modern features of the regime would necessarily prove incompatible with its apparently traditional patrimonial underpinnings. As we shall see, the patrimonial character of the regime, deriving largely from Soeharto's ability to bestow patronage in return for loyalty (or, equally important, use the sanction of withholding it where necessary), became an increasingly prominent feature of the system of government he created and personally controlled in virtually all its key aspects. As such, far from leading towards a crisis for his regime, it was one of the factors contributing towards its longevity.

Patronage and patrimonialism

Patronage and patrimonialism are distinct but closely intertwined concepts which need to be clarified before we go any further. The former is a fairly straight-forward term referring to a particular kind of mutual relationship, usually between a (relatively) wealthy patron and a needy or dependent client. It is not necessary to endow the term with much theoretical baggage, for we can usually recognise a pay-off or a patron-client relationship whenever we encounter one. They were often seen in traditional Southeast Asian societies, while latter-day variants of them are still to be found today both in Indonesia and in other countries nearby.

But the word patrimonialism is a very different matter, for it is a much more abstract notion referring to an entire socio-political system rather than a particular kind of easily recognisable relationship, such as patronage. Patrimonialism, as I will be using the term here, refers essentially to a system that is, first, based very largely on patronage, and second, on the granting of quasi-traditional fiefdoms to favoured subordinates, as well as, third, sustained largely by personal loyalties similar to those accorded to traditional rulers, although in more modern garb in recent times.[3] It is a more mesmerising word than patronage, having its own peculiar potency (due in part to its slightly mysterious, exotic quality, or because it is much harder to define or pin down).

Benedict Anderson had written, in the early years of the New Order period, about the 'marked consonance of the traditional Javanese concept of Power with the political structures and behaviour of the patrimonialist state' (Anderson 1972:36). He said of the pre-colonial Javanese state that it 'admirably fits Max Weber's model of the patrimonialist state', in that the government was 'an extension of the person of the ruler'. Officials held their posts and perquisites at his whim and they were paid in the form of 'benefices ... specified'. He noted the 'highly personalistic character of patrimonial rule [there], in which the corps of officials is regarded as an extension of the person of the ruler ... [and] proximity to the ruler, rather than formal ranking, is the key to power'. The re-emergence of the patrimonialist model in Indonesia in the mid-1950s (after the 'ration-legalist bureaucracy bequeathed by the Dutch' began to crumble due to financial problems) was, in Anderson's view, accentuated by the persistence of traditional ideas about government that were highly consonant with it (Anderson 1972:35–36).

Weber had analysed various forms of *Herrschaft* (authority, domination or, perhaps better, in Roth's term, 'rulership'), such as patriarchy, kingship, the 'routinisation of charisma', feudalism, the city-state and patrimonialism in his massive study of *Economy and Society*.[4] He introduced the word patrimonialism in a chapter on 'Gerontocracy, Patriarchy and Patrimonialism' in his section on 'traditional authority', noting that the first two of these are 'the most elementary types of traditional domination' where there is a complete absence of personal, patrimonial staff. Patrimonialism (and 'sultanism', its most extreme form) arise 'when traditional domination develops an administrative and military force that are purely political instruments of the master.' Weber adds 'We shall speak of a patrimonial state when the prince organises his political power over extrapatrimonial areas and political subjects—which is not discretionary and

---

3 Attitudes to authority, deference to superiors and a reluctance to express open opposition face to face even among equals are amongst the various so-called 'Javanese' qualities of mind which came to be widespread under the New Order political system and certainly helped to reinforce it. While they have been displaced to some extent in the *demokrasi dan reformasi* years (but by no means totally) I suspect that much of the tolerance of official corruption and patronage relationships that still prevails derives largely from that older cluster of values and attitudes associated with patrimonialism.

4 Max Weber, *Economy and Society*, New York 1968, 3 vols, 231 ff; this work first published in German in 1922, not long after Weber's death (and still unfinished) was a huge, wide-ranging survey of diverse types of state, semi-sociological and semi-historical in approach, covering many centuries from the pharaohs to medieval European city-states, Middle Eastern sultanates and others. According to Roth, 1968, pp.194–206, Weber's goal was to try to discover 'how the systems really work', as well as to theorise about their socio-political dynamics and the differences between them. It seems that Southeast Asian kingdoms, sultanates and principalities were utterly unknown to him.

not enforced by physical coercion, just like the exercise of his patriarchal power' (Weber 1968:1013). (By the latter he meant a situation where the authority of a patriarch was never challenged.) Originally, patrimonial administration 'was adapted to the satisfaction of the purely personal, primarily private needs of the master'. However, in more complex societies, such as the city-states of medieval Italy, the patrimonial ruler had to draw the privileged strata to his side by reserving key positions in the standing army for them and creating an army of professional soldiers, equipped with supplies and revenues that were provided by the ruler. The army was dependent on the ruler, and vice versa.

In applying Weber's analysis of patrimonialism to the more modern world, we should avoid thinking of it in an essentialist way, as if there is some fundamentally distinctive feature that marks it out from other types of *Herrschaft*, in the way he had categorised them, and think of it instead as simply a cluster of characteristics that will be found in varying proportions, more so or less, in different polities or at different times. (Soeharto's regime became much more patrimonial in that sense in the latter part of his rule than in the years Crouch was analyzing, it seems to me.) The key features include the personal authority of the ruler (howsoever achieved), the traditionalist accoutrements of such authority, the hierarchical array of subordinate authorities reaching from the apex of the state to the lowest levels, and the patron-client relationships that tie them all together. Another of Weber's key observations, for our purposes, is that patrimonial rulers, like all traditional rulers, must endeavour to maximise their personal leverage over their subordinates in a constant tussle over who has ultimate control.

Indonesian patrimonialism in Crouch's account

Crouch had earlier made many references to the practice of patronage in both Sukarno's and Soeharto's regime in his 1978 book on *The Army and Politics in Indonesia* although without using the term patrimonialism or any mention of Weber (Crouch 1978). But he developed their relevance to Indonesia much more explicitly in his *World Politics* article with a fuller analysis of the patrimonial and neo-patrimonial features of the Indonesian political system under Sukarno as well as Soeharto, citing works by Roth, who had co-edited Weber's major work on the subject, and Eisenstadt, who had applied his ideas to the newly modernising nations. Yet Crouch avoided becoming caught up in the theoretical complexities of Weber's thinking on the subject. His focus was more on the persistence of traditional features of modernising polities and how far their 'modern' features had replaced or modified the traditional elements in the post-independence Indonesian socio-political system, citing Geertz's (1960) and Ann-Ruth Willner's (1966) writings on that theme. Although Indonesian society had experienced great social change, with the Indonesian Communist Party (Partai Komunis Indonesia, PKI) mobilising wide popular support among the masses in the 1960s, the prominence of traditional features of both the New Order and Sukarno's 'Old Order' still seemed 'to hark back to the traditional patrimonial polities of earlier Javanese empires.' (Crouch 1979:573)

However, what Crouch concentrates on in his 1979 article is perhaps the most striking feature of modern Indonesian patrimonialism: the allocation of lucrative fiefdoms from which the President's subordinates could derive their funds for both official and private purposes, under both Sukarno and Soeharto. The expansion of Soeharto's authority, says Crouch, was backed at first by his growing capacity to use coercion against resisting groups, but later the main means was through the distribution of patronage.

> He was able to reward loyal supporters and win over potentially dissident officers with appointments to civilian posts that offered prospects of material gain. Control over the machinery of patronage ... was thus the key factor that enabled Suharto to win and maintain the support of the armed forces for his leadership. (Crouch 1979:577)

Under the New Order, in Crouch's words, 'the enforced political isolation of the masses ... was a factor favourable to the emergence of a new patrimonial system ... [and] patrimonial politics again took the form of a struggle for influence within the elite.' (Crouch 1979:576). With the PKI eliminated and the masses effectively excluded from political activity by the de-politicisation processes of the 1970s, patrimonialist politics 'again took the form of a struggle for influence within the elite' which Soeharto also kept within bounds through the distribution of patronage. Hence the new regime 'bore a strong resemblance to the patrimonial model. Political competition among the elite did not involve policies but power ... and the distribution of spoils.' (Crouch 1979:578)

Although facilitated by the elimination of the PKI, this was not an entirely new development, however, for Sukarno too had maintained a patrimonial regime during his Guided Democracy years (1959–65). 'In the patrimonial atmosphere of Guided Democracy, army officers—like most other officials—had used their [official] position to further their private interests'.

Whether or not they had been able to do so in the Sukarno years to the same extent as they did under Soeharto, or as such a central feature of Sukarno's political system, may be debateable. But Crouch is surely right in his view that Sukarno had to rely on the distribution of favours to his followers to maintain a balance between them because he was unable to exert much coercive power against them. Like the sultans in the patrimonial states of the past, Sukarno had managed to keep the courtiers jostling among themselves for his favours in order not to become too dependent on any one of them ... But Sukarno's courtiers were backed by modern organizations and he had no way of effecting a reconciliation between the interests and organizations they represented in the nation. (Crouch 1979:574)

That last point is important, for it touches on a key reason Crouch advances for his underlying belief that 'patrimonial ritual and the distribution of fiefdoms proved insufficient to hold together a polity that was sharply divided' under Sukarno. It may have seemed to be patrimonial, he says, but the disintegration of his regime in 1965 revealed that it was not. Yet that observation was surely an oversimplification. The collapse of Sukarno's Nasakom regime after the Gestapu coup attempt of September 1965 had little or nothing to do with its patrimonialist features but was due primarily to the destruction of the political balance that he had previously been able to maintain between the contending (modern) political forces, PKI on one side and the anti-Communists, principally the Army, on the other. And it was not patronage and fiefdoms that he provided to the PKI (or withheld from them) but political protection, which was crucial for it.

Crouch seems to have viewed Soeharto's New Order as basically similar to Sukarno's regime because of its patrimonialist features; hence he concluded that Soeharto's regime would eventually suffer the same fate as Sukarno's, for a similar reason, an inevitable clash between the traditional and the modern. Yet while he leaves us in no doubt about the crucial patrimonial aspects of the New Order, he did not assert bluntly that the New Order was a patrimonialist system. On the contrary, he says quite explicitly in his concluding sentence that while the regime may have appeared to be a patrimonial one and bore a strong resemblance to Weber's patrimonialist model, 'Indonesia's apparently patrimonial structures have been built on non-patrimonial foundations, with the result that patrimonial-type stability is not likely to endure.' (Crouch 1979:587)

In his view, the New Order regime was not exclusively a traditionalist and patrimonial regime, but one that also had many modern features, especially in its reliance on economic growth for legitimacy.

> The New Order government's dependence on economic growth seems to require an administrative system based on the bureaucratic values of predictability, regularity, order and rationality—in contrast to patrimonial favouritism and arbitrariness. As a result, basic conflicts over policy and the nature of the regime are becoming increasingly important. (Crouch 1979:579)

Crouch asserted that after the 1974–75 financial disasters in Pertamina and Bulog, Soeharto's ability to go on relying on patrimonialist formulae seemed to be coming under threat. He referred to 'the emerging conflict within [the army] with ideological overtones involving contrasting perceptions of government', the holders of patrimonialist benefices being pitted against a group of 'reform-minded officers' aligned with the economic technocrats pushing for a Weberian 'rational, predictable' legal and administrative structure favourable to the growth of production-oriented capitalism. Although doubtful that these pressures would be strong enough to result in 'the establishment of a Weberian legal-rational order in the immediate future', he expected there would be an increase in political conflict within the military elite and a breakdown of Soeharto's essentially patrimonialist system. Hence his conclusion, that 'patrimonial-style stability is not likely to endure' because the government will find itself forced to 'give greater emphasis to straightforward repression and less to the buying-off of dissidents.' (Crouch 1979:586–87). The system could not survive just on the basis of 'patrimonial favouritism and spoils.'

The later course of events in the 1980s did not bear out that prediction, however. During that decade, repression diminished (albeit slightly) rather than intensified. The rift between 'reform-minded officers' and the old-timers who held patrimonial benefices largely disappeared into the sands of time, as virtually all of them became drawn into the system in varying degrees. We heard almost nothing more of any challenge to the regime by them in the later years of the New Order. And the Soeharto regime continued to survive and flourish for roughly twenty years after Crouch wrote his article. It is even arguable that he might have remained in office much longer if the Asia-wide 'financial meltdown' of 1997–98 had not suddenly disrupted the Indonesian economy severely through the abrupt withdrawal of short-term foreign capital (an externally generated shock-wave, not primarily a domestic one), plunging the country into a crisis which shattered his authority terminally. But how far that crisis and his overthrow were attributable to the patrimonialist character of the regime or to other factors in the brittle political structure prevailing in 1997–98 is a contentious question to which I will return shortly. It was no doubt one of the many factors involved in the witches' brew of troubles which came to a head in May 1998 and left Soeharto with no option but to resign. But the assertion Crouch had made in his article that the New Order could not survive on the basis of 'patrimonial favouritism and spoils' alone seems to depend on an assumption that patrimonialism and real modernisation were incompatible, which I regard as a moot point, to say the least.

That view reflects the arguments that were in contention in the 1970s about the political dynamics of traditional as against modernising polities which we need not go into here. Crouch seems to have assumed that because of its highly mobilised mass organisations (prior to 1965, at least), modern ideologies and a politically conscious, influential corps of military officers, Indonesia now belonged at the modernising end of that spectrum, where there was no longer any place for a patrimonialist system of government. My own view would be that while we may all have hoped that was the case, hindsight reveals to us that the reality was very different. While there is no doubt that patrimonialism is an unhealthy pathology in a truly modern system of government it is surely an overstatement to call it incompatible with modernisation? Other modernising, or rational-legal regimes have been able to tolerate the persistence of patrimonialist elements to some degree. Soeharto was able to maintain them and rely on them to preserve his regime until the economic crisis reached its peak in early 1998.

The post–1979 entrenchment of the patrimonial system

The title of Crouch's 1979 article referred to patrimonialism and military rule, not specifically to it as the basis for President Soeharto's personal authority or rulership. In fact he does not say much at all in it about the great personal ascendancy Soeharto was building up within the New Order power structure even before 1979, partly, I suspect, because that ascendancy was not nearly as striking as it became in the decades following; in fact, it did not become at all securely established until after the troubled years 1975–78. In later years, when the senior officers military came to be more fully under Soeharto's control and his personal authority was unchallenged, the focus on him would no doubt have been much sharper.

In fact it is worth recalling that Crouch's article appeared just when the New Order regime was changing gears, as we might say, from its initially rather tentative search for a political format (Feith's apt phrase of 1968) to one which became far more set in its ways, more patrimonialist, powerful, personalised and later even 'sultanist'. After about 1980–81 any overt challenge to the authority of the president was a very risky course to embark on, as several generals discovered to their cost.[5] It is often forgotten now, when the New Order period is viewed in retrospect as one long continuum of Soeharto's dominance, that in fact his position had seemed far from secure in 1975–76 when there was a great deal of speculation about his possible political demise.

The changes that occurred after about 1979–80 were far-reaching. It was not just that Soeharto stared down the group of senior generals associated with the

---

5   The Petisi 50 group of generals who issued a strongly critical statement about the President's policies in 1980 were very abruptly repudiated and sidelined; see David Jenkins, 1982.

Petisi 50 group and had no further trouble from them, as well as imposing tight discipline over university students through the tough regulations imposed by Daoed Yusuf, his hard-line Minister for Education; it was also that the second oil boom of 1979–80 and the healthy state of the economy in the following years provided him with vastly greater financial resources than ever before which enabled him to allot lucrative fiefdoms to subordinates who were loyal to him, while punishing any whom he suspected of disloyalty by keeping them away from any of the government's now ample honey-pots. Moreover, he curbed any tendency for rival clusters of power to develop, far more effectively than he had been able to do earlier. His control over the military became much tighter as the 1945 Generation of senior officers gave way to the Magelang-trained younger generation with no experience of the revolution, hence greatly in awe of him. The Consultative Assembly (Majelis Permusyawaratan Rakyat, MPR) declared him 'Bapak Pembangunan' in 1983 and the FAO honoured him personally in 1984 for Indonesia's achievement of rice self-sufficiency. His performance legitimacy, which had been under a cloud during the late 1970s when the Green Revolution seemed likely to be derailed in its prime by the 1975–76 *wereng* (brown hopper) plague, was beyond question in the early 1980s, despite momentary hiccups due to oil price falls in 1981–82 and 1986, which were soon cured by the staunch economic policies of his technocratic ministers.

The most striking feature of the patrimonialist system of governance that developed in the 1980s, however, was not just the use of patronage to maintain the loyalty of the president's immediate subordinates but the way he ensured the dependent status of all officials and civil servants by keeping their official salaries and allowances too low to subsist on without resorting to 'unconventional finances' or various forms of corrupt practice. The salary levels of civil servants (*pegawai negeri*) were raised by only trivial amounts. That meant they were all dependent on the connivance and approval of their superiors right up the line to the president himself. Yet it was no longer the case that Indonesia was too poor a country to be able to spare the funds needed to pay more adequate salaries to civil servants. Because they were so poorly paid, they were in effect being kept in a condition of virtually complete dependence on the benefices handed out by the government as additional rewards for their obedience and loyalty. While it had perhaps been understandable that Indonesia's governments had earlier lacked the revenues needed to pay their civil servants and military personnel adequate salaries; that was no longer the case by the late 1980s when the funds available were vastly greater. So their high degree of dependence on the largesse made available from on high was simply maintained. I cannot help suspecting that this was deliberate policy on Soeharto's part, for it must have enhanced his control over the entire state apparatus immensely.

The growing political stature of Soeharto in the 1980s (greatly enhanced by the fact that the economy began to achieve steady growth as the Green Revolution took off and manufacturing industry at last began to develop strongly) may help to explain the resilience of his regime beyond the crisis point which Crouch earlier seemed to expect. In the 1980s, as the patrimonialist aspects of the New Order political system became more and more apparent with the emergence of big conglomerate corporations headed almost entirely by 'crony capitalists' (nearly all Sino-Indonesians) with good connections to the palace, so too did the president's personal predominance within it. As already mentioned, he now had immense financial resources under his control from both the regular budgetary sources (rapidly increasing oil and tax revenues, due in part to a major revamping of the fiscal system in 1983) as well as from what were initially called 'irregular revenues' or later 'off-budget' funds derived mainly from state corporations and other government agencies, not to mention straight-forward bribes paid by private businessmen in return for licenses, concessions and privileges. Control over both economic resources and political power came to be highly concentrated at the apex of the political system, to a degree that had previously been unknown in Indonesia, even under the strongest Dutch governors. So the fiefdoms which Soeharto could allocate to his most loyal subordinates, both civil and military, were now more lucrative and extensive than ever. Anyone who hoped for access to such riches had to be sure to keep on the right side of the president and his state secretary, who kept a close eye on the distribution of all major contracts and benefices. The few who dared to criticise the government in public were utterly excluded from the gravy train.[6]

Even the 'crony' businessmen who had begun to amass huge conglomerates through their contacts with the palace in the 1970s and 1980s were made well aware that it did not pay to try to become too independent of the president or his family. A few tried to do so to a modest extent; but William Suryajaya, who was second only to Liem Sioe Liong/Sudono Salim in the 1980s and tried to keep some distance from the palace after having his fingers burnt in 1974 for being too close to Soeharto's wife, Ibu Tien, was punished very blatantly in 1992 as the price to be paid for such presumption.[7] The most spectacularly wealthy conglomerates that emerged in the 1990s, on the other hand, were all very closely connected with him or his family. There were simply no alternative sources of political protection or patronage of comparable magnitude to Soeharto, unlike in the Sukarno era, when there was still a degree of pluralism in the system.

---

6 Retribution against dissident generals in the later New Order period took the form, according to General Sukendro, that 'all your lifelines should be cut'. Ali Sadikin said that 'they have cut us off from everything'— bank credits from state banks, the right to tender for state contracts, exit permits to travel abroad, even the opportunity to write for newspapers. Jenkins, 1982, p.187.
7 On the emergence of the conglomerates in the 1980s, see Robison, 1986, pp.131–75; Mackie, 1990, pp.71–95; Schwarz, 1986, pp.98–132.

Moreover, the patrimonialist character of the entire socio-political system extended down through its lower levels, with governors, district heads (*bupati*) and subdistrict heads (*camat*)—and even mere village heads—exercising the same sort of powers of control and patronage in their subordinate offices. No other local official or even a wealthy local businessman could afford to get badly off-side with the president's men. Power flowed down from the top during the last twenty years of Soeharto's rule not up from below (as it had done to some extent amidst all the tumult of 1966–67). The prime reason for that was his ability to keep all his officials, potential rivals and alternative power centres in a position of utter dependency.

Even the threat of regional dissidence which had plagued Indonesia under Sukarno was curbed by maintaining a tight rein over regional finances so that local officials were heavily dependent on the revenues they received from Jakarta, hence on the president's goodwill, as in the classic patrimonialist model. The 1974 law on Decentralisation and Local Autonomy enacted by Soeharto would be more accurately described as a law to centralise control over the provinces and to minimise local autonomy, thereby keeping them in a state of almost complete dependence over the next quarter-century.

Adam Schwarz has mentioned another key aspect of Soeharto's 'patrimonialist style of rule' as it related to tensions between the Chinese capitalists and their pribumi rivals:

> No matter how large and powerful the ethnic Chinese businessmen become, they represent no political threat to Suharto because they come from a relatively small minority. But economically powerful pribumi businessmen, freed from reliance on government largesse, would be a different story…. [and] could well outgrow a need for Suharto's favour and become a potent political faction. Whether Suharto views his actions in these terms is hard to say, but the top pribumi businessmen certainly see it this way. (Schwarz 1986:127)

***

A brief comparison of the Indonesian political system with those of Thailand, Malaysia and the Philippines over recent decades will serve to highlight one of the main reasons why the Soeharto regime can appropriately be characterised as patrimonialist whereas the latter three cannot. Since the 1970s, no leader in any of those three countries has held anything like the unassailable and continuing power that Soeharto did. That durability enhanced his power as the sole source of the most lucrative patronage available to any of them enormously. While the others all utilised patronage to the extent they could get away with it, they had nothing like the long-term dominance over the country that Soeharto achieved which made him the supreme patron and source of both offices and lucrative fiefdoms, with no rivals or threatening subordinates. Mahathir came closest to matching him in longevity (along with Marcos, discussed below) but he had serious rivals with followings in the United Malays National Organisation (Pertubuhan Kebangsaan Melayu Bersatu, UMNO) and some patronage capacity as ministers—Musa Hitam, Razaleigh and Anwar Ibrahim—whom he could never disregard entirely until after Anwar was shafted in 1999. And both the parliamentary structure, the judiciary and the bureaucracy imposed constraints on his naked use of patronage of a kind that Soeharto never had to bother about. In Thailand, prime ministers (and the parties behind them) came and went so frequently that none had sufficient opportunity to build up the vast networks of dependents among the wealthy Sino-Thai business groups through patronage that Soeharto created via the crony conglomerates. In that respect there was far more pluralism in both the Malaysian and Thai systems than in Indonesia, financial as well as political. The Philippines was a very different story, mainly because it is the one country in Southeast Asia with a substantial propertied class of about 200 wealthy landowning families who have exerted great political influence in Manila ever since independence, as well as immense economic clout in their regions, to a degree that is not replicated in any nearby nation. Marcos could not simply defy or override those interests even during the martial law years between 1972 and his overthrow in 1986 (indirectly caused by the murder of Aquino in 1973, plus mass opposition in Manila) but had to manipulate and accommodate them. Whether or not his regime was more venal, dictatorial or patronage-based than Soeharto's, an arguable question, it could certainly not be described as similarly patrimonialist.

A striking feature of the socio-political and economic structures that have developed since World War II in Thailand, Malaysia and Indonesia (but not the Philippines) is that there is a substantial disjunction between political and economic power in all three of them—as also in Singapore along very different lines. That is due in large part to the economic dominance of the local ethnic Chinese business class in each, coupled with its lack of anything like comparable political influence (except to some degree in Thailand since the late 1980s, where there have been more Sino-Thai prime ministers than ethnic Thai, something that would be inconceivable in Indonesia). That is a situation conducive to patrimonialist or 'sultanist' or patriarchal rule, as in so many pre-modern societies, but against the grain of most modern capitalist countries. It has been avoided in Thailand and Malaysia for rather special local reasons grounded in the historical position of the Chinese minorities there and the pluralist features mentioned above. But patronage is a more prominent feature of the political and economic landscape in Indonesia, widely accepted as a tolerable means of helping to create or support the small emerging class of pribumi businessmen. While that is also true of the other two, it is less marked and less politicised there.

I suspect that patronage will remain a continuing feature in all three countries, Indonesia especially, until an indigenous capitalist class emerges which starts to see virtue in the idea of level playing-fields and avoidance of special privileges on the basis of patron-client relationships. That will probably not be soon.

***

Did the patrimonialist character of Soeharto's New Order contribute to the longevity of his rule—or was it, on the contrary, responsible ultimately for the collapse of his regime in 1998? Or both? The answers to these questions must surely be that it was certainly one among a number of factors that contributed to its longevity and also one among those that brought about its final collapse. How great a part, or small, it played on either of these issues could be argued at great length, but I will try to give two brief answers.

As a factor that accounted for its longevity, I would say that it undoubtedly enabled him to retain the loyalty of his subordinates through the use of carrots rather than sticks. And he certainly had a lot of carrots at his disposal during the latter part of his long reign. The lack of any effective opposition to him from within the elite prior to the 1998 crisis must be attributed largely to that. On the other hand, there were other factors that contributed to the longevity of his rule. His 'performance legitimacy' was surely one of the most important, both in his early years when he quickly pulled Indonesia out of the economic and political chaos of the late Sukarno era and steered it towards recovery and ultimate prosperity, as well as in the boom years of the early 1990s which brought unprecedented wealth to large numbers of Indonesians. The fact that he was able to deliver the goods in bad times as well as good, even amidst falling oil prices and bad rice harvests, won him grudging acceptance even among his enemies. Another factor was the persistent hope that the improving political and social conditions that he had brought about and the gradual emergence of a semi-autonomous urban middle class would be followed sooner or later by progress towards a more democratic system of government. This seemed to be borne out by the three brief years of 'openness' (*keterbukaan*) between 1991–94—until they were abruptly ended by the banning of *Tempo* and *Editor* on absurdly trivial grounds. There was to be no return to that more liberal phase of government until after Soeharto had fallen. And there were growing expectations by the 1990s that his next term in office would turn out to be his last; so no one wanted (or dared) to take the risk of trying openly to dislodge him.

Can the collapse of his regime in 1998 be attributed in a way to its patrimonialist character? Only as a very indirect background factor, I think, insofar as it helps to account for the rigidity of the regime in its final months and for the public dissatisfaction that swelled suddenly and unexpectedly into a tidal wave of rejection of Soeharto's iron grip on the presidency in May 1998. Any explanation of how the end came must take account of a number of other elements in the equation that had an effect, some very short-term in their significance, others more deep-seated and persistent. The most important factor, of course, was the catastrophic collapse of the economy after the mid-1997 'financial meltdown' (*krismon*) which in itself could perhaps have been handled successfully had it not been for the obvious favouritism shown by Soeharto towards his children and their economic interests over the following months. But that was the sin of nepotism, not patrimonialism. It certainly magnified the collapse of public confidence in the competence of his government itself and in the value of the rupiah which fell precipitously, plunging the country into ever deeper economic turmoil. And the fact that the financial crisis occurred just before the March 1998 MPR session to elect or re-elect the president created an exceptionally volatile political climate. But the train of events which followed the shooting of four students at Trisakti University on 12 May and the mass rioting in Jakarta next day when his legitimacy and authority crumbled terminally had little to do with the patrimonialist character of the regime as a direct cause. If anything, the reverse; it was the fact that Soeharto could no longer exert anything like his former sway even over his closest ministers—and their refusal to join the new cabinet he was trying to cobble together in his final days—that made him realise the game was up.[8]

Conclusion

By characterising the New Order as patrimonialist, Crouch provided a more convincing explanation of its basic dynamics than any previous analyst had done. Modernisation theory, which had exercised a big influence on studies of the developing countries in the early 1960s—in particular on Herb Feith's writings on Indonesia as that time—lost much of its earlier appeal during the Vietnam war decade, especially in the United States.[9] So there was a theoretical vacuum waiting to be filled. Mortimer had earlier made a strong case for 'bringing class back in' to our explanations of the socio-political dynamics of Indonesian politics in the mid-1960s, but neither his approach nor the dependency theory and neo-colonialist interpretations that became fashionable after the sharp increase in transnational capital inflows of the early 1970s provided a convincing basis for new interpretations of the power structures underpinning Soeharto's regime along those lines (Mortimer 1973:54–68; Mortimer 1982).

---

8   On the fall of Soeharto in May 1998, good accounts are given in O'Rourke, 2002; and Aspinall, 2005.

9   Herb Feith revealed the early stages of his disillusionment with 'modernisation theory' in his famous reply to Harry Benda's review of his book in the *Journal of Asian Studies*, 1965, later in an unpublished 1969 article on 'The Study of Indonesian Politics: A Survey and an Apologia', both included in Anderson and Kahin eds, 1982, pp.41–53.

Benedict Anderson turned that approach on its head by 'bringing the state back in' a few years later, with an emphasis on its relative autonomy from class alignments (Anderson 1983). Nor did the various interpretations of the New Order in terms of 'bureaucratic authoritarianism' which cropped up in the 1980s as alternatives to structural-functionalism. None of those approaches helped to account for the extraordinary degree of personal ascendancy Soeharto was able to establish from about 1980 on, when he came to dominate the political scene completely for nearly two decades—primarily, I would argue, because of the increasingly patrimonialist character of the regime he created in those years. Without wanting to claim that Crouch had provided us with anything that can be compared with the grand theorising represented by the Almond and Coleman school or dependency theory, I think it can be said that he threw more light on the basic character of the Soeharto regime than any other analyst.

The Legacy

7 The Habibie Presidency: Catapulting Towards Reform

DEWI FORTUNA ANWAR

President B.J. Habibie was an unlikely reformer. As a technology specialist and President Soeharto's hand-picked vice-president, he did not seem to possess the necessary trackrecord or credibility to oversee reform. After the resignation of President Soeharto in May 1998, critics regarded President Habibie's government as a continuation of the New Order *status quo*. They depicted his reforms as nothing more than insincere and half-hearted efforts to gain popularity and cling to power in the face of intense public pressure. Yet several years after the collapse of the New Order and Indonesia's often painful journey through *reformasi*, it can be seen that many of the laws, regulations and other changes introduced by the Habibie government were in fact fundamental in nature. The Habibie government laid the foundation for Indonesia's democratic transition, its move toward decentralisation and many other features of the new Indonesia. President Habibie also allowed self-determination for East Timor, paving the way for its subsequent independence.

Far from being a reluctant reformer, President Habibie seized a brief political opportunity to introduce a slew of far-reaching reforms that Indonesia had long needed but could not carry out under the New Order, and which might have been more difficult to carry out once Indonesia returned to 'normalcy'. Yet looking at Habibie's educational and working background before becoming Soeharto's favoured aide, one should not be too surprised at Habibie's enthusiasm for political reform. He spent the best part of his youth and young adulthood in Germany where he had first-hand experience of living in a democratic society with a federal system of government. During his tenure as Minister for Science and Technology Habibie travelled widely, so he was fully aware of how the international community, notably western countries, viewed New Order Indonesia, particularly in relation to the East Timor problem. It was, therefore, not entirely unexpected that when Indonesia faced imminent collapse and he was under tremendous domestic and international pressure to institute drastic changes to rescue the country from the post-Soeharto upheaval, Habibie reached out to the West to help Indonesia in carrying out comprehensive political reform. For years various western governments have criticised Indonesia's lack of democracy, poor human rights record and continued occupation of East Timor. Jakarta's centralised control over the entire country had also been blamed for regional restiveness. Unlike Soeharto who was highly suspicious of the West and regarded democracy and human rights as manifestations of 'western values' incompatible with Indonesian cultural identity, Habibie did not seem to have any discomfort with 'western values' and once he became president immediately embraced the concepts of democracy and human rights as universal values. Habibie's support for wide-ranging regional autonomy could also be partly attributed to his experience of living in Germany where the federal system of government provides extensive rights and autonomy to the *Lande* or state governments, allowing them to flourish without weakening the unity of Germany. As a scientist Habibie could also see that the majority of developed countries are those that have adopted democratic systems of government which allow their citizens freedom of thought and expression.

In this chapter, the author, who served as one of President Habibie's assistants, looks at the dynamics of the Habibie presidency, focusing on some of the major reforms carried out and highlighting Habibie's open style of leadership, which contrasted sharply with that of his mentor, Soeharto. The chapter also discusses some of the problems encountered in the reform process. Since the writer was an insider during the period of the Habibie government, this contribution does not pretend to be a fully objective and critical scholarly analysis, for it relies as much on personal observations, experience and recollections, as on written documents.[1]

Accelerated evolution and constitutionalism

One key to understanding the record of the Habibie presidency, which lasted from May 1998 to October 1999, was that the president viewed himself as a strict constitutionalist. He was fond of characterising the rapid changes that he was overseeing as 'accelerated evolution' rather than revolution. Many of the student protestors and other radical reformers in 1998–99 were demanding revolutionary change and the discarding of the entire system inherited from the New Order. Habibie, by contrast, argued that Indonesia should avoid another costly, disruptive and unpredictable revolution, like those of 1945–49 and 1965–

---

1   When B.J. Habibie was elected vice-president in March 1998, the writer was appointed to a newly created position of assistant to the vice-president on Global Affairs. Not long after President Soeharto resigned on 21 May 1998 and Habibie had assumed the presidency, the writer was moved to the State Secretariat, occupying the position of assistant to the Minister for the State Secretariat on Global Affairs. The minister at the time was Akbar Tanjung. When Akbar Tanjung was later preoccupied with running for the Golkar Chairmanship, the writer was also appointed as a presidential spokesperson, having already acted unofficially in this capacity from the first day of Habibie's presidency.

68, since past achievements could be lost without guaranteeing satisfactory outcomes. Furthermore, revolutionary changes could delay institutional consolidation and open the way for more revolutions in the future. For these reasons, President Habibie always said he favoured evolution and step-by-step transformation of the existing system. As Indonesia's reform process had stalled for over three decades, making the system unable to respond to fundamental global and domestic changes, evolution needed to be accelerated. In his arguments Habibie used scientific and engineering examples to illustrate his point about the merits and demerits of evolution and revolution. He argued that a revolution, due to its burst of energy, could become random and unpredictable with uncontrollable consequences, while an evolution is always a planned and systematic approach so that the results can be predicted and anticipated. To speed up the evolutionary process it must be accelerated, but still follow a clear blueprint.

This opposition to revolutionary and unconstitutional change lay at the root of Habibie's rejection of the views of those who wanted to dismantle the Consultative Assembly (Majelis Permusyawaratan Rakyat, MPR) and the House of Representatives (Dewan Perwakilan Rakyat, DPR), and replace the government with some sort of unelected 'revolutionary' council (Budiman 1998:76). Habibie recognised that the existing MPR, DPR and his presidency lacked popular legitimacy in the wake of the mass public demonstrations that forced President Soeharto to resign. He also agreed with the emerging post-Soeharto consensus that the 1945 Constitution, the very foundation of the political system, did not sufficiently protect political and civil liberties; gave too much power to the executive branch; denied the people the right to elect their leaders directly, and therefore would have to be amended.

Where President Habibie disagreed with his more impatient critics was that he believed that in order to manage Indonesia's systematic transformation and safeguard its future, particularly to ensure that economic recovery was not jeopardised by prolonged political chaos, all changes—even those to the Constitution itself—had to be made according to a constitutional process. If the Constitution and existing laws stood in the way of reform, then these had to first be amended, revoked or replaced, but they could not in any way be disregarded or deliberately violated.

Within months of coming to office, the president and his advisers had come to the conclusion that in order to enable the reform process to move forward, one of the first steps was to remove the barriers to constitutional amendment. In the past President Soeharto had often invoked the 1945 Constitution to justify his undemocratic policies, and he had made the Constitution into a sacred text that could not be amended easily, since amendments could only be done through a referendum.[2] At the same time, Habibie recognised soon after he took over the presidency that political stability and economic recovery could only be attained if the legitimacy of the government were not in dispute. In order to avoid prolonging the political uncertainty and erosion of public confidence in state institutions, Habibie decided to cut short his presidency by almost four years and bring the general elections forward from 2003 to 1999. These and other fundamental changes could only be done by convening a 'Special Session' of the MPR, which took place in November 1998, six months after Habibie came to power. Despite massive student demonstrations to disrupt it, leading to violent clashes with the security forces, the 1998 Special Session succeeded in passing several important decrees which made it possible for the reform process to proceed both constitutionally and at an accelerated pace. This Special Session, despite being derided by supporters of *'reformasi total'*, became a major milestone in Indonesia's reform effort, the starting point for the fundamental changes which followed.

Amongst the decrees passed by the Special Session were No 8, which revoked an earlier decree requiring a referendum to change the Constitution, thus making it possible for the MPR to amend the Constitution; No 13, which limited the president and vice-president to a maximum of two terms in office (Soeharto had been re-elected for seven consecutive terms), and No 14, which brought elections forward from 2003 to June 1999. The Special Session also passed a decree (No 15) on regional autonomy, which later enabled the Habibie government to introduce the wide-ranging decentralisation package. Other important decrees included one on Human Rights and another ending Pancasila indoctrination courses. A number of these key decrees were later incorporated into constitutional amendments, thus vesting them with even greater constitutional weight.

One can only speculate on the political and economic direction that Indonesia would have embarked upon if the demonstrators had succeeded in disrupting the 1998 Special Session of the MPR, thus preventing an orderly political transition.[3] Indonesia might have been plunged into another period of political emergency and ad hoc experiments, which may or may not have led to greater democratisation. Many critics who have been dissatisfied with the

---

2   Decree MPR RI No IV/MPR/1983 stipulates that any amendment of the 1945 Constitution can only be done after a referendum approves each and every particular proposed amendment, which made it almost impossible to amend it.

3   The author was a member of the MPR from 1998 to 1999 and took part in the Special Session of November 1998 and thus experienced first-hand the extremely tense period surrounding it. Most members of the MPR stayed at the Hotel Mulya and were bussed to the MPR Building. Just before the opening session news broke out that the demonstrators were about to storm the building and every one was asked to get back on the bus to return to the hotel. We had to wait for some time on the bus, and then at the hotel till nearly midnight, before we were returned to the MPR building to continue the opening session. The determination of the demonstrators to disrupt the MPR Session helped to add a new urgency to the proceedings, MPR members fully realised that if the relevant decrees were not revoked, amended, replaced or passed as bases for future legislation and action, Indonesia's would enter a new period of uncertainty.

rather incremental changes taking place since then might well have preferred a revolutionary overhauling of the whole system, since a number of necessary reforms have since been stalled due to resistance from entrenched vested interests.

True to President Habibie's promise of rule-based accelerated evolution, the period of his government was one of extraordinary rule-making fervour. Between 21 May 1998 and October 1999, there were 50 laws passed, 2 Government Regulations in lieu of Law, 99 Government Regulations, 232 Presidential Decisions and 27 Presidential Instructions, making a total of 410 laws and regulations. These legislative and regulation-making productivities can be compared to the New Order period in which, during 30 years 122 laws, 510 Government Regulations in lieu of laws, 914 Presidential Decisions and 89 Presidential Instructions were passed (Asshiddiqie et al 1999). As a comparison in the DPR session period of 2003–04 there were 40 bills that were introduced as initiatives of the DPR and 17 bills that were introduced by the government, making a total of 57 bills. Of the 40 bills initiated by the DPR, 13 became law, while of the government-initiated bills 11 became law, making a total of 24 laws in two years. The 'Program Legislasi Nasional' has an ambitious legislation program, 248 bills for the period 2005–09, but there had been a backlog of legislation from the earlier period in the DPR. The laws and regulations enacted during the Habibie presidency covered a fairly wide spectrum, but most dealt with political, economic and financial matters.

There is some justification for the criticism that the Habibie government passed *too many* laws and regulations without sufficient time for rigorous discussion and scrutiny. The result was that a number of laws had confusing or contradictory articles. On the other hand, given the immediate need to carry out wide-ranging reforms in almost all aspects of public life, the frenetic pace of legislation was unavoidable, and it did provide a solid foundation for future reform.

Promoting civil liberties

Habibie spent most of his political career serving as Minister for Science and Technology in successive Soeharto cabinets. Before he became president Habibie stated openly on a number of occasions that he regarded President Soeharto as his mentor and 'political guru'. It was thus not surprising that many people were sceptical that he would rule any differently from his predecessor. In fact, Habibie demonstrated early in his presidency that he was a different type of leader. While President Soeharto ensured his unchallenged political control by imposing tight censorship of the media, limiting freedom of speech and association, imprisoning political opponents, and rejecting the very concept of human rights as being alien to Indonesian values, President Habibie did exactly the opposite.

The motivations for Habibie's actions can indeed partly be attributed to public pressure and his desire to win popular support. Yet the enthusiasm with which he carried out some of his reform initiatives, some of which were quite radical and even damaging to his immediate political interests, indicated Habibie's more personal interest and commitment to reform than is noted. If Habibie had been only concerned about winning public approval, he would probably have been more selective, introducing reforms that would be popular but avoiding those which would have negative consequences for his own political fortunes. Instead, Habibie did not shy away from introducing a number of important reforms, knowing that such reforms would limit or undermine his hold on power. His strong support for media freedom, despite the fact that he would become a primary target of criticism, the liberalisation of political parties which challenged Golkar's monopoly of power, and devolving power to the regions despite reservations from members of this government demonstrated Habibie's personal interest in the reform process.[4] On the East Timor issue it was quite clear that President Habibie was the prime mover in giving the East Timorese the choice of integration or independence since he did not want the East Timorese problem to remain a burden to Indonesia for years to come. In response to public pressure Habibie brought the general elections forward, thus cutting short his presidency creating the possibility of not being re-elected under the multi-party system. On bringing Soeharto to justice, however, it was clear that Habibie was very reluctant to do so. He would probably have earned some political mileage if he had put Soeharto on trial, but pressures from outside and from within his immediate circle notwithstanding, Habibie would not budge on the issue, saying that he would rather be unpopular than be '*durhaka*' or disrespectful towards Soeharto.

One of the first acts carried out by the Habibie government was to revoke all of the laws and regulations that had constrained freedom of speech, association and gatherings and to release political prisoners. Together with the DPR the government passed law No 9/1998 on Freedom of Speech in Public Places, while the president issued Presidential Decision No 83/1998, which ratified the ILO 'Convention No. 87 Concerning Freedom of Association and Protection of the Right to Organise'. Of even greater importance in guaranteeing freedom of speech was the 1999 revocation of the draconian 1963 anti-subversion law.

---

4 When criticisms against the government and the president became too vulgar (*kasar*) there were sometimes comments from certain members of the cabinet or visitors to the president that media freedom was 'kebablasan' or gone overboard. President Habibie and his Minister for Information, Junus Josfiah, often defended the press, saying that media freedom is important. On debates about regional autonomy Habibie showed some preference for a more federal arrangement, such as decentralising the police.

Throughout the New Order, there had been numerous political prisoners, ranging from high-ranking military officers to politicians, labour activists, intellectuals and women activists. President Habibie signed about a dozen Presidential Decisions releasing all political prisoners, including giving amnesty to the imprisoned East Timorese leader, Xanana Gusmao.[5] Not only did living political prisoners receive amnesty and have their rights rehabilitated, those who had died were also rehabilitated. President Habibie even awarded the late Lieutenant General H R Dharsono, who died after a long imprisonment for criticising President Soeharto, with the Bintang Maha Putra Utama, the highest award in the Indonesian honours system, as recognition of Dharsono's contribution to Indonesian independence.

The most notable reform carried out by the Habibie government in promoting civil liberties was undoubtedly in the area of media freedom. Soeharto had controlled the media not only by threatening journalists with imprisonment if they wrote articles to which the government objected, but through its control of publication licences (Surat Izin Usaha Penerbitan Pers, SIUPP). Not only were these licences difficult to obtain, which limited the number of print media options, but they could be revoked at the government's discretion, forcing editors to exercise stringent self-censorship.

President Habibie, enthusiastically aided by his Minister for Information, Lieutenant General Yunus Yosfiah surprised critics by his extremely liberal attitude towards media freedom, both printed and electronic.[6] The requirement to obtain SIUPP before starting a publication was rescinded, so that within a very short time literally hundreds of new newspapers, tabloids and magazines appeared. The government also gave almost untrammelled freedom to media reporting, and the Minister for Information no longer acted as a media watchdog or called editors to reprimand them on the contents of their publications. Although President Habibie was daily criticised, lambasted and sometimes lampooned by the media, he generally reacted with good humour, recognising open criticism was an outcome of the democratic processes he had initiated. The Indonesian media became one of the freest in Asia.[7] President Habibie was also noted for his personal openness and accessibility. Unlike his immediate predecessor, who hardly ever talked directly to the press, Habibie frequently

---

5   Xanana's release from prison came later after President Habibie offered the two options solution to the East Timor problem.

6   Yunus Yosfiah was better known for his role as a young officer in the Indonesian invasion of East Timor, during which a number of Australian journalists were killed. As a tough military man he was considered an unlikely reformer, yet he proved to be an enlightened Minister for Information, strongly supportive of media freedom.

7   Of course, media freedom did not automatically lead to good quality media. Many of the new publications were forced to close down due to market competition, not because of government action.

gave interviews to both foreign and domestic journalists.[8] This was probably the single most important action which helped to transform the image and character of the presidency. Under Soeharto the presidency was seen as remote, cold, inaccessible and shrouded in secrecy, and thus beyond public control. By exposing himself and his office to media scrutiny, Habibie helped to demystify the presidency, making it more transparent and closer to the people, and thereby easier to criticise and control.

Political liberalisation

Free general elections, in which political parties and candidates compete without fear of government intimidation and voters are free to exercise their choice, are prerequisites of democracy. Under the New Order, the government limited the number of political parties, and regulated their activities, while general elections were not free. Only two political parties, the Islamic United Development Party (Partai Persatuan Indonesia, PPP) and the Indonesia Democracy Party (Partai Demokrasi Indonesia, PDI) were allowed to exist to act as ornamental proof that Indonesia was not a one-party state. In effect, the government's own Golkar, not strictly regarded as a political party, was the only party allowed to win the majority of votes at every election. By controlling the political parties, the elections and other political recruitment processes, the New Order government had been able to pack the DPR and the MPR with pro-government appointees and semi-appointees, which in turn ensured the successive re-election of Soeharto as president every five years. The MPR and the DPR primarily served as rubber stamps for the executive, endorsing all government policies without any pretence of checks and balances.

As explained above, the 1998 Special Session of the MPR brought forward general elections from 2003 to 1999. Two laws were passed as preparation for these elections, No 2/1999 on Political Parties and No 3/1999 on General Elections. The government invited members of the public, including members of academic institutions and non-governmental organisations, to participate directly in the drafting of these new laws. Some such people made presentations at the presidential office. The new law on political parties removed all of the New Order restrictions on political parties, including the 'Asas Tunggal' doctrine whereby all parties were required to adopt Pancasila as their 'sole foundation'. Under the new law, Pancasila remained the sole ideology of the state, but

---

8   The writer was often asked to arrange media interviews with the president. They mostly took place on Saturdays, in the beginning usually at Bina Graha and later at the Merdeka Palace or at times at Habibie's private residence. Habibie was at first reluctant to talk directly to the press, but was later convinced that it was better for journalists to obtain first-hand information on what the president and the government had done and was trying to achieve.

political parties were free to have different political ideologies and platforms (except communism, which was still banned). As a result of this liberalisation, within a short time over 200 parties registered at the Ministry of Justice, though in the end 'only' 48 parties qualified to contest the elections in June 1999. The law on general elections also tried to ensure more democratic and fairer elections than had taken place under the New Order. It ended government control of the electoral process, giving the task of managing the elections to the newly formed National Elections Commission (Komisi Pemilihan Umum, KPU) which was then mostly made up of party representatives. The government also allowed independent domestic and international election watch groups to monitor the whole election process.

Many people, both at home and abroad, were sceptical of the Habibie government's ability to plan and carry out general elections under these new rules in the very short time available. It was undoubtedly a mammoth undertaking: within six months political parties had to establish themselves throughout the country, while the KPU had to register voters and prepare complex ballot papers for over 300 districts. The balloting itself had to be completed within a few hours in a single day in such a vast country, where many areas were difficult to reach.

Without strong international financial support and technical assistance it is doubtful that Indonesia would have been able to carry out its first truly democratic general election since 1955 so successfully. Here, too, President Habibie's personal role was significant. The president talked to many world leaders, including the US President, Prime Ministers of Britain and Australia, and the United Nations Secretary General, asking them to help Indonesia in its democratic transition. The response was overwhelming. Several governments, international organisations and international NGOs seemed to compete with each other in offering financial support and various forms of technical assistance. Indonesia initiated a process that would later be used as a model for other countries. In order to avoid competition and overlap amongst the donor countries and organisations providing electoral assistance, the government asked the United Nations Development Program (UNDP) to coordinate all of the assistance and activities. Initially the UNDP was hesitant to undertake this task, since it had not previously been involved in managing general elections. President Habibie was, however, insistent that the UNDP perform this coordinating function, in part because this would avoid giving particular donor countries too much prominence. The direct involvement and visibility of the UNDP, an organ of the United Nations, in the elections was more acceptable to nationalist sensitivities than if one or two western countries were to be seen running the show, a situation which could have weakened the legitimacy of the elections in the eyes of critics.

Although external pressure forced Habibie to bring the elections forward in order to preempt the demands of the radical elements who wanted '*reformasi total*' by forming a 'revolutionary government', once sold on the idea Habibie tried to make the elections as democratic as possible within the shortest time. Some senior politicians who had pressed for immediate general elections thought that Habibie was being unrealistic believing that the preparations could be done within six months.[9] In the end Habibie confounded all sceptics who doubted the elections could be run on time without organisational fiasco or violence. As it turned out, the general elections were on the whole peaceful and deemed to be fair and democratic.

One result of the elections was the sharp decline in Golkar's vote, though it still managed to come second after the then hugely popular Indonesian Democratic Party of Struggle (Partai Demokrasi Indonesia—Perjuangan, PDI-P). This showing for Golkar was itself a major victory, remembering the political climate in which some student activists and others were calling for the party to be banned. No party won an overall majority. Many Habibie supporters at the time believed that if pooled together, the votes obtained by Golkar and all of the Islamic and Muslim-based parties, would still constitute a majority in the MPR, giving Habibie a chance to retain the presidency. This was not the case, for a number of the Golkar members of the MPR joined the PDI-P, the National Awakening Party (Partai Kebangkitan Bangsa, PKB) and other anti-Habibie factions in rejecting President Habibie's Accountability Speech during the MPR Session in October 1999. The military faction was also believed to have voted against President Habibie, as a mark of their disappointment over the loss of East Timor. As a result, Habibie withdrew his candidacy and threw his support behind Abdurrahman Wahid.[10]

During this period Habibie's conduct in the face of political adversity was significant. It could not have been easy for President Habibie to listen to the speeches that were critical of his government and of him during the 1999 MPR Session. During these early days of Indonesia's democratic transition and the excitement which came after overthrowing a long-term dictator, the behaviour of the DPR/MPR members was often lacking in graciousness. Many of them refused to stand up and some booed as President Habibie came into the MPR Chamber, while speeches lambasting him at times used vitriolic language. Nevertheless despite the pain and effort it must have cost him, Habibie attended all sessions and sat through these political attacks. When people close to him asked Habibie not to subject himself to such public humiliation, telling him

---

9   One of the senior politicians was Professor Emil Salim who during one of his visits to President Habibie's residence openly voiced his scepticism.

10   Many Habibie supporters blamed Golkar's Chairman Akbar Tanjung and his close associates for betraying Habibie. For an account of the political manoueverings in the MPR session leading to the election of Abdurrahman Wahid, see Mietzner, 2000, pp.39–57.

he did not have to listen to the responses to his accountability speech, Habibie answered that acting in this way was part of the political education of the public regarding how a leader of a democratic country should behave. Open criticism of the president was part and parcel of the democracy that Indonesia wanted to nurture; Habibie was willing to undergo personal indignity to help the process along. In another important gesture, Habibie attended the inauguration of President Abdurrahman Wahid, assisting Wahid to walk to his chair. Habibie remarked afterwards that this was to demonstrate to the Indonesian people that in a democracy, victories and losses are commonplace, so that it is not necessary to cling to power through all means or to see defeat as a shame or disgrace.

Radical decentralisation

Another important reform introduced by the Habibie government was wide-ranging regional autonomy, regarded by many observers as one of the most radical shifts from centralism to decentralisation undertaken by any country. The New Order's over-centralisation, in almost every aspect of national life, had been the main grievance in the regions. Not only were the social, political and economic activities of the regions tightly regulated and controlled by Jakarta, most of regional wealth was also taken by Jakarta.

Law No 22/1999 on Political Decentralisation and law No 25/1999 on Fiscal Decentralisation and the sharing of revenue have been the subject of many studies so they will not be discussed at length here (Aspinall and Fealy 2003). Law No 22 gave wide-ranging powers to regional governments at the district/mayoralty level, the second tier of regional governments, rather than to the first tier, the provinces. Law No 25 allowed regional governments to retain substantial amounts of the revenue they collect, thus giving them greater financial independence and responsibility.[11] Under law No 22, the central government retains power in five key areas, namely defence and security, foreign policy, fiscal and monetary affairs, the judiciary and religious affairs; authority on all other matters is transferred to the regions.[12] In short, the new decentralisation policy fundamentally transformed relations between the central government and the regions, changing the character of the Indonesian state.

This policy was introduced after what was, given the time constraints, a highly consultative process. The government carried out extensive discussion

---

11   For instance, the regions can now retain 80% of income from forestry and mining, leaving only 20% for the central government. For oil the division is 85% for the central government and 15% for the producing regions, while for natural gas the income accruing to the central government is 70%, leaving 30% to the regions after taxes. See Jimly Asshiddiqie et al, 1999, p.121.

12   The right to regulate religion was not devolved to the regions to prevent possible discrimination against religious minorities in regions in which one particular religion is dominant.

in drafting the bills, sending teams overseas to study the experiences of other countries and inviting national and international experts to provide input. The task of drafting the bills was given to a group of academics from the Institute for Government Studies (Institut Ilmu Pemerintahan, IIP) under Professor Ryaas Rasyid, a well-known specialist on local government. Although the political climate at the time was strongly in favour of regional autonomy, the draftspeople and many members of the cabinet insisted that autonomy should only be given to the second tier of government, the district/mayoralty level. Ostensibly this was to bring government and public services closer to the people; but the real reason was based on fear that giving autonomy to the provinces, which were larger and stronger administrative units, would lead to federalism.

President Habibie's personal role in this policy shift has been little commented upon by observers. Throughout the discussions, he showed his strong interest in, and support for, regional autonomy. Indonesia's regional autonomy laws in fact contain important characteristics which are similar to a federal system, notably the transfer of all powers to the regions except in specific areas which are reserved to the central government. During a presentation of the draft regional government bill at Wisma Negara to several cabinet members and officials of the State Secretariat, observed by the author, the president intervened to directly answer many questions officials asked of the bill draftspeople; in his answers he often explained how the German *Lande* system worked. At a cabinet meeting discussing the separation of the military and the police (another major achievement of the Habibie government), also witnessed by the author, Habibie suggested that police in different provinces could have different uniforms, underscoring the different characteristics of each province.[13] This suggestion was quite radical in the Indonesian context, and was perhaps also derived from the German example. When someone remarked that establishing separate police forces in each province would be akin to federalism, the president did not pursue the matter further.[14] In fact, however, he envisaged that at some future date each region would have its separate regional police and civil service (Asshiddiqie et al 1999:120).

---

13 A number of first echelon officials, including the author, were invited to attend cabinet meetings, to take notes.

14 Like the military, the Indonesian police currently have a unified national organisation under the chief of police who is now directly under the president. The police have strongly opposed suggestions that they be put under the Minister for Internal Affairs, which would also make them fall under the jurisdiction of the regional governments. Such practice is common, even in unitary systems.

Paving the way for East Timor's independence

The most radical and controversial reform carried out by President Habibie was allowing self-determination to the people of East Timor, providing them the choice between accepting special autonomy within Indonesia or rejecting it. President Habibie regarded a settlement of the East Timor problem as part of his government's democracy and human rights agenda, but also as a way to free Indonesia of the long drawn-out East Timor issue once and for all. Habibie argued on a number of occasions that the rights of over 200 million Indonesians should take first priority, and that the East Timor problem should not be allowed to detract from attempts to resolve Indonesia's many other problems. Although his desire to resolve the conflict peacefully came to grief when violence broke out after the ballot results were announced, history will record that his bold decision removed one of the most difficult legacies of the New Order government, even if it did cost him his presidency.[15]

Indonesia's annexation of East Timor and its integration into the Republic of Indonesia in 1976, after the departure of the Portuguese colonial administration, had never been recognised by the United Nations and the majority of its members. Indonesia's forcible integration of East Timor, and the widely reported human rights abuses carried out by the military there, became a major stumbling bloc in Indonesia's international relations and badly tarnished the country's image, particularly in the West.

As Minister for Science and Technology for most of the New Order period, Habibie had almost nothing to do with East Timor. However, once he became president, the East Timor issue immediately came to the top of his agenda, particularly as leaders and ambassadors of western countries and journalists raised it at meetings. Habibie's first public statement about his plan for resolving the East Timor problem came at his first interview as president, given to the BBC correspondent in Jakarta, and aired on 9 June 1998, less than three weeks after he became president. In response to a question, Habibie announced that he would give special autonomy to East Timor. He did not elaborate what the special autonomy would entail in the interview, but immediately afterwards he instructed Foreign Minister Ali Alatas to develop the concept and to revive the tripartite talks on East Timor between Indonesia, Portugal and the Secretary General of the United Nations. The governments of Indonesia and Portugal had agreed to carry out regular talks to reach an agreement on East Timor under the

---

15   The margin between the Yes and the No vote on President Habibie's Accountability Speech at the MPR General Assembly in October 1999 was very narrow (322 votes to 355). After he lost this vote, Habibie withdrew his nomination for re-election as president, opening the way for Abdurrahman Wahid to win. It has been suggested that the military faction's vote against Habibie due to the loss of East Timor, tilted the vote against him.

auspices of the United Nations Secretary General, but Portugal pulled out of further meetings after the 1991 Santa Cruz incident, when Indonesian troops fired on demonstrators in Dili, killing many people. Habibie and his advisers hoped that the special autonomy offer would forestall East Timorese demands for independence and prompt Portugal to recognise Indonesia's jurisdiction over the territory.

The special autonomy initiative received enthusiastic international support. The tripartite meeting between senior Indonesian and Portuguese officials and the UN Secretary General in October 1998 discussed a model of enlarged autonomy for East Timor that had been drafted by the UN Secretary General's office. Bilateral relations between Indonesia and Portugal improved considerably.

Indonesia's decision to offer special autonomy to East Timor, however, took an interesting turn towards the end of 1998. For Indonesia, the offer of special and enlarged autonomy was seen as a final solution for the East Timor problem, under which the territory would receive privileges not enjoyed by other provinces, such as having a completely separate police force and its own provincial symbols. Despite the generous provisions of the autonomy package, however, it became clear that pro-independence East Timorese groups, as well as Portugal, viewed the special autonomy offer merely as an interim solution, the final solution being a referendum for self-determination at a later date. For Indonesia, allowing special autonomy as only an interim solution was not acceptable, because it would prolong the uncertainty concerning the final status of the province.

Two events took place in December 1998, which helped to shape President Habibie's decision to give the East Timorese the option of choosing between special autonomy and separating from Indonesia. The first event was Habibie's disappointment with Bishop Belo's refusal to meet the him in December, as had originally been agreed. Habibie had already met Belo on 24 June 1998 at the president's office in Bina Graha. At that meeting Belo expressed the grievances of the East Timorese population, such as those about restrictions on the people's freedom of movement. Habibie promised to address the grievances and asked Belo to meet him again after the MPR Special Session. At a cabinet meeting on 23 December, the president informed the cabinet that he was due to meet with Bishops Belo and Nascimento. He requested the Foreign Minister and the Minister State Secretary to accompany him at the meeting, and instructed the Coordinating Minister for Political and Security Affairs to coordinate meetings to prepare an analysis of the extent to which the government had delivered on its promises to Belo, who was also expected to report on whether his demands to the president had been met. Yet, in the end Belo failed to meet the president, claiming he was too busy. The snub was deeply felt by Habibie as can be read in his memoir, *Detik-Detik yang Menentukan* (2006). Habibie clearly felt that Belo had little faith in his sincerity to make fundamental changes in East Timor and at the same time this probably also made him impatient with the whole East Timor issue.[16]

The second trigger was the now famous letter from Australian Prime Minister, John Howard, addressed to President Habibie. In the letter Howard reaffirmed Australia's support for East Timor being part of Indonesia. However, Howard also suggested that special autonomy should include a review mechanism after ten years or more, similar to the Matignon Agreement provided by France to its colony, New Caledonia. President Habibie took exception to Howard's suggestion that East Timor's position within Indonesia was in any way similar to that of New Caledonia vis-à-vis France. At the same cabinet meeting on 23 December 1998 in which he prepared to meet Bishop Belo, President Habibie responded to Howard's letter, explaining that East Timor was not an Indonesian colony, for it enjoyed the same rights as all other provinces, and that East Timorese could occupy high-ranking government positions, whereas subjects of a French colony could never do the same in France. Habibie also pointed out that East Timor was integrated into Indonesia through an MPR Decree (No 6 of 1978), in response to the Balibo Declaration, in which, as he put it, the people of East Timor requested to be part of Indonesia.[17] Although the president refuted it, Howard's letter undoubtedly triggered new thinking on his part about how to reach a solution of the East Timor problem.

The president sent copies of Howard's letter to the Coordinating Minister for Politics and Security, the Foreign Minister, the Minister for Internal Affairs, the Minister for Defence and the Minister State Secretary with a covering instruction to these ministers to study what alternative solutions should be available if the East Timorese rejected special autonomy. In the covering note, Habibie asked whether if, after 23 years of being part of Indonesia, the people of East Timor were still not content, would it not be wise, even democratic and constitutional, for East Timor to part from Indonesia peacefully and with honour. Habibie's 'disposition' to his ministers, suggesting that the East Timorese should be given the alternative to separate peacefully from Indonesia if they have been so dissatisfied after being part of Indonesia for 23 years, paved the way for the 'two options' formula that were later offered by the Indonesian government to resolve the East Timor question. Reports that President Habibie did not consult the relevant ministers before he announced his 'two option' solution for East Timor are thus not accurate.

---

16   At one point President Habibie betrayed his impatience with the East Timor problem by saying that East Timor has nothing but rocks.

17   The credibility of the Balibo Declaration has long been questioned internationally, but it was used by the Indonesian government to refute charges that it had annexed East Timor illegally. Material in this and the preceding paragraph are derived from the author's personal observations of the cabinet meeting.

On 27 January 1999, there was a full cabinet meeting on politics and security, in which the East Timor issue was one of the main agenda items. As was usual during the Habibie presidency, all of the relevant ministers had met two days earlier to prepare their reports for the meeting; while the cabinet meeting itself was attended by all of them, although General Wiranto, the Minister for Defence and Commander of the Armed Forces arrived slightly late, since he had attended a parliamentary hearing in the morning. President Habibie opened the meeting and asked General Faisal Tanjung, the Coordinating Minister for Politics and Security, to present his report. Faisal Tanjung reported that at the earlier coordinating meeting, everyone had agreed to consider two options for East Timor, and Foreign Minister Ali Alatas made a presentation, accompanied by a written document, in which he outlined two separate options. The first was Special Autonomy for East Timor as a final solution, without the promise of any future referendum. The second option, which would come into effect if the first was rejected by the East Timorese population, was to bring the East Timor issue to the MPR which would then issue a decree separating East Timor from Indonesia, without any intermediate process. Minister Alatas elaborated on the implications of a second option victory, such as the fate of East Timorese who wished to remain Indonesian citizens. Wiranto, who joined the cabinet meeting later, agreed that the East Timor problem could be solved once and for all by giving the East Timorese the two options. He added a caveat that all past decisions on East Timor should not be faulted, to prevent the sacrifices made by Indonesian soldiers in the fulfilment of their duties there being rendered futile (personal notes, 27 January 1999).

Given the gravity of the subject being discussed, the president invited all other cabinet members to express their views, and almost everyone did. It was the longest discussion on any subject at a cabinet meeting during the Habibie presidency (during which period cabinet meetings often dragged on for hours). The discussion was heated and quite emotional, but no one objected to giving East Timor the two options, thus opening the real possibility that East Timor would separate from Indonesia. President Habibie made his own views clear during the meeting. For instance, he said that the MPR decree on the integration of East Timor could be revoked, and he also stressed that the military would not object to such an outcome, since it was loyal to all decisions made by the MPR and the government. He also said the tripartite talks should be continued, underlining Indonesia's position that special autonomy would be final, with no future referendum. But he added that the Indonesian delegation should convey that the only alternative, should special autonomy be rejected, was to revoke the MPR decree integrating East Timor into Indonesia. He stressed that East Timor was part of Indonesia only through an MPR Decree, unlike other provinces which make up Indonesia based on the 1945 Constitution. He said the government would advise MPR members to look at the possibility of issuing

a decree separating East Timor from Indonesia and, finally, observed that on
1 January 2000, East Timor would no longer be part of Indonesia, and that
Indonesia would enter the new millennium as it was at the 1945 Proclamation
for Independence. These remarks made it clear that Habibie expected the East
Timorese to opt for separation from Indonesia, and that he actually welcomed
such a prospect (personal notes, 27 January 1999). Finally, after almost three
hours of deliberation, the meeting made the fateful decision to give the two
options to the people of East Timor: either accept special autonomy as a final
solution, or reject it and separate from Indonesia. The decision was announced
to the outside world immediately after the cabinet meeting, by the Minister for
Information, Yunus Yosfiah and Foreign Minister Ali Alatas.[18]

The details of the special autonomy package, the preparations for the ballot and
the violence which followed it have been subjects of numerous studies and cannot
be discussed with justice in this short chapter. On 5 May 1999, an agreement
was signed in New York by the parties to the tripartite talks which became the
basis for the ballot that took place on 30 August 1999. Preparing and organising
the ballot was mainly the responsibility of the United Nations which created
the United Nations Mission in East Timor (UNAMET). At Indonesia's insistence,
responsibility for maintaining security and order remained in Indonesia's hands.
The woefully inadequate police were put in charge of security, in order to prevent
the military's involvement in the run-up to the ballot, though there were clear
signs of security threats from both pro-integration and anti-integration forces.
Although the government in Jakarta anticipated some violence in the aftermath
of the ballot, it must be admitted that the government underestimated the level
of violence that would ensue. There was probably some degree of complacency
in Jakarta after the hugely successful and peaceful general elections in June
1999, which many observers had predicted would be a blood bath. President
Habibie held the mainstream nationalist views that no foreign soldiers would be
allowed to operate on Indonesian soil.

The violence that broke out immediately after the UN Secretary General
announced the results of the ballot caught the government unprepared. Jakarta
blamed the Secretary General for making a precipitate announcement and thus
triggering the violence; President Habibie had apparently asked for a 72-hour
delay in publicising the results in order to allow the Indonesian government to
increase its security measures. International observers blamed the Indonesian
military for not reining in the pro-integration militias that had been created
earlier by the military to support East Timor's integration with Indonesia. Perhaps
Indonesia should not have been so adamant in refusing to accept international

---

18   The 27 January 1999 meeting is explained in some detail here as there have been reports that Foreign
Minister Ali Alatas was away at the time and was taken by surprise by the decision. These reports were
inaccurate. The author was present at the press conference.

security forces to help maintain security during the ballot, given the fact that the Indonesian military would prove incapable or unwilling to control the pro-integration militias. Whatever the cause, the outbreak of violence clearly damaged Indonesia's credibility in general and President Habibie's credibility in particular, both at home and abroad. After intense international pressure, the government was forced to accept the presence of multi-national troops to restore order. Aware of public sensitivities on the presence of foreign, and especially white, soldiers in East Timor when the province was still formally part of Indonesia, Habibie asked a number of ASEAN leaders to send troops. Due to time constraints, however, the United Nations could not send a fully funded Blue Beret international peace-keeping force, and no ASEAN country was really in a position to send and financially support a large number of troops. It was only Australia, the country nearest to East Timor, which had the capacity to send the necessary troops and lead the multi-national force. The presence of Australian troops in East Timor triggered an Indonesian nationalist backlash against Australia, for many Indonesians blamed Australia for their support of the East Timorese independence movement. President Habibie, however, did not voice any objection to Australia's role vis-à-vis East Timor.

In many respects the East Timor problem was the most difficult issue that the short-lived Habibie presidency had to face. President Habibie was criticised at home for letting East Timor become independent, and from abroad, for failing to prevent violence. Many observers argued that the loss of East Timor and the perceived international humiliation that Indonesia had to suffer as punishments for allowing the violence in East Timor was the single most important reason President Habibie's accountability speech was rejected by the MPR. Nevertheless, while the East Timor issue may have been decisive in Habibie's loss of support among some of the military delegates in the MPR, it was quite clear from the outset that the PDI-P, PKB and some Golkar members had already made up their minds to reject Habibie regardless of the East Timor ballot outcome. Habibie's desire to resolve the East Timor problem stemmed from a genuine desire to apply democratic and human rights principles in East Timor as in other parts of the country. He also felt that the East Timor problem had for too long become an obstacle to Indonesia's overall development and reform. He took the decision mainly to free the next president to focus on solving other difficult national problems. Habibie made it clear that he would be happy with whatever option the East Timorese decided upon, and that he would honour their choice. Although Habibie may have lost the political support he needed to remain president shortly after the East Timor ballot, and some critics vilified him for 'losing' East Timor, in retrospect letting East Timor go was undoubtedly one of the wisest decisions Habibie made for Indonesia and for East Timor. Indonesia was able to move forward without the constant distractions of East Timor hampering its every step, especially when dealing with western governments, and soon after Indonesia and East Timor were able to develop normal bilateral relations as close neighbours. This would probably be remembered in later years as one of Habibie's most important legacies.

Conclusion

Habibie ascended to the Indonesian presidency under very unpropitious circumstances and was president for just over 500 days. Yet, during that short time his government passed numerous laws and regulations which laid the foundation for Indonesia's transition from authoritarian rule to democracy. Although most were passed in haste and thus contained flaws, it is likely that if they had not been passed during the Habibie period they would not have been passed at all. Unlike his successors, President Habibie inherited from the New Order a strongly centralised government apparatus and a legislature which he could control. Later governments consisted of cumbersome coalitions and had to deal with fractious and less productive parliaments. Yet President Habibie was not only the heir to an authoritarian and effective regime, he also proved to have a democratic spirit. Unlikely though it may seem, history will show that President Habibie, Soeharto's hand-picked vice-president and successor, would become the main architect of Indonesia's democratic transition, its new civil liberties' landscape, radical decentralisation and even the independence of East Timor. These policies have been controversial and given rise to new problems, yet all of them have fundamentally transformed the face of Indonesian politics. Though far from perfect, Indonesia is now recognised as the world's third largest democracy.

8 Semi-Opponents in Power: The Abdurrahman Wahid and Megawati Soekarnoputri Presidencies

EDWARD ASPINALL

Indonesia's transition between authoritarian and democratic forms of government was marked by a curious combination of circumstances: the most far-reaching reforms were carried out by a leader from the old authoritarian regime; once critics of that regime came to power, reforms slowed down.

As Dewi Fortuna Anwar explains in the preceding chapter, most of the major structural reforms that occurred during Indonesia's transition took place during the brief presidency of Habibie. Habibie, of course, had been a prominent member of the New Order elite. After he fell, Indonesia was ruled in quick succession by two individuals, Abdurrahman Wahid and Megawati Soekarnoputri, who had been (with qualifications explained below) prominent leaders of opposition, or at least of oppositional sentiment, during the preceding New Order regime.

Yet Abdurrahman's and Megawati's governments achieved relatively little in terms of substantive reform. The release of political prisoners, the lifting of restrictions on political parties, trade unions and other political organisations, reform of the electoral system, the removal of the military from formal politics, and political decentralisation: all of these were achievements, or at least initiatives, of the Habibie period. During the succeeding two presidencies, there were some adjustments to Habibie's reform blueprint, but in some areas reform also stalled.

There are many different ways to explain the vicissitudes of the Indonesian transition and the relatively limited progress of political reform after Habibie. The fast accumulating journalistic and scholarly literature points to a number of culprits. Most analysts stress contextual factors and sources of authoritarian resistance. In the Indonesian public debate at the time, many commentators pointed to resistance by 'status quo' forces. Some scholarly works echo this approach, emphasising the obstacle to reform represented by a recalcitrant military and bureaucracy (e.g. Barton 2002:382–84). Hadiz and Robison (2004), in a more sophisticated version of this argument, stress the resilience and reconsolidation of oligarchy. Others blame the severity of the economic crisis that Indonesia faced, as well as the degree of violence and ethnic, separatist and other forms of conflict that Indonesia was experiencing (e.g. ICG 2000). Yet another strand of analysis stresses the tenacity of the culture of corruption and patrimonialism (e.g. McLeod 2005; Mackie in this volume).

One common view is that the really sharp break, and a decisive defeat for *reformasi*, came with the collapse of Abdurrahman Wahid's presidency in July 2001. In this view, Abdurrahman came to power as the counter-*reformasi* forces were reconsolidating. Aroused by his reformist views, they rallied their forces, sabotaged his government and eventually defeated him. Megawati's government, by contrast, made peace with the forces of reaction and even came to embody the counter-*reformasi* impulse (see Barton 2001; Kingsbury 2002:297; Vickers 2005:212).

This chapter presents a different interpretation. It stresses the similarities and continuities between the Abdurrahman and Megawati presidencies rather than the differences. It emphasises how reform was undermined from *within* government during these presidencies, including from the very top, as a consequence of leaders' coalition-building choices and styles of political behaviour. These choices and styles, it is further argued, may in turn be related to a legacy of the New Order period that is not often emphasised: the lasting effect of the methods the regime used to deal with potential opponents. Building on an argument about the nature of political opposition under the New Order developed elsewhere (Aspinall 2005), it is here suggested that the New Order encouraged a distinctive 'semi-oppositional' style in civil and political society, that both Abdurrahman and Megawati were products and exemplars of this style, and that many of the vicissitudes of their presidencies can be explained by this dynamic.

The New Order and its legacy

A kind of revisionism has taken hold of scholars since the New Order regime fell. During the New Order years, some observers arguably took some of the regime's legitimating claims too seriously (see van Klinken 2001 for one critique). Since the regime fell, by contrast, there has been a reverse tendency. Now scholars emphasise the violence of the regime (e.g. Anderson 2001), its criminal nature (Lindsey 2001), and its use of repression, to the exclusion of all else. At least in one section of the Indonesian studies field there is a new orthodoxy that violence and exclusion were the essence of the New Order.

It is undeniable that repression was fundamental to the New Order. However, it was only one half of the means by which the regime managed potential opposition. For the majority of political actors the regime was, at least by its final decade, not especially violent. Setting aside the large numbers the security forces killed in anti-separatist operations in East Timor, Aceh and Irian Jaya, where nationalist ideology and guerilla organisation gave a special force to opposition which was absent elsewhere, the number of people directly killed in political violence by agents of the state in the final years of Soeharto's rule between 1990 and 1998 was relatively low. Of course, as Heryanto (2006) has argued, the memory and threat of violence was inculcated into the fabric of citizens' daily lives and could thus be debilitatingly effective without always being overt. Even so, the exclusive focus on violence and repression misses much about the New Order, and thus fails to capture important aspects of its legacy.

As I have argued elsewhere (Aspinall 2005), one key to the New Order's longevity and success was the way it combined violence (and the threat of violence) with co-optation and toleration. The regime did not merely prohibit threatening forms of political action and ideology, it also allowed a relatively wide variety of organisation and representation of societal interests—political parties, the societal organisations or *ormas*, NGOs and the like—so long as they did not fundamentally challenge the regime and adapted to its rules.

This situation inculcated a distinctive form of political behaviour even in most political actors who sought to remain independent from or even challenge the regime. Following Linz, this form of political behaviour is known as *semi-opposition*. Semi-opponents were, in Linz's words, 'those groups that are not dominant or represented in the governing group but that are willing to participate in power without fundamentally challenging the regime.' (Linz 1973:191; also Aspinall 2005:6–7, 145–76). Semi-opponents worked within regime-sanctioned bodies like parties and *ormas*. They learned how to express criticisms in ambiguous language, how to work within regime structures while endeavouring to maintain some degree of autonomy, and how to carefully read the signs emanating from the regime's leaders in order not overstep the ever-changing line separating tolerated political behaviour from that which was suppressed. The combination of repression with toleration created a dominant political culture of compliance, compromise and moderation.

This culture was especially strong among the representatives of the old *aliran*, the major socio-cultural streams which had dominated Indonesia's political life before the rise of the army in the late 1950s and mid-1960s. The most obvious were the modernist Muslims of Muhammadiyah, with about 20–25 million followers by the late New Order and the traditionalist Muslims of Nahdlatul Ulama (NU), around 30–35 million. The Sukarnoist nationalists—many of whom were drawn from the Javanese nominally Muslim cultural variant or *'abangan'*, or who were members of minority religious communities—were more loosely organised but equivalently numerous. They were represented primarily through the regime-tolerated political party, the Indonesian Democracy Party (Partai Demokrasi Indonesia, PDI).

Significantly, the leaders of each of these three currents, respectively Amien Rais, Abdurrahman Wahid and Megawati Soekarnoputri, became the major political figures of the immediate post-Soeharto years. Their prominence was not fortuitous. Semi-oppositional forces were in advantageous positions when the New Order collapsed. They had managed to preserve a political apparatus throughout the New Order years, albeit mostly by compromising with the regime. Partly as a result, they had also been able to retain mass constituencies. More radical opponents of the regime, by contrast, had been isolated, repressed and prevented from gaining access to the public. Moreover, because semi-opponents were not from the inner core of the regime or implicated directly in its failings, they were now able to present themselves as a political alternative to it. This was especially the case because during the New Order's final decade, as political tensions had increased, some of the chief semi-oppositional leaders and their organisations had become more independent and had more openly criticised the regime.

The obvious exemplar of this trend was Megawati Soekarnoputri, daughter of Indonesia's first president, Sukarno, an embodiment to many Indonesians of Sukarno's populist spirit. In a sign of erosion of the regime's political control mechanisms she had attained the leadership of the PDI because of her grassroots support in 1993. She was subsequently removed from her post on Soeharto's orders in 1996, conferring on her much public admiration as a victim of the New Order. Amien Rais, who became chairperson of Muhammadiyah in 1995, was also becoming by 1996–97 a leading public critic of Soeharto. Abdurrahman Wahid, the head of NU, had also been critical of the government during its last decade and narrowly avoided being unseated in a government-organised plot to remove him as NU leader in 1994. From 1996–97, however, Abdurrahman assiduously courted Soeharto and his circle in order to ensure that NU and his own leadership were no longer undermined.

In the first post-Soeharto election in 1999, 64 per cent of the vote was won by parties which either had themselves formerly been in a semi-oppositional relationship with the New Order, or were linked to mass organisations which had been in such a relationship. These parties were the new incarnation of Sukarnoist nationalism, Megawati's Indonesia Democracy Party—Struggle (Partai Demokrasi Indonesia—Perjuangan, PDI-P) winning 34 per cent of the vote; the party of Abdurrahman Wahid's wing of the largest Muslim organisation in Indonesia, NU; the National Awakening Party (Partai Kebangkitan Bangsa,

PKB), 13 per cent; the party of modernist Muslims led by Amien Rais, the National Mandate Party (Partai Amanat Nasional, PAN) 7 per cent, as well as the United Development Party (Partai Persatuan Pembangunan, PPP), 11 per cent, an Islamic party that had been created by and tolerated by the New Order. More radical forces espousing '*reformasi total*' were entirely unable to organise and become a credible electoral force.

Politics in the post-Habibie period were thus dominated neither by former New Order stalwarts nor by former unbending opponents of the regime, but instead by its former semi-opponents. They brought with them the habits and political outlook that had been inculcated in them during the New Order years. The remainder of this chapter looks at the effects by focusing on Indonesia's second and third transitional governments, those of Abdurrahman Wahid and Megawati Soekarnoputri.

The Abdurrahman Wahid presidency (October 1999–July 2001)

Abdurrahman Wahid has long been an intriguing figure in Indonesian politics. Unusually liberal-minded for such a senior member of Indonesia's political elite, let alone for an *ulama* from a blue-blooded Nahdlatul Ulama dynasty, he had also confounded many Indonesian democrats in the final years of Soeharto's reign by realigning with the president's camp and opening his NU constituency up to Golkar and the President's daughter Siti Hardiyanti Rukmana or 'Tutut' (on this see Aspinall 2005:197–98). Yet when he came to power he surprised observers with the radicalism of some of his political rhetoric and associations. For instance, he called for the unbanning of Marxism-Leninism and apologised to victims of the anti-Communist 1965–66 massacres. He publicly associated with individuals like the left-wing author Pramoedya Ananta Toer who had long been *persona non grata* in elite culture and politics.

His actions were also more than merely symbolic. He initiated efforts to overhaul government policy and structures in key areas which, had they been successful, would have transformed Indonesian politics even more fundamentally than had Habibie's reforms. There is insufficient space to explore his agenda in detail, but we can mention two illustrations. First, Abdurrahman initiated plans to begin a major restructuring of the military's territorial command structure, the very foundation of the military's institutional autonomy and pervasive political influence. In order to achieve this goal he cultivated and attempted to promote an outspoken military officer, Agus Wirahadikusumah, who antagonised conservative members of the officer corps with his bold plans for military reform (Mietzner 2006).

Second, Abdurrahman brought a bold approach to the handling of regional, especially separatist, unrest. In Aceh, after first promising a referendum on independence (he immediately and confusingly backtracked), he initiated negotiations with exiled Free Aceh Movement (Gerakan Aceh Merdeka, GAM) rebels, a step previously rejected by the Habibie administration. Abdurrahman took a leading personal role in initiating negotiations (indeed, he even personally telephoned a leader of a minority GAM faction in Sweden and offered him Aceh's governorship in exchange for a peace deal: interview with Husaini Hasan 13 June 2004). His approach bore fruit in the form of a preliminary peace deal, the 'humanitarian pause' of mid-2000. On Papua, he was no less bold, making a famous visit to the province on new year's day 2000 when, at dawn, he renamed the province Papua (previously, it had been called Irian Jaya, a term resented by many locals). He even funded the Papuan People's Congress later that year, an event which became an important forum for expression of Papuan grievances and nationalism (Chauvel 2003:27–32). His approach to these conflicts was marked by naiveté and inconsistency, but it also marked a dramatic break with past practice and antagonised many in the security establishment.

Yet almost nothing came of these ambitions. The debacle of the Abdurrahman Wahid presidency has been discussed thoroughly elsewhere (Liddle 2001; Aspinall 2002; Malley 2002; Mietzner 2001, 2004). Having constructed a fragile coalition to win office, Abdurrahman set about dismantling it almost immediately he came to power. By sacking ministers from the parties who had supported him and publicly taunting their leaders, he invited confrontation with the legislature and political parties. By its end, his presidency had degenerated into farce. Most of the parties which had earlier backed his presidential bid turned against him. Abdurrahman responded by making increasingly erratic and inflammatory comments about friends and foes alike and threatening, but proving unable, to dissolve parliament and rule by decree. Eventually, he was forced from office by impeachment on 23 July 2001.

Abdurrahman's presidency left very little lasting legacy of reform. One could argue that the Helsinki Agreement of August 2005, which may become the foundation of a lasting peace in Aceh, was the culmination of his efforts to begin negotiations to the conflict there. The special autonomy laws for Aceh and Papua that were signed into law by Megawati shortly after Abdurrahman fell, were also largely negotiated during his presidency, although the prime movers here were forces in parliament rather than in the executive. In both cases, it is likely these outcomes would have happened regardless of Abdurrahman's presidency. Certainly, by its end, Abdurrahman's reform plans were in disarray. Security forces were returning to repression in both Aceh and Papua. Plans to restructure the military had stalled.

The point here is not simply that Abdurrahman's reform policies generated resistance from establishment forces who were ideologically opposed to them or who stood to lose from them. There certainly was such resistance, as might be expected. What was striking about Abdurrahman's approach, was how little relationship there was between his coalition-building and coalition-destroying efforts on the one hand and his reformist vision on the other. He made little effort to construct a broad coalition in favour of reform or to build a consistently reformist government. Ministers were sacked and appointed, with a few exceptions, not on the basis of how they would contribute to reform, but on the basis of whether they would advantage Abdurrahman in factional terms.[1] Eventually, Abdurrahman Wahid himself made no efforts to preserve his own reforms, preferring to make concessions willy-nilly to his opponents in the attempt to shore up his own position. For instance, on the question of Aceh policy, he approved a return to military operations in the form of an April 2001 Presidential Instruction. Likewise, he willingly sacrificed Agus Wirahadikusumah and other reformist officers when it became necessary to strengthen his position in the military (Tentara Nasional Indonesia, TNI). Indeed, Abdurrahman eventually himself tried to bring the TNI back into the political arena, by ordering it to support a decree dissolving the legislature and allowing emergency rule.

In conclusion, during Abdurrahman's presidency what might have been a period of dramatic democratic transformation and consolidation was wasted. The reform momentum that still animated Indonesian politics at the end of the Habibie period was dissipated and diverted into endless petty disputes about Abdurrahman's behaviour, political representation and power-sharing. The public mood, previously strongly in favour of reform, became increasingly alienated from and indifferent to politics. Abdurrahman Wahid, lionised by many observers as the true champion of democratisation, is better viewed in retrospect as its antithesis.

The Megawati Soekarnoputri presidency (July 2001–October 2004)

In the mid-1990s, Megawati Soekarnoputri had become a potent symbol of resistance to Soeharto's rule, with minimal effort. She put forward no philosophically elaborate democratic program, but simply called for the regime

---

1   For example, Laksamana Sukardi, the PDI-P Minister for state enterprises, was widely viewed as both competent and relatively clean, and was replaced early on in Abdurrahman's term by the Nadhlatul Ulama politician, Rozy Munir. This move was generally seen as enabling the president and NU to more readily access the massive resources available to the ministry (*Straits Times*, 27 April 2000).

to respect what it said were its own principles of rule-based government and constitutional propriety. In particular, she argued that the decision of the PDI to choose her as leader should be respected. This minimalist vision was both her strength and weakness. It allowed her to expose the regime's hypocrisy when Soeharto ousted her in 1996, but led to a strategic dead-end thereafter. As a result, Megawati and her followers played little role in the mobilisations that toppled Soeharto in 1998.

The important point, for current purposes, is that when Megawati came to power over the wreckage of the Abdurrahman presidency in July 2001, in conditions where a basically democratic institutional framework was already in place, it turned out that she was also ill-equipped to become either a visionary or even an effective reforming president. Her presidency, therefore, while not the fully fledged Indonesian Thermidor that some of her detractors suggested, did embody an ebbing of the *reformasi* tide.

Megawati's conservatism was obvious in many fields. Unlike Abdurrahman, who tried to appoint at least some noted reformers to key posts, Megawati curried favour with hawkish military men and former New Order stalwarts. She backed the reappointment of New Order era governors in the provinces, often against the wishes of the local branches of her own party. Especially disillusioning for her supporters was her patronage of Jakarta governor, Sutiyoso, the very man who as Jakarta military commander in July 1996 had organised a violent military assault on Megawati loyalists who were protesting against her ouster as PDI leader. As president, Megawati was also personally close to military officers, notably Army Chief of Staff General Ryamizard Ryacudu, who were very warlike on separatist conflicts and generally hostile to reform. She oversaw a dramatic return to authoritarian policies in Papua and Aceh, including (after a largely military-engineered collapse of another peace deal) the declaration of military emergency in Aceh in May 2003, under which all manner of gross abuses were committed.

The reform process did not entirely grind to a halt during Megawati's presidency, however. Some important legislative changes and institutional initiatives did occur, such as the establishment of a new anti-corruption body (Komisi Pemberantasan Korupsi, KPK), and the passage of the fourth amendment to the Constitution which provided, among other things, for the direct election of the president (Megawati first opposed this, but later acceded to it). In these cases, however, the initiative mostly came from forces within parliament and would likely have occurred whatever executive government was in power. Sympathetic commentators often say that Megawati succeeded in restoring stability and predictability to the government after the chaos of the Abdurrahman period, which is really another way of saying that she made few positive reforms. Others point to successes in restoring security, such as successful police action against the Bali bombers after October 2002 and peace deals in Maluku (late 2001) and Central Sulawesi (early 2002). In these cases, too, however, the chief initiative came from Megawati's subordinates. As president, Megawati was not simply conservative, she was also passive and aloof. She took little interest in policy development, provided little more than general statements of principle to guide her ministers, and allowed her trusted lieutenants to take the lead in setting the government agenda.

Coalitions of opportunity

How did the legacy of the New Order pattern of semi-opposition impact upon the generally disappointing reform outcomes of the Abdurrahman and Megawati presidencies? If space permitted, it might be possible to develop several different lines of argument. For example, Megawati's personal conservatism was itself arguably a product of years of political socialisation under the New Order.[2] Her chosen vehicle for political action in those years, the PDI, was for much of the New Order an ineffective plaything of the government that lacked ideological independence. It might also be possible to emphasise the inculcation of a patrimonial political culture under Soeharto, whereby even office holders in the semi-oppositional political parties and mass organisations could expect material rewards for demonstrating loyalty to the government. When the leaders of such organisations later took political office it was unsurprising that many of them viewed ministries and other government bodies as ripe for exploitation. The resultant culture of corruption helped slow democratic reform.

The remainder of this chapter, however, will focus on just two New Order legacies. The first concerns the attitudes to political coalition building which resulted from the New Order years, the second to the personal styles of the leaders who rose to political prominence through the semi-oppositional route.

Both Abdurrahman Wahid and Megawati Soekarnoputri's governments were effectively grand coalitions of all the major political parties represented in parliament, plus the Armed Forces, with the addition of non-party professionals and bureaucrats. Abdurrahman's first cabinet of 35 members included four ministers from Golkar, as well as five from the TNI (six, if the military commander, who sat in cabinet meetings was included). Megawati's cabinet was based on a similar formula, and included several individuals who had earlier

---

2 Though as Angus McIntyre, 2005, pp.139–50 notes, a large part of Megawati's psychological formation also occurred prior to the New Order, and many of her public statements suggest a nostalgia for her father's Guided Democracy institutions and arrangements. (My thanks to Greg Fealy for this point.)

served under Abdurrahman.[3] So marked has been the power-sharing tendency that one observer (Slater 2004) has described Indonesia's national governments as being based on a 'party cartel' system.

It is possible to point to various origins of this tendency toward broad coalitions. One early antecedent is Sukarno's Nasakom (Nationalist-Religious-Communist) cabinets of the Guided Democracy period, as well as his even earlier discussions about the need to blend all the elements of Indonesian politics into a single form. More immediately, broad party coalitions were of course partly a response to the extremely fragmented nature of the political map after the 1999 elections. Any president who wanted to secure a workable majority in the parliament had to ensure that he or she had the support of several political parties. Yet the coalition building which took place was curiously unselective. In many transitional democracies, coalition-building choices are often dictated by parties' role in the former non-democratic regime. For example, in post-communist countries in East and Central Europe, former communist parties were routinely excluded from coalition governments during at least the early phases of democratic transition. In Indonesia, by contrast, there was almost complete disregard for party origin, ideology or democratic potential. The *aliran*-based parties of former semi-opponents, which claimed to embody the new spirit of *reformasi*, shared power more or less equally with individuals and forces that had been the main supports of the Soeharto regime.

Other patterns would have been possible. An opportunity to create an anti-New Order coalition had arisen between the first post-Soeharto election of June 1999 and the People's Consultative Assembly (Majelis Permusyawaratan Rakyat, MPR) session of October 1999 when Abdurrahman was elected to the presidency. During this period, many critical intellectuals, student and NGO activists argued for a '*reformasicoalition*' built around the major parties representing the biggest of the old semi-oppositional *aliran*. Megawati's PDI-P, Abdurrahman Wahid's PKB and Amien Rais's PAN together commanded 262 of the 550 seats in the DPR, and had a majority of 320 if the PPP was included; in the MPR the numbers were tighter, but the old semi-oppositional forces still had a theoretical majority. Despite considerable agitation in favour of such a coalition, including from the grassroots of these parties, Abdurrahman Wahid instead came to power by first securing the support of a 'central axis' (*poros tengah*) of Islamic parties and then by successfully wooing the military and the dominant Habibie wing of Golkar (Mietzner 2000). To secure this outcome, he made promises of cabinet seats and other important government posts, and also pledged to protect the corporate interests of the military and other key players (Mietzner 2004:191).

---

3   With a little more modification, notably the exclusion of Megawati's PDI-P, Susilo Bambang Yudhoyono's government since 2004 has also been based on the same essential formula.

Abdurrahman's construction of a coalition of opportunity, with the sole aim of securing the presidency for himself, had a dramatic effect on the political dynamic in Indonesia. As I have argued elsewhere (Aspinall 2002), it blurred the line between Indonesia's authoritarian past and its democratic future. Most obviously, it did this by bringing individuals and political forces opposed to reform into the highest level of government, where they could sabotage reform from within. For example, key political posts including the Coordinating Ministry of Political and Security Affairs, and the Home Affairs Ministry, were reserved for military men, with the result that TNI retained the ability to dictate the pace of its own reform.

More generally, Abdurrahman's strategy greatly complicated and blurred the political map. Previously, forces in civil society such as student groups and NGOs had been able to push forward Indonesia's political transition because they believed they had a clear target: governments representing the 'status quo', first under Soeharto and then under Habibie. Such groups now found it hard to say whether the government represented reformist or ancien regime interests, and many of them became disoriented or split as they debated whether or in what way they should support the new president and his government (e.g. *Kompas*, 7 March 2001; 7 June 2001). To make matters even more complicated, Golkar under Habibie and Akbar Tanjung had done an effective job of presenting itself as a force favouring reform: it was Golkar's Slamet Effendy Yusuf and ex-Golkar leader Jacob Tobing who drove the main constitutional reforms through the MPR. Especially in the later phases of his presidency, Abdurrahman tried to appeal to the activist groups by depicting himself as a victim of Golkar and other reactionary forces. However, by then it was too late; many of them had lost faith in the president or become entirely disillusioned from the official politics.

Equally fundamentally, the major political parties were no longer aligned for or against the government per se (though they quickly developed positions on Abdurrahman himself). Now, each party was represented inside government and had little incentive to compete to present a more convincing reformist face to the public. Bereft of the disciplining effects of either being in opposition *or* fending off opposition, they instead became preoccupied with struggling for position and resources inside government. We do not know what would have happened had the government which came to power in October 1999 been based on a *reformasicoalition*, but it surely would have imparted a very different political dynamic to the following years.

For the purposes of the argument presented here, it is important to stress that the tendency toward building grand coalitions was itself a natural product of the previous regime's semi-oppositional culture. Under the New Order, individuals who aspired to lead the major parties and *ormas* were required to cultivate links with patrons and protectors within the regime. Even when

Megawati Soekanoputri alienated Soeharto and his camp in the 1990s, she and her followers strove to cultivate links with sympathetic elements in the officer corps. She received invitations to speak at officer training courses, and a congenial officer from the state intelligence agency (Badan Koordinasi Intelijen Negara, BAKIN) accompanied her wherever she went on party business and was popular with her retinue (field notes, June 1995). In the late 1980s and early 1990s, Abdurrahman Wahid tried to secure political advantage and advance the cause of reform by identifying himself with military officers who were becoming disillusioned with the president; he was personally close to the senior general L. B. (Benny) Moerdani. In 1996–97 he had hastily realigned Nahdlatul Ulama toward president Soeharto and his family. To continue the contrast with post-communist transitions: individuals like Vaclav Havel or Lech Walesa viewed the former ruling parties and their leaders across a gulf of hostility; in Indonesia, the new democratic leaders were long used to seeing their equivalents as potential allies. They simply continued this habit when they came to power.

Politics of personality

A second legacy of the New Order semi-oppositional background can be found in the personal styles of the first two post-New Order leaders themselves. Abdurrahman and Megawati had in some ways very different, almost diametrically opposed, personal styles. Whereas Abdurrahman was hyper-energetic, reckless and earthy in his approach to politics, Megawati was passive, cautious and aloof. Yet underpinning these great differences was a similar inflexibility of political style. Despite the many compromises they had made as semi-opponents during the Soeharto years, once they became president, both seemed to share an utter conviction of the rightness of their own course and an unwillingness to compromise, even on trivial matters, when their personal prestige was affected. It is surely more than a coincidence that Indonesia's first two post-New Order presidents shared similar flaws as political leaders.

Their personalities contributed to their political failings, and to the problems of Indonesia's political transition. Abdurrahman's contempt for the coalition partners who had delivered him the presidency has already been remarked upon. His recklessness, indeed, the delight he apparently took in antagonising both friends and foes led to the destruction of his government and succeeded in making himself, rather than political reform, the major issue in post-Habibie politics. Megawati, by contrast, embodied a kind of arch passivity which was similarly destructive. Abdurrahman's opportunism has already been noted as one key cause of the stillbirth of the '*reformasicoalition*' dream of 1999; Megawati was equally responsible. Between June and October 1999, Megawati made almost no attempt to court potential allies or reassure them of her intentions. Instead, she alienated other party leaders by acting as if she believed the presidency was hers by right, merely because her party had won a plurality of the vote. As president, she seemed equally unconcerned about the views of even her most loyal supporters, as her willingness to ride roughshod over them in gubernatorial races demonstrated. Criticisms of her by members of the public brought outbursts of petulance, such as when she angrily condemned student protestors who burned her image or effigy during demonstrations (McIntyre 2005:248). Eventually, even her close supporters admitted during the 2004 presidential elections that her unsympathetic public image was a liability, and they tried to soften it. In summary, Abdurrahman and Megawati's personalities played a major role in crippling their presidencies, forestalling reforming coalitions and thus in damaging the reform process itself.

Abdurrahman's and Megawati's personalities were produced by the distinct political cultures of their respective milieux, and by the special places both occupied therein. The two were similar, however, in how they came to prominence and in how they were viewed by their followers. Both became leaders not largely because of what they said or did, but because of who they were. Megawati's father, the republic's charismatic founding president, had been the focus of cult-like veneration both before and after his death. Megawati was wholly unremarkable as a parliamentarian before she was elevated to head the PDI on a wave of Sukarnoist nostalgia in 1993. (Aspinall 2005:145–76; McIntyre 2005:155–75; Brooks 1996). During fieldwork in the mid-1990s, I attended several PDI public functions where party supporters greeted Megawati's banal utterances with evident rapture. One can only imagine the aggrandising effect such a reception must have had on her sense of herself; certainly Megawati developed an obvious sense of entitlement by the late Soeharto years.

Abdurrahman Wahid, as grandson of the founder of Nadhlatul Ulama and son of K. H. Abdul Wahid Hasjim, its revered chairperson and Minister of Religion in the 1950s, had similarly aristocratic credentials within the traditionalist Islamic *aliran*. Unlike Megawati, he had shown signs of real intellectual ability when young, and was catapulted at a relatively early age to head NU in 1984. His great oratorical and intellectual capacities marked him out from other members of his extended family, who failed to capture such high office in NU. Unlike Megawati, he was the standout figure among his cohort and the lineage alone was not enough to make him NU leader.[4] Even so, his family background did contribute to the mystique which surrounded him. By at least the early 1990s many of Abdurrahman's followers venerated him as a wali or saint, strove to kiss his hand at public events, and believed that his more peculiar actions and utterances were simply beyond the ken of ordinary people (Fealy 2001). Being surrounded for many years by people—and not merely by a thin layer

---

4   My thanks to Greg Fealy for this point.

of sycophants, but a massive social constituency—who believed that whatever he did was correct even if they could not understand it, must largely explain Abdurrahman's imperviousness to criticism and the recklessness of his political behaviour while in office (although as McIntyre (2005:252) points out, the effects that two strokes had on his cognitive powers likely also played a part).

It is not only in Indonesia, of course, where populist leaders come to power because of their dynastic credentials or because they are viewed by followers as mystically embodying popular aspirations. However, to return to the chief argument of this chapter, the New Order political dynamic helped to push such individuals forward, because it blocked pathways for different types of leaders. Under the New Order, it was not possible to become a prominent critic of the regime by serving a lengthy political apprenticeship in a modern political organisation, convincing first one's own followers and then a broader public of the rightness of one's political vision and the acuity of one's political skills. The New Order system was designed precisely to prevent such alternative leaders from emerging. Instead, Megawati and Abdurrahman became leaders because they were seen by their followers as embodying their own diffuse sentiments and aspirations. They were adored not for the actions or utterances, but for what they symbolised. The end result was that Indonesia's political transition was steered by individuals who, when they came to power, had already accumulated the hubris, inflexibility and arrogance that one often only sees in ageing political leaders who have long enjoyed the fruits of office.

Conclusion: was the New Order really to blame?

The argument so far advanced in this chapter has been relatively straightforward: Indonesia's democratic transition has been influenced by the legacy of the preceding authoritarian regime. It has been marked not merely in the obvious ways of there being remnants of New Order power (the army, oligarchy, bureaucracy, etc) which obstruct reform, or patterns of New Order political behaviour (patrimonialism, repression, corruption, etc) which erode it. The trace of the New Order was also visible at the heart of the first post-authoritarian governments. The way that the New Order regime dealt with potential opposition, by combining repression and selective tolerance, left a lasting impact on Indonesia's democratic leaders. Those forces and leaders who were able to seize the political initiative when the old regime collapsed brought with them the political habits that had been inculcated in them by the experience of semi-opposition.

In conclusion, however, it might also be apposite to question the argument so far developed in this chapter. As noted at the outset, there is a tendency in much of the scholarship of the post-New Order era to ascribe whatever observers feel to be negative features of the new political system to the 'legacy of Soeharto' (or some such phrase). The argument presented thus far in this chapter is a version of this approach, albeit one which focuses specifically on the effects of the semi-oppositional pattern of politics of the New Order years.

Obviously, we cannot write the New Order period out of Indonesian history. The political system which has developed in Indonesia since 1998 has a direct connection to the preceding 33 years. But it is also striking that many of the phenomena we see in post-Soeharto Indonesia also have much deeper historical roots, and are similar to phenomena which occurred during Indonesia's earlier period of democratic rule in the 1950s. For example, when considering the record of Abdurrahman Wahid's government, including the extreme pragmatism Abdurrahman exhibited when forging political alliances, and the willingness of members of his retinue to see ministries and other state institutions as sources of patronage, there are striking parallels with the political behaviour of Nahdlatul Ulama in the 1950s and early 1960s. In that period, NU became known for the extreme flexibility, bordering on opportunism, of its political alliances, and for its corruption, with the Ministry of Religion becoming a virtual NU fiefdom (Fealy 1998). Likewise, it is also possible to detect many similarities between Megawati Soekarnoputri's behaviour when in power and that of the right-wing of the Sukarnoist Indonesian National Party (Partai Nasional Indonesia, PNI) in the 1950s and 1960s.

In short, in some crucial respects, the politics of post-Soeharto Indonesia are strikingly reminiscent of the earlier democratic period in the 1950s, especially in the tendency toward formation of broad and opportunistic coalitions, and the ubiquity of the patrimonial style. Similarities with Guided Democracy in the 1960s—especially the tendency toward unity governments—are also obvious. These observations point toward other research agendas, which would involve placing post-Soeharto Indonesia in longer historical perspective. They also perhaps suggest that we need to re-think the New Order period itself in more fundamental ways.

In the past, it was customary to view Indonesian politics as being marked by a sharp break in 1965–66 when the New Order regime was established. Before that time, the major schism in Indonesian politics was between the left, centred on the communist party (Partai Komunis Indonesia, PKI) on the one hand, and the other major political forces, including the parties and the military, on the other. After the destruction of the PKI and the murder of its adherents in

1965–66, so the conventional wisdom holds, the main axis of politics shifted. A government dominated by the military and bureaucracy now subjected all pre-existing civilian forces to its dominance.

But given the ease with which the semi-opponents of the New Order years transformed themselves into coalition partners of their erstwhile rulers after 1999, it is perhaps more appropriate to view the New Order in retrospect as a project of a broader spectrum of the Indonesian elite. Modernist and traditionalist Muslims and Sukarnoist nationalists were incorporated into that regime in subordinate positions, but they had a stake in it nonetheless. They recognised its legality, accepted its rules, agreed with much of its ideology and valued the order and economic benefits it produced. As events since 1999 have shown us, they were certainly not so alienated from it that they rejected all of its legacy once they were able to take power for themselves.

9 The Legacy of the New Order Military in Local Politics: West, Central and East Java

JUN HONNA

Post-Soeharto scholarship regarding the Indonesian military (Tentara Nasional Indonesia, TNI) has largely concentrated on two areas of military politics: first, institutional reform at the national level, such as the elimination of the socio-political section in the military organisation and military neutrality in national elections; and second, the military involvement in political violence in remote areas.[1] Such studies leave an important question untouched: civil-military relations in the everyday politics of 'non-conflict' areas where most citizens live. How have democratisation and decentralisation re-shaped local elite politics and civil-military relations? What legacies of the New Order military remain consequential for political dynamics at the local level? This chapter tries to answer these questions by focusing on political developments in West, Central, and East Java.[2]

The focus of this chapter is on the period between the two general elections in 1999 and 2004. This was the first phase of Indonesia's democratic transition, and the one in which New Order legacies were most clearly defined. We first look at the re-shaping of local power elites in the three provinces immediately after the 1999 general elections, then the changes brought about by decentralisation policies from 2001 and the attendant rise of new political strategies for diverting funds from development projects and maintaining political power. Finally, we focus on the gubernatorial elections in 2003 as a case study to elucidate the theatre of civil-military politics and its contribution to the fortification of local civil-military elite collusion.

---

1   For scholarship on military reform, see, for example, Honna, 2003, Chapter 7, and Mietzner, 2006. Military violence in remote areas is well analysed in Sukma, 2004, and Davies' unpublished paper.
2   I thank Edward Aspinall for his invaluable comments on the manuscript. For a more extensive version of the argument used in this chapter, see Honna 2006

Although the power of the military to dominate and direct local political and economic affairs has clearly declined since the end of the New Order, the analysis presented in this chapter suggests that the TNI remains an important player in even the relatively economically advanced regions. Local military actors have adroitly adapted to the new institutional framework, taking advantage of political competition between civilian elites and the rise of new privatised forms of violence to both promote themselves as neutral arbiters in local political contests and to secure access to political resources. In acting in this way, however, local military elites are not serving ideological ideals or obeying commands from the centre. Instead, local TNI officers have a high degree of autonomy and they are very flexible. They take action in order to maintain and defend the military's distinctive political, economic and other corporate interests. In this sense, they have become merely one among many players in post-Soeharto local politics, albeit one which the new civilian political elites are almost invariably eager to accommodate.

The 1999 elections and the re-shaping of local elites

Local politics during the Soeharto era were controlled by the trinity of Golkar, the military and bureaucracy.[3] Jakarta's central government distributed development budgets to local governments which then allocated these funds to various projects. Local business groups were instructed to affiliate with Golkar if they wanted to participate in these projects. This traditional 'concession regime', consisting of Golkar, local bureaucrats and business elites, became deeply embedded in the local political economy during the three decades of Soeharto's rule. The military played a watchdog role, using coercion to repress social forces which threatened the concession regime. During elections, Golkar's dominance was secured by the military, bureaucrats and business elites.

This structure of local dominance faced a serious challenge in the 1999 general elections, following the wave of support for democratisation and *reformasi* that had precipitated the fall of Soeharto in 1998. The elections resulted in the victory of Megawati Soekarnoputri's Indonesia Demokrasi Party of Struggle (Partai Demokrasi Indonesia—Perjuangan, PDI-P) which obtained 34 per cent of total votes at the national level, and defeated Golkar (22 per cent)—its first electoral defeat since the beginning of the New Order. The 1999 elections also brought about the collapse of Golkar dominance in local parliaments, where PDI-P now emerged as the leading party in 13 provincial parliaments. In the provinces which are the focus of this chapter, PDI-P came first in Central Java

---

3   On the role of the military in the New Order polity, see Crouch 1978.

44 per cent) and West Java (33 per cent) and ran a close second (34 per cent) to the National Awakening Party (Partai Kebangkitan Bangsa, PKB) (35 per cent), in East Java. PDI-P also won majorities in 76 out of 99 parliaments (about 80 per cent) at the regency level in the three provinces. This sweeping electoral victory of the PDI-P effectively ended the dominance of Golkar and forced modification of established concession regimes at the local level. The power shift in local parliaments compelled local governments to form new alliances with new political elites in distributing the benefits of concession businesses and development projects. It also encouraged businesspeople to work closely with PDI-P politicians, many of whom were also local entrepreneurs. In this way, the centre of the local politico-economic power shifted away from Golkar to the PDI-P.

The 1999 elections also influenced the position of the military in local politics in these provinces. The military's regional commands which had uniformly supported Golkar during the New Order era had to adapt to the new environment. In places where Golkar retained parliamentary supremacy, the military maintained existing ties, while where the PDI-P won the elections, regional military commands had to forge new alliances in support of the new local concession regime. This dynamic led to the collapse of the military's uniform nation-wide political orientation and forced military commands to respond to local political developments. Unlike in the past, local commands now had greater institutional flexibility and discretion in adjusting to everyday local politics. This trend was reinforced by the financial problems being experienced by military commands, precipitated by the bankruptcy of many military businesses following the 1998 Asian economic crisis. In consequence, many commands that had relied on 'subsidies' generated by these military businesses were forced to develop their self-financing capacities. In the new era, this meant deepening ties with local elites who had access to economic resources.

For instance, the Siliwangi Military Division (Kodam III/Siliwangi), which oversees West Java, is widely known to have business partners, including local timber traders who are deeply involved in illegal logging in West Java. In forests near the Citarun River in Bandung and the Cimanuk River in Garut, for example, illegal logging is conducted by local gangs and dealers who depend on the security apparatus to transport logs.[4] It also appears that a human trafficking

---

4   Interviews with a local journalist from *Pikiran Rakyat* (Bandung), 21 June 2004 and a member of the local environmental NGO, DPKLTS (Dewan Pemerhati Kehutanan dan Linkungan Tanah Sunda), 22 June 2004. Stories about this kind of illicit trade do not appear in local media because of pressures brought to bear on editors.

syndicate in Indramayu, the illicit drug trade in Bandung, and a youth gang specialising in vehicle theft in Bandung are generating opportunities for protection rackets operated by local military commands.[5]

In Central Java since 1998, the Diponegoro Command (Kodam IV/Diponegoro) has been facing agitation by local civil society groups demanding the return of land seized by the military in the wake of the military-orchestrated killings and persecution of alleged communists in the mid-1960s. These mobilisations have been organised mostly by the families of former communists, whose land was confiscated, along with a younger generation of liberal-minded and leftist activists affiliated with Nahdlatul Ulama (NU), the largest Muslim organisation in Indonesia, who have been pioneering a process of reconciliation with vicitims of the 1960s killings and repression. To protect land that has been used by the Kodam Diponegoro for its business activities, the local military elite has sought political protection, leading to a new alliance with PDI-P politicians (interview, 13 January 2004). At the same time, Kodam ratcheted up its propaganda campaign *'bahaya ex-tapol'* (danger of ex-political prisoners) and relied on its intelligence services to approach *kiai* (Islamic teachers) and persuade them to not join the land campaigns led by young NU leftists.

In East Java, the Brawijaya Military Division (Kodam V/Brawijaya) and the Eastern Naval Fleet Command long profited from real estate and protection rackets involving industrial areas and red-light districts in Surabaya.[6] These activities depended on the co-operation of the local government and parliament which, after the defeat of Golkar, required the military to switch its attention to the new dominant political forces in East Java, namely the PKB and the PDI-P.

Decentralisation and new patterns of elite bargaining

The next wave of change in the pattern of concession hunting among local elites resulted from the introduction of another reform, decentralisation. Decentralisation legislation, passed in 1999 and implemented in 2001, transferred

---

5   West Java political actors generally believe that these operations are conducted or at least managed by local *prema*n (hoodlums) affiliated with powerful ethnic associations, namely Angkatan Muda Siliwangi (AMS) and Gabungan Inisiatif Barisan Siliwangi (GIBAS). However, the organised vehicle theft, is monopolised by a group of high school drop-outs who call themselves Briges (Brigadir SMA 7) after their high school.

6   It is well-known that the sex industry in Surabaya, perhaps the largest in Indonesia, operates under army and navy protection. Large entertainment and amusement places are said to be protected by the navy, while short-stay hotels and street prostitution is controlled by the army. This 'gentlemen's agreement' in favour of the navy is accepted by the army because it overwhelmingly controls the real estate business in East Java. Interviews with two local journalists (24 June 2003) and the director of a gender-issue NGO (25 June 2003) in Surabaya.

management of local economic resources from the central government to local governments, especially at the regency/city level. As a result, competition over these resources intensified among local elites. In the three provinces of West, Central and East Java, escalation of intra-elite contestation typically centred on regional governments' development projects. Local bureaucrats spoke of 'good governance' and 'administrative transparency' in project implementation, but in many cases tenders and bids were orchestrated and manipulated behind the scenes, allowing for the diversion of state funds to bureaucrats, politicians and their allies.

A new government ordinance in 2000 required local leaders (governors, district heads (*bupati*), and mayors) to submit annual 'accountability reports' (*laporan pertanggunjawaban*) to examination by local parliaments. If local councillors voted to approve the reports, local leaders would remain in office; if they withheld approval, the leaders would lose office before completing their term. This new rule meant governors, *bupati* and mayors greatly intensified their efforts to woo and co-opt majorities in their local assemblies and resulted in a redistribution of largesse away from central authorities to local rent seekers. Local government heads typically approached members of the leading faction in the local parliament, and took 'necessary measures' to successfully shepherd their accountability reports through the approval process. Such measures typically involved allocating contracts for government projects to companies linked with faction leaders and extracting slush funds from the routine budget as 'operational funds' for faction members. If the region was rich in economic resources, the proportion of locally acquired revenue (Pendapatan Alokasi Daerah, or PAD) in the government budget was high as was the level of corruption, including bribery of local councillors.

For example, in Bandung city, the government allocated eight per cent of PAD for the city council in fiscal year 2002. This was almost twice the level in the Soeharto era and part of a 400 per cent increase in total government expenditure for the city council since 1997.[7] According to civil society organisations, increases in the local council budget were principally aimed at co-opting it (interviews 29 March 2004; 30 March 2004). Meanwhile, members of Bandung's political community believe that about half the value of any government contract is transferred to whomever mediates between the contractor and government (typically, the mediator is a politician or bureaucrat) as a kickback. Local NGOs tried to monitor murky aspects of city budgets, including expenditures for the city council, with limited success. As one local NGO leader explained

---

7   For the budgetary problems in Bandung, see Haryadi and Sumindar, 2002.

> It is extremely difficult to conduct research on how the budget is actually used, because it involves the problem of tenders in public projects and procurements. Once we touch on these issues, we are confronted by endless intimidation (interview 30 March 2004).

Central Java is a stronghold of PDI-P; the towns of Semarang, Solo, Kudus, and Cilacap are known as PAD-rich districts where local governments manage 'operational funds' in abundance. Moreover, in Central Java, 20 out of 35 local government heads (*bupatis* and mayors) between 1999 and 2004 were PDI-P-affiliated, meaning that in these places the party dominated both executive and legislative branches. Indeed, in the regencies of Semarang, Grobogan, Tegal, Pemalang, Banyumas, Kebumen, Magelang, Kendal, Batang, and Kudus, *bupatis* were simultaneously the heads of local PDI-P branches. In such places, PDI-P leaders before long began behaving like local kings (*raja lokal*), who reigned the concession regime. The PDI-P itself became the site of the most vigorous lobbying regarding local development projects.

These new dynamics in legislative and executive politics influenced civil-military interactions at the local level. Many heads of local governments now enjoy wider discretion in allocating economic resources, having at their disposal large amounts of 'tactical funds' which were used to maintain or buy support from salient bureaucratic networks, including local military institutions. As Mietzner argues, the executive branches of local government found it advantageous to cultivate good relations with TNI, given the fractious and fickle nature of local legislatures (Mietzner 2003:254). Politically savvy regents and governors knew it was important to co-opt the TNI, as it held a block of parliamentary seats which could cast the deciding vote during approvals of accountability reports (until 2004, the TNI and police were allocated ten per cent of seats in local legislatures). Unlike many civilian councillors who were susceptible to lobbying from pressure groups, councillors in uniform tended to follow instructions from local military headquarters. Therefore, local government leaders often found it relatively straightforward to secure votes in a local parliament by lobbying the territorial command. TNI elites in local commands in turn understood the value of the swing vote, and offered support in return for policy rewards.

For example, the reward could be budgetary allocation for projects—such as land development and transportation business—linked to local military enterprises. The other important reward could be the extension of TNI's access to the administrative decision-making process. Here, the role of the Regional Leadership Assembly (Musyawarah Pimpinan Daerah, Muspida) should be highlighted. Muspida was a New Order-era institution which combined local leaders of executive government and key local security officials, aiming to discuss regional political issues under the leadership of governors, *bupatis* and mayors.[8] Interestingly, Muspida has not only survived into the post-reform era as one of the few channels through which the military can exercise a direct influence on local political affairs, but it is also expanded in some regions by including more military officers—such as commanders of Military Sub-District Commands (Komando Rayon Militer, Koramil) and strategic battalions—in the assembly. As one *bupati* explained

> the military is crucial for political stability here, and I have successfully incorporated TNI in my administration by giving it more say in Muspida, which is now called Muspida++.[9]

The term Muspida++ refers to the expanded version of the assembly, and it is this political initiative of *bupati* that has helped them co-opt TNI into the administration, which in turn has increased TNI's direct influence on the everyday local governance after the New Order.[10]

In sum, between 1999 and 2004, local military elites effectively exploited the political vulnerabilities of local leaders who now enjoyed wider discretion in using economic resources. The new framework provided ample opportunity for the military to draw on its intelligence, political and security strengths to take advantage of decentralisation, forge new alliances and develop new methods for resource extraction.

Military politics in gubernatorial elections

The advantages conferred on the TNI by this situation were evident during elections of top local executive positions. The 2003 gubernatorial elections in West, Central and East Java were excellent examples of how local military commands adopted virtual king-making roles in this new context.[11]

In West Java, the gubernatorial election was conducted in May. The balance of party politics favoured the PDI-P, which formed the largest faction in

---

8   Muspida was formulated by Soeharto's presidential decree in 1986. At the regency level, the New Order Muspida was typically constituted by *bupati*, the commander of Kodim (Military District Command), the head of resort police, the chief of district public prosecutor, the head of district court, and the speaker of the local parliament.

9   Interview with Samsul H. Siswoyo, *bupati* of Jember, East Java, 26 June 2003. In the case of Jember, Muspida during the New Order invited only the Kodim Commander from the military, but after the 1999 elections and under the leadership of post-New Order *bupati*, not only Kodim Commander but also battalion commanders were invited to provide policy input to Muspida.

10   In Central Java, the similar Muspida expansion can be found in Semarang where the mayor has incorporated many TNI officers in what he calls 'Muspida+'. Whether it is Muspida+ or Muspida++, there seems to be the same political aim, that is, giving local TNI a more say in the administration.

11   Until 2005, elections of local leaders were always carried out within local legislatures, rather than by direct elections by voters, a new system which began to be implemented in 2005.

the provincial parliament. From the outset, PDI-P's central and provincial executives wanted to nominate Rudi Harsatanaya, the head of PDI-P's West Java chapter and a long-time Megawati loyalist since the 1980s. This decision, however, provoked strong resistance from local elites who saw Rudi, a Chinese Sumatran, as not representing the Sundanese community. Sundanese power brokers blocked Rudi's nomination, and organised a statement of opposition to his nomination by seven PDI-P kabupaten branches. The anti-Rudi lobbying was led by two of the ethnic associations discussed, Angkatan Muda Siliwangi (AMS) and Gabungan Inisiatif Barisan Siliwangi (GIBAS), which called for 'a Sundanese governor for Sundanese society'. The prominent Sundanese leaders, Mashudi and G.P. Solihin, who were also both retired three-star generals, former commanders of Kodam Siliwangi, *and* former West Java governors, forcefully lobbied the local elite. Mashudi privately consulted with the Commander of Kodam Siliwangi, Major General Iwan Ridwan Sulandjana, himself a Sundanese (interview 29 March 2004; 22 June 2004).

In the face of such pressure, Megawati's party headquarters finally decided to withdraw the nomination of Rudi and joined a coalition with PKB which nominated as governor retired Major General Tayo Tarmadi, ex-commander of Kodam Siliwangi, in the expectation of securing the support of Siliwangi generals. However, it was predicted that the military would never support Tarmadi because he was unpopular, corrupt and would behave disrespectfully towards the current Siliwangi commander (interview 28 April 2003). These circumstances all benefited Golkar. The retired Major General Nurhaman, the head of Golkar's provincial branch had strong ties with local military elites in the Siliwangi Command. Backed by Mashudi and Solihin, Nurhaman worked effectively to convince TNI that it would be beneficial to support Danny Setiawan, the Golkar nominee for the governor's post (interview 22 June 2004).

The election was by a vote of all 100 members of the provincial legislature. Tarmadi expected to secure the 30 votes from PDI-P members and 12 from the PKB faction, totalling 42 votes. Golkar calculated that its own 21 votes and 27 from other parties would give it at least 48 votes. It was also believed that it could exploit the PDI-P's internal rift through vote buying (interview Heri Akhmadi 27 May 2003). The situation thus seemed to favour Setiawan. Satisfied with this turn of events, the TNI faction which had 10 votes in the provincial and district parliament (Dewan Perwakilan Rakyat Daerah, DPRD) decided to abstain from voting in the name of 'political neutrality'. By refraining from casting its votes, the TNI sent a clear message that it preferred Setiawan the civilian bureaucrat, to Tarmadi, the ex-military officer. Abstaining also helped to avoid an open breach with the PDI-P, still the dominant party in West Java.

Thus, the Siliwangi Command adroitly assessed the political situation and secured its institutional interests without actually using its leverage or aligning itself openly with any of the rival civilian elites.

Two months later, in July 2003, another gubernatorial election was conducted in East Java. The incumbent Imam Utomo (also a former Kodam commander in East Java) was nominated by PDI-P for re-election and he was challenged by PKB which nominated Abdul Kahfi, a retired police brigadier general. The latter was 'recommended' by former president and PKB senior Abdurrahman Wahid, ignoring the preference of many NU leaders in East Java who wanted to form a coalition with PDI-P. The PKB held 33 seats in the 100-member DPRD against the PDI-P's 31. The third largest party, Golkar, had 11 seats and decided to support PKB. A coalition of small parties, also with 11 seats, supported PDI-P. Thus the power balance in the parliament was roughly equal, as one local politician put it, 'It was TNI which had the casting vote' (interview Achmad Ruba'ie 25 June 2003).

The fact that Utomo was a former Brawijaya Commander (1995–97) would not automatically guarantee support of the current commander, Major General A. D. Sikki. On the other hand, senior military officers in East Java found it hard to accept Abdul Kahfi because, in the TNI leadership in East Java, there was an institutional memory of 'bad times' during the Abdurrahman administration. The Brawijaya Command had been irritated by Abdurrahman who had relied on intelligence provided by *kiai* and repeatedly intervened in personnel matters involving Resort Military Command (Komando Resort Militer, Korem) commanders. Also in the last days of his presidency, Abdurrahman mobilised his militant supporters in East Java to fight against troops. The bad blood from this standoff explains the Kodam's hostility to Abdurrahman's nominee as governor, Abdul Kahfi, and their active lobbying against him.

Finally, the logic of *preman* politics also pushed TNI to defend Utomo. Powerful Madurese ethnic associations, such as Ikatan Keluarga Madura Indonesia (IKMI) and Ikatan Anak Buah Madura (IKABRA), were active behind the scenes in silencing NGOs which opposed Utomo's re-election. Ethnic *preman* circles were eager to block Kahfi's advance because they believed that he was close to a Jakarta gambling king who threatened to encroach on their turf.[12] It was this underworld territorial war that encouraged IKMI and other *preman* groups, such as Forum Komunikasi Putra-Putri Purnawirawan ABRI (FKPPI) and Pemuda Panca Marga (PPM), to campaign for Utomo, including by intensively lobbying the Brawijaya Command itself.

---

12 According to a DPRD member who was a leader of Utomo's campaign team, Kahfi's main financer was Tommy Winata. Anonymous interview, 24 June 2003.

Four days before election day, General Sikki gathered the local TNI top brass as well as FKPPI and PPM, and issued a political statement that Kahfi was not really a candidate of PKB, but rather of Abdurrahman Wahid. Those who attended this meeting at the Utami Hotel got the message that Kodam was behind Utomo. On 17 July 2003, Utomo was duly re-elected, gathering 17 votes on top of the expected 46, thanks largely to the support of TNI and the split within the PKB. As in West Java, local military elites assessed the civilian power balance, identified their institutional interests and acted accordingly. Here too they collaborated with local pressure groups to engage in political lobbying.

A week after the re-election of Imam Utomo, there was another gubernatorial election, this time in Central Java. This province was the second largest stronghold of PDI-P after Bali, and therefore it was expected that whoever won the party's support would win the election. Thus, Mardijo, the head of PDI-P's Central Java chapter and a long-time party loyalist, decided to mount a challenge to the re-election of incumbent Mardiyanto by nominating himself as the PDI-P candidate. However, Megawati's party headquarters told him to withdraw and instructed PDI-P to join forces with PKB in supporting Mardiyanto. Mardijo felt disgraced and decided to run for election anyway, a decision that led Megawati to dismiss him as provincial branch head. As a result, PDI-P, the largest party in Central Java, was split between those who supported Mardijo and those who obeyed Megawati's instruction to abandon him. Again, the contest among civilians effectively opened a space for politicking by the Kodam generals.

The split within the PDI-P was helpful to chief-of-staff of Kodam Diponegoro, Brigadier General Salim Mengga. At first, Mengga was torn between Mardijo and Mardiyanto, as the former represented the dominant concession elite (the PDI-P) in Central Java, while the latter had been his superior in 1997–98, when Mengga served as socio-political adviser under Mardiyanto as Diponegoro Commander. Megawati's decision to oppose Mardijo's ambitions solved Mengga's dilemma, giving him free rein to support Mardiyanto.

The role of NU in this election was also vital for Kodam. For five years, the Central Java NU had enjoyed good relations with Mardiyanto. Many *kiai* favoured Mardiyanto's re-election, which would facilitate further inflows from the development budget for their *pesantren*s. They opposed Mardijo, who had patronised the most militant segment of PDI-P's paramilitary wing, called Komunitas Marhaenisme (Komar). Komar's aggressive expansion in the underworld of Semarang and Solo had infringed on turf formerly controlled by NU vigilante corps (Banser). Frustrated Banser leaders lobbied *kiai* and NU executives to complain about this situation to Mardijo. NU thus favoured Mardiyanto in the gubernatorial election, and it was Muhammad Adnan, popularly called Gus Adnan, Chairman of the Central Java Branch of NU, who became the main broker involved in consolidating support for Mardiyanto. In order to cement its relationship with Mardiyanto, NU—via PKB—nominated the non-partisan Ali Mufiz, Deputy Chairman of NU's Central Java Branch, as his running mate.

Having secured this political arrangement, NU approached Kodam Diponegoro, promising that NU would maximise co-operation with TNI and the police to maintain social order after the elections. Mengga and his top brass welcomed this approach as they also were unhappy with Mardijo's Komar. Komar was thought to be involved with radical anti-TNI leftists who were demanding the return of lands seized by the New Order army in the 1960s, as discussed above. Quelling this movement was an institutional imperative for the Diponegoro Command, which stood to lose a great deal if it was forced to return the land in question. To avoid this scenario, it sought the support of NU for its campaign of 'vigilance' against ex-political prisoners. It was in this context that the local military elite joined forces with NU in supporting Mardiyanto's re-election. The voting in the DPRD was conducted on 24 July 2003. As anticipated, the PKB and TNI voted for Mardiyanto while PDI-P, although split between the two candidates, also favoured Mardiyanto propelling him to victory with 62 votes.

All three gubernatorial elections in Java demonstrate TNI's active political participation. There was no instruction from TNI headquarters in Jakarta to support either incumbents or candidates from the leading party, as was the case during the New Order. Rather, Kodams were given autonomy to support candidates who would maximise the interests of Kodam. In each case, TNI relied on its informal networks involving religious, ethnic and retired military elements. Generals proved adroit at manipulating civilian political competition and using their power to ensure their institutional interests were not compromised by electoral outcomes. In fact, these elections strengthened ties between local TNI and civilian elites.

Politics of *preman* and the out-sourcing of violence

As competition intensified among local political elites 'civic protest' became a covert means of lobbying for concessions and graft. Local legislators often used the strategy of mobilising 'local residents' to protest against projects in fields like land zoning and allocation, village or community development, and even welfare. The very politicians who orchestrated the demonstrations could then point to them as evidence of 'civil unrest' requiring establishment of special parliamentary committees (*pansus*) to discuss the problematic government project in question. Government officials in charge of the project had no choice but to 'consult' with the politicians who raised the issue. What typically happened was that these politicians then acted as 'mediators' in resolving the problem, making lucrative deals in the process. In exchange for 'calming' local residents, officials ensured that project contracts were allocated to companies connected to the 'mediator'.

This manipulation of protest to facilitate deals with government officials became a favoured and effective means of fundraising by local politicians, who exploited the need for post-Soeharto local governments to show they respected the concerns of citizens. Astute politicians organised various types of 'resident groups' prepared to pounce on any opportunity to shake down the government. Such groups came in the form of resident forums, youth groups, labour associations, farmer assemblies, environmental NGOs, ethnic delegations, religious representatives, to name a few. Political power increasingly came to be measured in terms of the scale of 'mass protests' that a politician could mobilise and the number of groups that he or she controlled. As one prominent politician claimed, 'access to local concessions now depends on how many corps (*pasukan*) you can prepare to demonstrate your importance to the government' (interview Ade Komaruddin 9 October 2003).

Manufacturing protests requires manpower. Since the economic crisis of 1997–98, which boosted the number of unemployed youth, recruitment of protestors has become easier, but it still requires mass brokers with the networks and muscle to get people onto the streets. Such brokers could be ethnic leaders, informal leaders of customary (*adat*) communities, religious teachers or, most importantly, local hoodlums (*preman*). Elite politicians with connections to the right brokers need only make a phone call to organise a mass protest. Indeed, many prominent local politicians work with several different brokers and thus enjoy the power to command the 'voice of the citizen' in very flexible ways.

During the New Order period, various *preman* groups, most infamously Pemuda Pancasila (PP) and PPM, enjoyed official sanction and in return performed coercive activities for the regime, such as strikebreaking. Since the end of the New Order, diversification of underworld power has been discernible, most notably with the growth of local ethnic groups, political party-affiliated youth organisations, and religious vigilantes. The proliferation of such organisations and their embrace of *preman* tactics has resonated with local power elites' increasing need of for mass mobilisation as a practical weapon in the everyday competition for concessions. In West, Central and East Java local politicians built alliances with *preman* in order to orchestrate 'popular' protests and hence tap into government economic resources.

In West Java, the capital city of Bandung and industrial areas of the northern coast have been hotbeds of *preman*. Here, a 'youth' organisation AMS, which was established by the West Java military command in the 1970s, is acknowledged as the most powerful *preman* group. AMS has regional branches in all West Java regencies and in the neighbouring province of Banten, and its structure resembles that of a military command, with its agents placed in many villages and districts for industrial workers.

This network, which links local elites and grassroots activists in a clientelistic way, has effectively countered many civil society organisations which attempt to promote mass solidarity based on the class interests of labourers and farmers. Several Bandung-based NGOs have endeavoured to organise both industrial workers along the north coast and agricultural employees in the southern area of the province (where many regencies, like Garut, Cianjur, Sukabumi, Ciamis and Tasikmalaya, remain relatively impoverished). These attempts, however, have been constantly blocked by the *preman* in the area who intimidate workers and villagers collaborating with NGOs from Bandung. Here, civil society movements trying to promote a class-oriented interest representation, based on 'horizontal' social solidarity, are countered by an elite model of organising the masses based on 'vertical' solidarity.

It is not only the AMS which has been significant in maintaining the elite's vertical model of mass mobilisation. A group which splintered from AMS in 2001, Gabungan Inisiatif Barisan Anak Sunda Siliwangi (GIBASS), also enjoys wide influence in Bandung.[13] Members of GIBAS have helped the city administration resolve many 'problems' that could not be solved by legal means, such as eviction of street vendors and slum clearance for development projects. Both AMS and GIBAS claim to be safeguarding the ethnic interests of the Sundanese people, and their local networks are made available to prominent Sundanese political elites.

East Java is the heartland of NU power and influence. During the Abdurrahman Wahid presidency (1999–2001), East Java's underworld was largely taken over by NU's vigilante corps, Banser. The rise of the Abdurrahman presidency in 1999 encouraged Banser to expand its underworld activities, but his impeachment and replacement by Megawati in 2001 facilitated the emergence of a PDI-P-affiliated vigilante corps, Banteng Muda Indonesia (BMI), in the *preman* sector. BMI's aggressive expansion of protection rackets, ranging from traditional cockfights and secret lotteries (*toto gelap* or *togel*), to brothels and industrial extortion, ignited a public furore over its brutal methods. According to one local politician in East Java, BMI successfully took over major underworld territories previously controlled by Banser, except for places directly controlled by *pesantren* (interview Machmud Sardjujono 26 June 2003). BMI expanded its influence partly by allying with powerful Madurese ethnic associations, namely

---

13 GIBASS was later renamed as GIBAS by dropping 'Sunda' from the original name. GIBAS is said to be more 'militant' than AMS.

IKABRA and IKMI. These groups found that BMI not only had few qualms about engaging in underworld business but also enjoyed direct access to the central government. The *preman* territory of East Java was, in this way, wrested from Banser by BMI, a process that relied on Madurese *preman* leaders whose reputation for aggressiveness and coarse behaviour was an obvious advantage in doing this sort of business.

Industrial areas in the Surabaya Bay, for example, have long been a playground of these ethnic *preman* groups. Since the end of the New Order, they have often been hired by enterprises to engage in strikebreaking and union busting and to evict poor residents to make way for development projects initiated by the city administration. They also have sent hit-men and kidnappers to terrorise NGO activists campaigning against evictions. As one local official put it,

> It is stupid to kill NGO activists, because it is enough to make a phone call to them and then say 'I am now in front of your son's primary school'… You know this is not Jakarta where any tiny event like this may make news in the print media' (interview June 2003).

It is widely believed locally that top clients of IKABRA and IKMI include people from the inner circles of Imam Utomo, the Governor of East Java, Major General A. D. Sikki, the commander of Brawijaya Military Division, and some 'charismatic' Islamic teachers (*kiai khos*) linked to local politicians.

The growing political role of *preman* illustrates how decentralisation and democratisation initiatives have been captured by local elites in ways that have consolidated clientelistic practices in the post-Soeharto era. In particular, ethnic identities such as those of the Sundanese and Madurese have become very effective tools for political mobilisation, as they structurally bind local power elites and people in 'vertical solidarity' against the 'horizontal' model employed by the civil society movement. The ensuing atmosphere of intimidation and violence has largely muted the influence of local NGOs, media and other agencies which try to monitor the activities of the political elite and hold them accountable.

In this way, the utility of violence in political process is no longer dominated by local military commands, and political elites have increasingly relied on civilianised violence organised by *preman* groups. Importantly, TNI's withdrawal from direct political violence has effectively given the local military a relatively free hand in dealing with political competition among civilian elites. For civilian political elites, such a transformation of TNI is welcome, and these aspirants to political office almost inevitably seek support from the TNI, which is in turn in the position to weigh different offers and carefully calculate who are most suitable as strategic partners. Thus, it can be argued that, by out-sourcing violence to the *preman* proxy, TNI has effectively enhanced its bargaining power in the civilian local political competition.

Conclusion

This chapter has been concerned with the first phase of democratic transition in Indonesia, which lasted from the first post-Soeharto general elections in 1999 to the second in 2004. During this phase, the post-Soeharto *reformasi* movement promoted several significant democratic projects, including the 1999 elections themselves, decentralisation, civic participation in politics, and elections (not appointment) of local government heads. What was the political impact of these projects in Java and how did the TNI respond to the changing rules of the game and the shifting political landscape? Focusing on these questions enables us to clarify the legacy of New Order military in non-conflict areas.

Clearly, the democratising impact of the 1999 elections on elite politics was immense. They ended three decades of Golkar dominance. In about eighty per cent of all district and municipality DPRD in the three provinces new power elites affiliated with PDI-P became dominant, leading to the re-shaping of local concession regimes. In the face of this power shift, local military commands were given greater autonomy to adjust local alliances with civilian elites for the sake of securing their institutional interests.

Decentralisation also greatly modified the pattern of concession hunting among civilian elites. Access to increased resources and greater budgetary discretion led to more widespread corruption. Local legislators used their power to demand annual accountability reports from government heads to siphon off maximum benefits from development projects. The *modus operandi* of collusion has become pervasive and more sophisticated, outstripping the monitoring capacity of local anti-corruption NGOs. In order to share in the spoils of government, the territorial commands skilfully mobilised their bargaining power vis-à-vis local leaders. Revivified Muspida was one means by which civilian leaders used to buy political loyalty from the TNI.

In response to the growing role of civil society organisations, the political elite increasingly relied on *preman* brokers to mobilise mass support and to tap into concession projects. Patrimonial identities, such as those based on ethnicity, religion and kinship were used to counter class-based horizontal social solidarity. With some exceptions, this 'civilianisation' of violence reduced TNI's traditional role in containing civil society, helping the military to burnish its image and focus its institutional resources on securing its own interests. Thus, the out-sourcing of violence to *preman* bolstered TNI's credibility at the price of extensive gangster involvement in democratic processes and institutions.

These developments came together in the 2003 gubernatorial elections held in the three provinces in Java. It was expected that the election of governors would increase political accountability and improve local governance. Yet these elections considerably bolstered the political bargaining power of local military elites who skilfully exploited civilian competition for power and money, tactically collaborated with dominant social forces, and shrewdly developed ties with electoral victors.

It can be concluded that the legacy of the New Order was still very strong in local politics in West, Central and East Java during the first phase of democratic transition. This initial phase of political *reformasi* has now passed, but it continues to shape the direction of the second phase of political reform and democratic consolidation that began in 2005. Since 2005, local leaders have been popularly elected (see Mietzner in this volume), meaning also that the system of presenting annual accountability reports before local parliaments has ended. Also with the 2004 general elections, TNI's parliamentary seats were abolished. There are signs that these reforms are significantly altering the pattern of civil-military relations, with a further reduction of the military's influence on politics at the local level. At the same time, however, the legacy of the New Order system of pervasive military influence still lingers. The territorial structure of the military remains intact, military commanders still have access to local political decisionmaking through the Muspida structure, and the practice of self-financing of the local military budget continues at various command levels. The economic incentives created by self-financing continue to motivate local military officers to collude with business elites—including criminal entrepreneurs—who gain benefits from the political protection provided by local heads and parliamentarians. The institutional reforms enacted so far have not yet been sufficiently thorough to promote a truly robust civil society or to break local concession regimes.

10 The Political Economy of Reform: Labour after Soeharto

CHRIS MANNING

The dramatic changes of 1998 in the political and economic environment brought to the fore tensions between economic and social policy that had simmered near the surface for three decades under Soeharto. These strains were felt acutely especially in areas where the interests of large, disadvantaged, social groups were perceived to have been sacrificed in the quest for faster economic growth and crony business expansion. In several key areas where economic and social policy intersect, such as labour, agricultural policy and land rights, since Soeharto fell there has been a significant shift in favour of social groups disadvantaged during the New Order. This chapter focuses on one such group, wage workers in the formal sector.

Labour policy is one domain in which the rights of a significant social group, wage workers, were neglected in the interests of greater political and economic stability during the Soeharto period (see Hadiz 1997). It is no surprise therefore that labour reform was high on the agenda of the early *reformasi* governments led by Habibie and Abdurrahman Wahid in 1999–2001, and continued to receive close attention as the new democratic political format was consolidated under Megawati and Susilo Bambang Yudhoyono from 2001–07.

However, suppression of organised labour was not the only legacy of the Soeharto regime. It had also adopted a classic East Asian model of encouraging increases in exports and jobs in labour intensive industries, which contributed to poverty decline.[1] The spate of new jobs raised expectations for improvements in living standards among poorer sections of the community. At the same time, as manufacturing exports took off, the Soeharto government in its later years had sought to provide greater protection for wage workers, through minimum wages

---

1 The four 'Tiger' economies of South Korea, Taiwan, Singapore and Hong Kong all achieved significantly improved living standards partly through jobs created in export-oriented industries in the first 20 years of rapid economic growth (World Bank 1993).

and other labour legislation, partly in response to domestic and international criticism of Indonesia's labour rights record. The Soeharto legacy in labour policy is more complex and multi-faceted than is commonly recognised.

Dealing with the potential conflict between political transformation and greater freedoms on the one hand, and economic performance which provides jobs for the poor, is not a uniquely Indonesian dilemma (Haggard 2000). It is not surprising, therefore, that the post-Soeharto governments have faced difficulties in reconciling the labour reform agenda with broader economic development goals. Similar problems have been faced by other countries which have made the transition from autocratic to more democratic political systems, especially in Latin America during the late 1980s and 1990s (Cox-Edwards 1997).

However, it is argued in this chapter that the contradictions between social and economic policy have been quite stark in the case of Indonesia. They are particularly manifest in the policies of Indonesia's fourth president in the post-Soeharto era, Susilo Bambang Yudhoyono, elected for a first five-year term in 2004. Yudhoyono set ambitious targets for reducing unemployment as one of the main goals of his government. At the time of writing, six years into the term of the government's term in office, it seemed less likely to achieve employment goals than successive governments under the New Order.

Part of the dilemma for the government relates to how governments weigh up policies designed to promote the welfare of formal sector wage workers as against those seeking to support the interests of labour in general. These wage workers not only account for a minority of all employed persons in Indonesia (as in other developing countries), but can have quite different interests to those in small enterprises and the informal sector. Conflicts of interest arise from the impact that greater government-mandated protection of formal sector workers ('insiders'), as opposed to more decentralised collective bargaining, has on labour costs and job opportunities for 'outsiders', those mainly in the informal sector. In the East Asian context, a major avenue for improvement in living standards among outsiders in the early stages of development had been through providing them with access to formal sector jobs, mainly in internationally competitive, labour-intensive industries, such as textiles, clothing, footwear, furniture and electronics (Galenson 1992; Fields 1994).[2] Government-mandated protections of conditions for insiders already located in the formal sector can be a barrier to the entry of these outsiders.

The views of economists commonly diverge from those of many other social scientists on the social costs of different approaches to labour policy in Indonesia.

---

2 Note that these improvements are relative to less favourable jobs in many informal enterprises. By First World standards, of course, wages in the textile, clothing and footwear industries, are still very low, and have been a subject of widespread criticism by labour activists.

Other social scientists and lawyers, focusing on the denial of labour freedoms in the New Order period, have generally welcomed changes in the legislative framework since the downfall of Soeharto (eg Lindsay and Masduki 2002; Caraway 2006). They draw attention to more independent labour unions, an improved industrial relations climate and greater compliance with labour laws in the post-Soeharto era. In contrast, many economists have focused on a different set of variables, in particular the slow rate of investment and employment growth in the formal sector. They have drawn attention to the potentially harmful mix (from the point of view of job creation) of a more active union movement and extensive labour protection mandated by the government authorities. In the Indonesian context, it has been suggested that this has contributed to steeply rising labour costs and employment arrangements which are not conducive to job creation (World Bank 2005).

I take up some of these issues in the chapter. The second section of the chapter delves briefly into the relationship between political and economic reform, both in general and with specific reference to Indonesia. This sets the scene for a more detailed discussion of the political economy of labour policy in the third section. Three episodes are discussed briefly: the controversy over legislation on levels of severance pay and redundancy arrangements, the dramatic increases in minimum wages in 2000–02, and the half-baked and ultimately unsuccessful attempts to revise clauses in the 2003 Manpower Protection Act under Yudhoyono in 2005–06. In the fourth section, the discussion turns to labour outcomes, focusing on employment and drawing contrasts between the Soeharto and post-Soeharto years.

Political change and economic policy in Indonesia

Autocratic systems of government, like that of Soeharto, have a mixed economic record (Williamson 1994).[3] Nevertheless, autocratic governments have the means to implement far-reaching economic reforms, because they exert control over the political system—including electoral processes (if any), cabinet appointments, and the legislature—and dominate interest groups, the media and the bureaucracy (Haggard 2000). International experience suggests, however, that this is by no means a sufficient condition for success. Necessary characteristics include leaders with a long-time horizon and ability to select a team of economic

---

3   Economic reform is defined loosely to include policy changes which promote economic growth through more efficient allocation of resources, and increased savings and investment. Key elements of the policy mix include relatively stable and predictable macro-economic conditions, a more open economy and government policies which promote domestic and foreign investment in competitive industries.

advisers, often in key economics cabinet positions, with a strong allegiance to the leadership, such as in the cases of Chile and Singapore (Pinera 1994). A clear strategy is needed on the sequencing of reforms to promote sustained economic growth. Reform-oriented governments also need some luck. Exogenous domestic or international shocks to the economy can derail the reform process, although one measure of successful autocratic leaders is the capacity to devise strategies to cope with crisis.

An abrupt transition to a democratic regime, as occurred in Indonesia in 1998–99 has the potential to disturb many of the conditions which underpin economic expansion under a pro-growth autocratic government. This is especially true where the changes required to sustain growth threaten the livelihoods and economic standing of interest groups, or significant sections of the wider community. The government, especially if it is part of a coalition, loses many of the levers that ensure the successful implementation of economic reforms. It is no longer able to control electoral processes, or to ignore interest groups or censor what is printed in the media, given the necessity of preserving public support for electoral purposes. Unless it is supported by a strong professional bureaucracy, new democratic governments can find it difficult to stick to a consistent reform program, especially if key economic portfolios are held by coalition partners with a different policy priorities. In presidential systems, weak control over the legislature has the potential to slow or even halt economic reform programs.

Economic policies under Soeharto

Especially in the first two decades, Indonesia under Soeharto had many of the features of an autocratic government committed to economic progress (Bresnan 1994; Hill 2000). The close working relationship between the president and the closely knit group of technocrats who controlled economic portfolios was a key feature of the regime. It not only enabled the passage of economic reforms which stabilised the economy, and promoted agricultural development, population control, trade expansion and foreign investment, but also helped Indonesia deal with periodic economic crises, especially in the early years of the regime (Hoffman et al 2007). The widely documented control over the electoral process, political parties, the legislature, the media and other potential opposition groups (including organised labour), enabled the government to press forward with its sometimes unpopular economic agenda without significant challenge.[4]

---

4 The effectiveness of the autocratic model for economic advancement waned after the break up of the cohesive technocrat team from the University of Indonesia; serious fault lines emerged within the cabinet and in the bureaucracy in the 1990s (especially the 'technolog' challenge to a more open, competitive economic

Particularly relevant for our later discussion of labour policies, it is worth noting that Soeharto was no Pinochet when it came to explicit support for market-oriented economic policies, and nor were his 'Berkeley mafia' of US-trained technocrats as doctrinaire as the Chicago boys who managed the Chilean reforms (Pinera 1994). While the government initiated a raft of reforms (especially removing obstacles to trade and restrictions to foreign investment) that underpinned the export boom which occurred in the last decade of the regime, neither Soeharto nor his technocrats demonstrated a strong public commitment to a more open and competitive economy.[5] The reform package was sold to the public as 'deregulation' rather than the conventional program of economic liberalisation that it in fact represented. Soeharto himself was no supporter of liberal economics. He frequently stated his preference for state-imposed 'co-operative' forms of ownership and distribution on the grounds they were the 'appropriate form of enterprise' for Indonesians (Soeharto 1989:233).

Similarly, as we shall see, reform of quite extensive labour protection, which constrained labour market flexibility in an increasingly competitive international economic environment, was never part of the government reform agenda under Soeharto, as it was in Chile under Pinochet (Edwards 1997). To the contrary, protective legislation was even extended during the later Soeharto years, in response to criticism of the regime's poor record on labour rights.

Both the preference for co-operatives and protective government labour regulations were a reflection of the strong paternalistic streak and ambivalence with regard to market solutions that marked Soeharto's approach to public policy. The same mindset is reflected in policies adopted by subsequent, post-New Order governments, especially that led by Susilo Bambang Yudhoyono.

The politics of economic policy after Soeharto

The institutional environment changed dramatically with breathtaking pace of political reform after the fall of Soeharto: the first free elections in 1999, 'big bang' decentralisation in 2001, constitutional reform in 2002, the first direct presidential elections in 2004 and elections for district and provincial governments over subsequent years.

---

policy; see Azis, 1994). Added to this was increasing alarm at the extent of economic favours granted to members of the first family, which began to undermine public support for the entire reform agenda initiated in the 1980s.

5   Soesastro, 1989, refers to the strategy of 'low politics'—reform almost by stealth than through direct confrontation with potential opposition groups—adopted by the technocrat reformers, which helps explain the relatively trouble-free adoption of market-oriented policies in the 1980s. This was possible in an environment where reform packages were not vetted publicly in the media, or comprehensively in the political arena, in contrast to the post-Soeharto era.

After the initial three years of frenetic political change and sometimes chaotic economic policy making under B. J. Habibie and Abdurrahman Wahid, economic policy began to stabilise in the Megawati and then Yudhoyono presidencies. Several key patterns emerged. First, the power of the presidency and executive was weakened, and that of legislature strengthened.[6] Economic cabinet ministers now were obliged to negotiate most major regulatory changes in the parliament. Major pieces of legislation such as revisions to the tax and investment laws all took at least twelve months and often much longer to gain parliamentary approval.

Second, ministers appointed in successive coalition governments no longer spoke with a single voice, nor did their ministries pursue a consistent line on economic policy, in contrast to cabinet ministers during much of the Soeharto era. Cabinets now consisted of broadly based multi-party 'rainbow coalitions' (see Aspinall in this volume). Different policy agendas emerged, for example between the Finance and Trade and Industry ministers over trade policy under Megawati, and between the ministers of Agriculture and Industry, on the one hand, and ministers in the key economic portfolios—Finance, Trade and the coordinating minister of Economic Affairs—on protection for industry policy (Awiscahyono and Hill 2004; Basri and Patunru 2006).

Third, interest groups, including business and labour unions, now had much more access to decision makers in the parliament, and the bureaucracy, as well as cabinet ministers who were no longer protected by a powerful president. In addition, there was now constant public scrutiny of government performance from civil society groups and the media. Later we shall see that that freedom of the press, in particular, has been important in putting pressure on government in the area of labour policy.

Finally, decentralisation meant that the central government no longer controlled some of the key levers of economic policy. Some areas of labour policy, such as the setting of minimum wages, have been decentralised, even though most laws are still the prerogative of the central government.[7]

Two other features of the policy-making environment are also relevant for labour policy in the *reformasi* era. Firstly, the media, many parliamentarians and some cabinet ministers adopted a more nationalistic stance regarding foreign investment in certain sectors (such as mining) and international financial organisations (IFIs), such as the IMF and World Bank. The economic crisis had

---

6   The constitutional reforms of 2002 restored some authority to the president, even though she/he had much less absolute authority than during the New Order period, Ellis, 2007.

7   Indonesia is unlike some countries (such as India) where state governments can amend national labour laws for application within their own jurisdictions.

dented Indonesian policymaker confidence in IFIs, not least for their strong advocacy of market solutions when Indonesia was on its knees during the financial crisis (Johnson 1998; Robison and Hadiz 2004:148–49).

Second, much resentment about about corruption, cronyism and human rights abuses had built up under Soeharto and now meant that less credit was to be accorded in the public discourse and political arena for the achievements of the Soeharto government. Besides the well-known economic 'miracle', these accomplishments were in areas such as employment growth and poverty alleviation, which were much less in the political spotlight after the crisis than issues such as repression of collective rights. Galvanising public support for 'neo-liberal' economic reforms in areas such as trade reform, privatisation, or labour, was likely to prove a difficult task for the new post-New Order governments, precisely because of a widespread, popular belief that the Soeharto regime's economic policies had not benefited the poor significantly, if at all.

We now turn to labour policy in the new political environment.

Labour policy in the post-Soeharto era

Labour is one area where there were major changes in the institutional environment following the fall of the Soeharto regime. Most important was government recognition of the right to join trade unions and bargain collectively through ratification of ILO conventions and the Trade Union Law, No 21/2000, one of the first major laws passed after the fall of Soeharto just two years earlier. Multiple union structures were permitted in the form of national federations and larger confederations, after some 25 years when one government sanctioned union (Serikat Pekerja Seluruh Indonesia, SPSI or the All Indonesia Trade Union) was the only trade union organisation recognised by the government.[8] Five years after the crisis, the total number of union members was estimated at close to 10 million, and may have increased somewhat since then (Quinn 2003:26). Although this number is almost certainly an overestimate,[9] union activism was certainly on the increase in the post-crisis period. Workers were distributed over 60 union federations, and three major confederations that accounted for around over 80 per cent of all union membership. For economic

---

8   In response to heavy national and international pressure, independent company unions were permitted by the Soeharto regime in the 1990s. Alternative union bodies with multiple branches, most notably the Indonesia Prosperity Labour Union (Serikat Buruh Sejahtera Indonesia, SBSI), were also formed, despite official opposition, see Hadiz, 1997.
9   The true number of dues paying members is probably closer to 3–5 million with a union density of perhaps around 5–10 per cent among wage employees.

and social analysis, the most important implication from this expansion has been stronger pressures from trade unions for compliance with basic labour laws and standards, compared with the New Order period.[10]

Whereas under Soeharto, security officials, technocrats, politicians and businesspeople were appointed as Ministers of Manpower, several former trade unionists were appointed as Ministers of Manpower in post-Soeharto governments.[11] These appointments were symptomatic of a major shift in government policy towards greater support of labour rights and standards. Improved standards were promoted by the government through law No 13/2003 drafted by the Ministry of Manpower, and passed after long negotiations between the major union confederations and the employers organisation (Asosiasi Pengusaha Indonesia, APINDO) and presentations through 2001–02 by major stakeholders to the relevant parliamentary committee (Komisi VII). This law covers a wide range of labour protection issues, bringing together previous legislation scattered in a range of Ministerial and Presidential Decrees and government laws, as well as setting new standards in areas such as protection of female workers and procedures and compensation for lay offs and dismissals.[12]

The significance of these changes for the discussion in this chapter relates to the implications of a freer labour movement and an extensive set of regulations for adjustment of employment and wages to economic circumstances. Under Soeharto, regulations were extensive but compliance was low (Manning 1998). After *reformasi*, given greater compliance and more extensive regulations, one might reasonably conclude that Indonesia has one of the most regulated labour markets in the developing world, at least for larger firms in the formal sector. Developments after the fall of Soeharto stand in contrast to international trends in the directions of greater individual and collective bargaining in setting labour standards, especially in Latin America (IADB 2004).

The viewpoint that organised labour has gained through a combination of the new laws and greater compliance enforced by freer unions is a contested one. Caraway (2004) has argued that protective legislation inherited from Soeharto and enshrined in a single law in 2003 has provided a protective environment for labour employed in the modern sector. This applies especially to workers

---

10 See for example Suryahadi et al, 2003, on minimum wages which suggests higher levels of compliance with regulations in 2000 compared with before the crisis.

11 The two ex-union leaders who became Ministers of Manpower were Bomer Pasaribu, former Chairman of SPSI and an active member of Golkar, and Jacob Nuwa Wea, also an SPSI unionist but a strong supporter of the PDI-P before the downfall of Soeharto. The former was minister in an early Abdurrahman Wahid cabinet (1999–2000), and the latter in the Megawati government 2001–04.

12 The law deals with basic protection issues (such as hours of work, overtime, and minimum wages), protection of vulnerable workers (children, females, and contract and migrant workers) and basic principles for collective bargaining and industrial relations, including sanctions for non-compliance. Many of the issues have been subsequently regulated in implementing legislation, see Manning and Roesad, 2007.

represented by the now freer, smaller unions that are unable to match employers in collective bargaining. In contrast, others have argued the laws have facilitated wider use of flexible labour arrangements, especially the employment of contract workers under less favourable conditions compared with regular workers (Tjandra 2008; Tjandraningsih and Nugroho 2008).

While there is little disagreement about greater use of contract labour since the law came into effect, cause and effect are debatable. Tjandra (pp.1, 7) argues that the new laws allow for a 'high degree of flexibility' and in practice there are 'massive violations' of the law in regard to provisions requiring the appointment of contract workers to permanent positions after a given period of employment with the firm. Tjandraningsih and Nugroho (p.6) also focus on the greater flexibility in labour management practices since the labour law was passed in 2003, which they also attribute to the law: '…a direct effect of the legislation been the introduction of flexible industrial relations practices in the form of contract labour and third party labour recruitment practices on a very large scale.'

Besides holding the view that the law is less binding on employers than in the past, other explanations for this shift in labour practices include greater product market competition and introduction of new technology (eg, Tjandraningsih and Nugroho, 2008:5–6). The possibility that the attempt to limit the number of permanent employees in many firms, and flout the laws, is due to the *tightening* (not loosening) of labour regulation with regard to remuneration and dismissal is not countenanced. This is one of the main arguments implicit in this paper, although our focus is on the actors engaged in the process of reform, some of the political processes underpinning them, and the employment implications, rather than on an analysis of changing labour practices.

Three Labour policy episodes

Three episodes in labour reform in the post-crisis period illustrate some of the key features of the changed political environment and its significance for public policy in the post-Soeharto era: revisions to legislation concerning severance pay for laid off workers; large minimum wage increases in the period 2000–02 and attempts to revise the labour laws under the Yudhoyono administration in 2005–06.

In each of the above cases, the Ministry of Manpower and ex-Ministers with a labour union background, played a central role in promoting new initiatives, all involved vigorous public debates and media coverage, and the involvement of interest groups, both employer organisations and labour unions. Two—the minimum wage increases and the revisions to severance pay—had regional dimensions. Each was ultimately resolved in favour of wage workers.

All three areas of policy had been on the Soeharto government's political agenda in the 1990s.[13] Minimum wages were raised quite significantly during the late Soeharto years when they were revised annually, for the first time in all provinces across the country. Severance pay rates were also increased by regulation in 1996, and a new labour law was drafted by the government in the last years of the Soeharto government. As in the post-Soeharto years, the main actor was the Ministry of Manpower, but on that earlier occasion change was initiated, perhaps surprisingly, by a minister who was also a prominent businessman: Abdul Latief, who had been appointed by Soeharto to the cabinet for the 1993–98 period. As noted above, the main labour initiatives were in part a response by the Soeharto government (probably with the strong support of the president) to increasing national and international criticism of its labour policies, including 'exploitation' of low-wage Indonesian labour in foreign dominated, export-oriented industries.

The cost of laying off workers. The first example relates to rising costs of laying off workers and illustrates the extent of influence on policy exerted by mass action in the post-Soeharto years. In 2000, changes to severance pay arrangements (Ministerial Decision No 150/2000) were introduced by the Minister of Manpower and former SPSI union leader and prominent Golkar politician, Bomer Pasaribu (see Manning 1998:172–98). Ministerial Decision 150 raised the rate of severance and long service pay and extended coverage to new groups of workers. In response to strong representations made by APINDO, which objected especially to the payment of severance to workers dismissed for criminal acts, the legislation was initially overturned by a Ministerial Decision No 78 of 2001. But heavy media criticism of the reversal of the decision in favour of business and major demonstrations by workers in several cities (including the threat of violence by demonstrators in Bandung) led to an almost immediate reinstatement of the original decision by the Minister of Manpower.

A compromise was reached two years later in the above-mentioned law, No 13/2003 on Manpower. Unions accepted revisions to clauses which denied severance and long service pay to workers laid off for criminal offences, or who quit voluntarily, in return for further increases in rates of severance. For business this was a somewhat pyrrhic victory: severance rates were now very high by international standards (Manning and Roesad 2007).[14]

The Jakarta minimum wage. The second episode of contentious labour policy involved unilateral action by regional interests supported by a pro-labour Minister. At the end of 2001, Soetiyoso, the Governor of Jakarta sought a rise

---

13   See Manning, 1998, Chapter 7 for a detailed discussion of labour reforms during the Soeharto era.

14   In most countries, severance pay and long service leave is mandated at 4–8 months pay for workers dismissed after 5–10 years service. In the Indonesian case, they amount to close to 2–3 times this amount: 15–20 months pay for similar durations of employment, Manning and Roesad, 2007.

in minimum wages in the national capital for 2002 of just under 40 per cent in one year, which would have been one of the largest rises in workers' pay in Indonesian history. The increase was championed by Soetiyoso, in the year in which he was seeking re-election as Governor. The minimum wages were to apply only to the special region of Jakarta, but had important flow on effects for minimum wages in other provinces, especially neighbouring West Java.

In this case, the wage increase was challenged in the courts by the employers association APINDO, on the grounds that they were not based on the official guidelines for wage increases set out by the Ministry of Manpower, and would be harmful to its members. APINDO initially won the appeal in one Jakarta district court, but this ruling was subsequently overruled by another district court. In this case, this policy initiative was strongly defended by the Ministry of Manpower, under new Minister of Manpower, Jacob Nuwa Wea, a staunch Megawati supporter and former labour union activist in the Soeharto period. Jacob's appointment as Manpower Minister under Megawati was widely viewed as a move to try and shore up labour support for PDI-P leading up to the 2004 election.[15]

The controversy was widely reported in the Jakarta media, with most commentators supporting the increases. Most argued that Indonesia's wages were too low by international standards, although some reports included warnings from foreign chambers of commerce with regard to the potential impact of such major increases on labour costs and employment.[16] As in the case of dismissals, the issue was resolved in favour of organised labour, despite the potential threat to employment, which has been considered historically a key area of policy concern for organised labour.

Revising the Labour law. Finally, the case of the labour law revisions illustrates, once again, how vulnerable government was to mass action on the part of labour unions, and it also demonstrates the latter's suspicions of government-business reform agendas. The Ministry of Manpower made recommendations, during discussions with unions and employers in February 2006, for significant revisions of some of the more controversial clauses of the manpower law No 13/2003, including the level of severance pay discussed above and restrictions on the employment of contract labour.

The proposal for revision of the law was extensive, surprisingly so, for a Ministry which had drafted and promoted the original legislation only three

---

15   See, for example, Mardjono, 2002, who argued the case for high wages increases on behalf of the Ministry in a paper presented to the parliamentary committee on labour and social policies.

16   See Ford, 2004 for a discussion of some of these issues. The Korean Chamber of Commerce argued strongly that large wage increases were raising labour costs too quickly (see *Jakarta Post*, 24 August 2002), For arguments in favour of the wage increases, see for example articles by Ballinger and Keady (*Jakarta Post*, 18 January 2002, p.5).

years earlier (Manning and Roesad 2007).[17] It appears that the main initiative had come from government agencies concerned about slow economic growth. Revisions of the labour legislation had been incorporated together with other proposed legislative changes (including the tax, customs and investment laws) in the Economics Coordinating Minister's plans to improve the investment climate (Coordinating Ministry for Economic Affairs, 2006). The World Bank in particular had provided strong public support of reforms in all these areas during 2005, including co-hosting a major international conference in co-operation with the Indonesian Chamber of Commerce (Kamar Dagang dan Industri, KADIN), and opened by the vice-president, Jusuf Kalla, in November of that year (World Bank 2005).

The proposed reforms met with stiff opposition. All the major union confederations rejected the proposed changes to the labour law out of hand, partly because they felt that they were not sufficiently engaged in drafting the original draft proposal. The government was faced with increasingly vocal opposition, culminating in major demonstrations in Jakarta and in several other cities in April and May in 2006, the largest of which was reported to involve close to 100,000 people (almost certainly an overestimate) in Jakarta on 1 May, followed by a subsequent smaller demonstration involving some destruction of public property outside the parliament building in Jakarta several days later.[18]

Although the shows of opposition were not extreme by international standards, President Yudhoyono announced quickly in May that proposed revisions to the labour law were to be withdrawn from the national economic reform package, only several months after they had begun to be debated in the public domain. He appointed a 'Five University' team of experts (including economists, lawyers and sociologists) to examine options for labour reform. The team later recommended several changes to regulations to help promote employment.[19] Privately, however, senior government and KADIN officials conceded that any significant revisions to the labour law were almost certainly off the government reform agenda for the rest of the Yudhoyono's term of government.

These three cases of decision making over labour-policy issues demonstrate both breaks with political-economy processes under Soeharto, as well as

---

17   It covered all major areas which had been questioned by business groups, including severance pay rates, restrictions on the employment of contract workers and provisions with regard to minimum wages.

18   See *Jakarta Post*, 2 June 2006, 4 June 2006. Strikes in protest against the law led by the Confederation of the Indonesian Workers Union (Konfederasi Serikat Buruh Indonesia, KSPI) had begun in late March especially in the Bandung region and had become widespread in follow-up actions in early April 2006. See reports in *Pikiran Rakyat*, 24 June 2006 and *Jakarta Post*, 6 June 2006.

19   The committee was chaired by Professor Armida Alisjahbana of Padjadjaran University, Bandung. Its report was submitted to Boediono, the Economics Coordinating Minister in August 2006. It is noteworthy that all of the major union confederations declined to give submissions to the committee, which held a series of closed meetings with stakeholders from mid-May to July. However, some of the committee's recommendations were subsequently examined through union-employer discussions during 2007.

elements of continuity. Politicians and bureaucrats were now more responsive to political pressure through interest group representation, mass action and the media, than in the Soeharto era. While several senior officials including ministers in key economics ministries, believed that labour regulations were hurting employment, very few were prepared to state this publicly or to take the lead in challenging the Ministry of Manpower's strong support for greater government mandate protection of workers. Senior officials within the employment division within the national planning agency (Badan Perencanaan Pembangunan Nasional, Bappenas), had made consistent public representations for less rigidity in employment and wage regulations over the period 2002–04. But they privately acknowledged that the political odds were stacked against reform, especially after the new Manpower Act was passed in 2003. This was despite some compelling empirical evidence which suggests that regulations were harming employment.[20]

Fear of union and wider community backlash against any reforms which appeared to be against the interests of labour (in this case represented mainly by wage workers in the modern sector), meant that reforms aimed at reducing hiring costs and rigidity in employment and wages were too sensitive a subject for political leaders. Like the term economic 'liberalisation', labour market 'flexibility' remains a hot potato in the Jakarta political lexicon, as it does among many labour union and NGO leaders internationally. It should be no surprise, therefore, that none of the major political parties publicly supported winding back restrictive clauses in the labour law, or sided with business in its attempts to modify severance pay and minimum wage regulations.

Also, unlike in the Soeharto period, among interest groups the unions were quite effective, and the employers federation much less successful, in lobbying for changes in public policy. While the government had given a public commitment to employers organisations to reform labour regulations, as part of a strategy to improve the investment climate, it was not able to deliver on its promise.

However, there were also important areas of continuity in policy. The unions were able to gain public support, precisely because of an expectation that the country should continue to rely heavily on government-imposed labour market regulations to set standards, rather than collective bargaining. Paternalism persisted as part and parcel of the labour regime inherited from Soeharto, underpinned by a common belief that far-reaching government regulation was necessary to protect workers from rapacious employers which was, perhaps ironically, another legacy of the Soeharto period.

---

20 The results of these studies were reported in a Bappenas 'White Paper' issued in 2003, see Indonesia. Bappenas, 2003.

Employment in the New Order and post-New Order periods

This brings us to contrasts in the New Order and post-New Order periods in terms of employment. Employer interests were accorded higher priority in the New Order period, and the government pursued economic growth and employment objectives that extended beyond the interests of formal sector workers. Even though regulation was already extensive, and hence might have constrained investment decisions, employers could always find ways around the laws, either by buying the support of official labour union representatives, or by coercing workers who demanded better conditions of work that were in line with regulations (Hadiz 1997). De facto, the regulations did not matter nearly as much as in the *reformasi* period, and hence there was less conflict between regulation and job creation.

Three sets of data—trends in employment in manufacturing and the informal sector, and in unemployment rates—suggest Indonesia has struggled with jobs in the post-crisis period in precisely those areas where the more extensive labour protection laws and new industrial relations arrangements are important. Data on trends in each of these three areas are shown in Figures 10.1–10.3.[21] They are quite disturbing from the perspective of job creation in the formal sector, which was the major engine for improvement in labour incomes—both in terms of jobs and higher wages—in the Soeharto period (Manning 1998).

Figure 10.1 shows employment growth by major sector of the economy in the six years before the crisis, and six years after relative economic stability was achieved around the year 2000. Two major contrasts are apparent. First, employment growth has been minuscule in the more recent period compared with the late Soeharto era in manufacturing and services, the two sectors which employ a high proportion of wage workers.[22] The contrast was especially marked in manufacturing.[23] From 2000, at a time when the total labour force was growing at around one and a half million per year, less than a miniscule ten thousand new jobs (not even one per cent of all new jobs created) had been added to the total manufacturing work force of some twelve million people. This contrasts with some 350–400 thousand new jobs created each year in manufacturing in the first half of the 1990s.

---

21   The figures are calculated based on data recorded in the annual (more recently bi-annual) National Labour Force Survey (SAKERNAS).
22   These two sectors have the highest proportion of jobs in wage employment. In services, wage workers are concentrated in the public sector, in personal services (especially maids) and education and health services.
23   The figure shows growth rates in employment of less than 0.1 per cent per annum in manufacturing, 0.2 per cent in services in from 2000–01, compared with 6 per cent and 4 per cent respectively, per annum, over the period 1990–96.

Figure 10.1: Employment Growth, Indonesia 1990–1996, 2000–2006 (% p.a.)

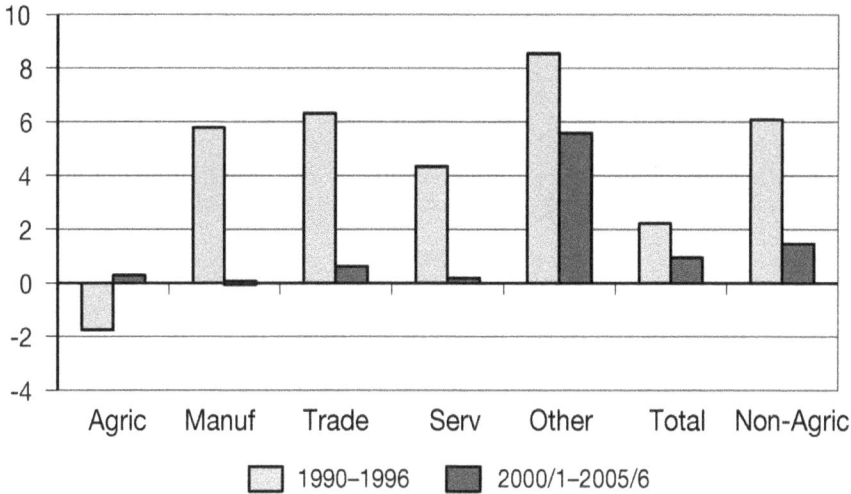

Note: Data for the second period are two year averages, owing to sharp annual fluctuations in several indicators.

Source: CBS (Central Board of Statistics), National Labour Force Surveys, Various Years.

Second, from the point of view of labour welfare, it has not just been the slow growth of jobs that is most alarming but the kinds of job opportunities that have dried up in recent times. Workers who had been attracted out of rural areas and into manufacturing and services in the pre-crisis period now sought new jobs back in low productivity agriculture, or in transport and construction (subsumed in the 'other' category shown in Figure 10.1). Output per worker in the agriculture sector still grew, but only at a little over half the pace recorded before the crisis.[24] Indonesia, which had begun to follow the classic East Asian growth pattern of improved living standards through the shift of workers out of agriculture and into higher productivity activities in towns and cities, now experienced a reversal in this trend in the post-crisis period.

Employment rose briefly in response to increased competitiveness of exports and then declined quite steeply in the labour intensive sectors, textiles, clothing and footwear, or the so-called TCF industries after the crisis.[25] Employment declined through to 2003, and was barely above levels achieved a decade earlier in these 'footloose' industries which tended to be vulnerable to both higher labour costs and more rigid employment arrangements. In contrast, new jobs in

---

24   From 1990–96, output per worker rose by just under 4.5 per cent per annum compared with under 3 per cent from 2000–01 (figures calculated from national accounts and labour force survey data).

25   Data on the industrial breakdown of employment come from the annual survey of large and medium manufacturing industries.

larger firms pre-crisis were concentrated in these competitive export-oriented industries, which had absorbed many rural workers during the export boom from the mid-1980s.[26]

Associated with the above, another important response to the scarcity of new wage jobs has been a trend towards more informal sector work.[27] This contrasts with the pre-crisis period when there was a marked shift away from agricultural and informal sector jobs in favour of more formal sector work (Figure 10.2).

Figure 10.2: Wage Jobs Outside Agriculture, and Agricultural and Other Non-Agricultural Jobs, Indonesia 1986–2004

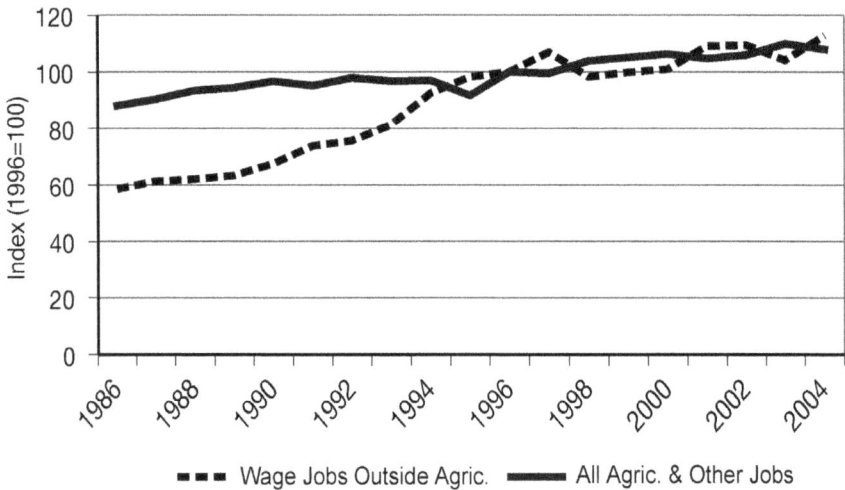

Wage Jobs Outside Agric.   All Agric. & Other Jobs

Note: Data for 1995 are interpolated.

Source: CBS, National Labour Force Surveys, Various Years.

Rising unemployment rates represent another piece of evidence, suggesting much more difficult employment circumstances after the crisis.[28] Compared with more developed industrial countries, unemployment is not as important as an indicator of labour market conditions in less developed in countries like Indonesia, where unemployment benefits are not paid and few can afford to be unemployed. Nevertheless, these figures are worth mentioning because unemployment figures featured prominently in the debates on the government

---

26   From the mid-1980s employment in the TCF industries more than tripled over a decade from some 400 thousand to 1.3 million workers.

27   The formal sector is proxied crudely here by wage employment in non-agricultural sectors.

28   It is useful to bear in mind that unemployment rates are not always meaningful as an indicator of labour market conditions in countries like Indonesia where the informal sector is the main refuge for people who cannot get formal sector jobs, and there is no government unemployment compensation scheme.

record in 2006–07 (bearing in mind that Yudhoyono made halving unemployment from just under 10 to 5 per cent one of his key promises during the election campaign in 2004).

After the crisis, unemployment did not recover as in most other East Asian countries. Rather the number of unemployed continued to rise steadily, and this helps explain why both formal sector jobs grew so slowly. Total unemployment reached double-digit figures by November 2005 for the first time in Indonesia's history (Figure 10.3). Just under half of all the unemployed were young, secondary educated people (mainly senior high graduates) aged 15–24, most of whom resided in urban areas, who might be expected to be queuing for formal sector jobs.[29] Around one third of urban youth, with some secondary schooling, as well as a surprisingly large number in rural areas, were unemployed in 2004–06.

Figure 10.3: Unemployment Rates in Indonesia, 2001–2006

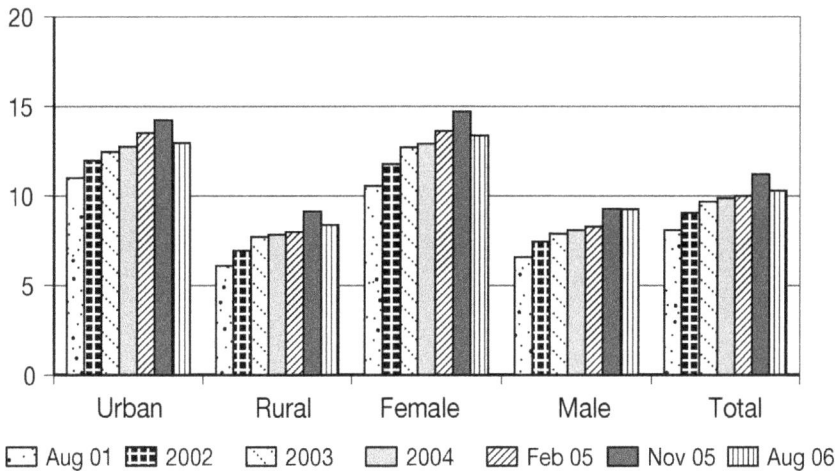

Source: CBS, National Labour Force Surveys, Various Years.

How much can we ascribe these trends in employment and unemployment to some of the labour regulations discussed in the previous section? Labour laws have certainly not been the dominant factor. A big part of Indonesia's employment problem since the crisis can simply be attributed to slower economic growth rates. Economic growth rates were half the rates recorded before the crisis, even after the economy had returned to relative stability by 2000 (Figure 10.4). In addition to labour regulations, a range of other factors have also been important. Uncertainties and the high cost of production in Indonesia relate partly to a less

---

29   These data are for 2004. The proportions of young educated among the unemployed have remained relatively stable since the crisis.

unfavourable investment environment than before the crisis—especially long delays in the investment approval process, lack of transparency, illegal taxes and customs, and deterioration in infrastructure.[30]

Nevertheless, slower growth rates notwithstanding, the number of new jobs created for a given increase in production (output) was still very much smaller than before the crisis. A one percentage increase in output created less than half the number of jobs after the crisis, compared with the pre-crisis period.[31] It is not only the rate of growth that has dented employment growth, but the growth that has taken place has not created enough jobs.

Figure 10.4: Growth Rates in Output (% p.a., constant prices)

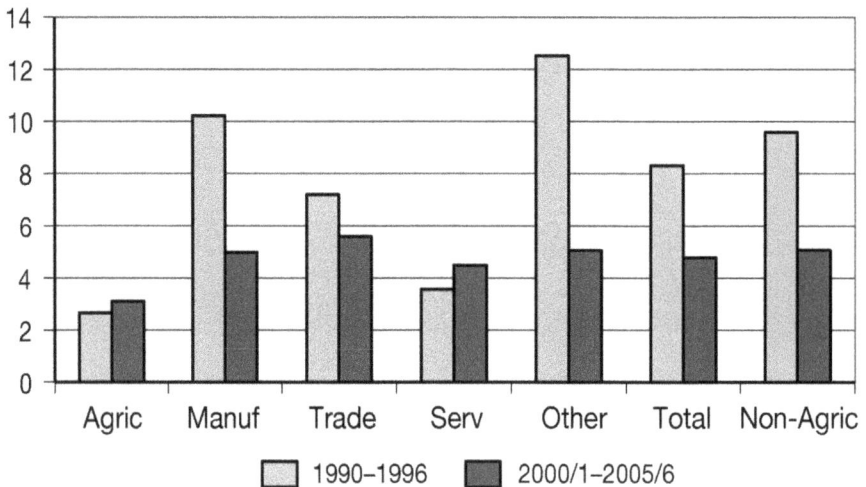

Source, CBS, National Accounts (reported in CIEC data base)

In the wider literature, this phenomenon is often referred to as 'jobless growth', and has been experienced by several developed, Latin American and other Asian countries such as Philippines, although not among the more rapidly growing Asian economies such as China and Vietnam (Asian Development Bank 2005). Technological change and import penetration from low cost producers such as China have been identified as the chief cause of jobless growth, although especially in Latin America, less flexible labour markets attributed to the regulatory environment (IADB 2004).

---

30 See the regular surveys economic developments in the *Bulletin of Indonesian Economic Studies* in 2005 and 2006 for detailed discussion of these developments.
31 In technical jargon, employment elasticities (which measure the percentage change in employment in relation to a one percentage change in output) halved in the non-agricultural sector over this period.

Although still fragmentary, research does suggest that the new, restrictive labour regulations have contributed to the disappointing employment record, especially in labour intensive industries. Three factors have been important. First, with regard to wage regulation, minimum wages rose sharply and appear to have underpinned a similar increase in wages in manufacturing over the period 2000–05 (national average), despite depressed conditions of demand for labour. There is some evidence that these increases especially affected the employment of less educated, younger and female employees (Suryahadi et al 2003). Minimum wages were already close to median (average) wages for urban employees by 2000, suggesting that they were more 'binding' on employees than in the past. In other words, employers were more likely to observe regulations after the crisis, when unions were in a better position to ensure compliance, than during the Soeharto era.

Second, the high costs of severance—the lump sum payment paid when workers are laid off—bolstered by increased minimum wages, effectively imposed a substantial increase in fixed costs of employment.[32] The increases compared with before the crisis were very high. Manning and Roesad (2007:66) report, for example, that severance costs almost tripled in three years in the period 2000–03. While some of these provisions were introduced before the crisis, few employers were considering laying off workers, in light of buoyant demand for labour at that time. The further increase in severance pay after the crisis occurred when many firms were already having to downsize, imposing additional costs. This provided the wrong signals to investors at precisely a time when severance pay rates and systems were being reformed in many other countries of the world, which were competing with Indonesia for investment (LP3E-UNPAD 2004).[33]

One reaction on the part of employers was to employ contract workers short-term or outsource some of their operations. For example, one survey of employment practices found that firms reportedly increased their use of fixed-term contract employment between 2001 and 2003, especially in manufacturing, as part of restructuring efforts (LP3E-UNPAD 2004: Figure 5.5). But subsequently provisions with regard to fixed-contract employment, and more importantly outsourcing of jobs, were also tightened in the new manpower law of 2003.[34] In this respect, Indonesian regulations are more restrictive than in several other Asian countries (Bird 2005).

---

32   The increase in minimum wages are important for severance costs since rates of severance are based on the level of wages paid to workers at the time they are laid off (calculated on a monthly basis, depending on years of service).

33   There were no major extension of regulations in other East Asian countries which compete with Indonesia; in general severance pay rates were much lower in these countries than in Indonesia, see Bird, 2005.

34   The main provisions relate to a reduction in maximum duration of fixed term contracts and the limiting of outsourcing to activities outside the 'core' production activities of firms. See Manning and Roesad, 2007 for details.

To sum up, despite public concern with the employment situation, the jobs situation worsened considerably after the crisis, much more than might have been expected if slower economic growth had been the only factor at play. The government responded by supporting workers in formal sector jobs, seemingly at the expense of employment opportunities for those without jobs, or who sought to move into formal sector jobs from the informal sector and agriculture. The policies backed 'insiders' who were a relatively easily identified group of regular wage workers with strong political support, at the expense of 'outsiders', most of whom were unorganised and worked in low and uncertain jobs in the informal sector and in agriculture. It is important to bear in mind that the newly created union bodies played an important role in the process, both through their active involvement in negotiations over the labour law, and in ensuring that regulations were complied with at the enterprise level.[35]

At the same time, it is important to note that labour unrest—which had been the main economic rationale for limiting union power in the Soeharto era—appears to have had a minor direct impact on employment. The incidence of strikes has remained low by historical and comparative standards (Quinn 2003). As far as actions in the labour sphere, extensive government controls seem to have been the main culprit.

Conclusions

This chapter has examined some political economy dimensions of economic and social policy making in Indonesia with special reference to labour. The focus has been on both continuities and changes in the design and implementation of policy in the post-Soeharto era, compared with that of the New Order. One legacy of the Soeharto era was a strong sense of injustice suffered by wage workers as a consequence of repressive labour policies. Another was a tendency towards state-directed paternalism in setting labour standards that were wide-ranging compared with most other East Asian countries. At the same time, the changed political circumstances under successive democratic governments after the crisis, led to greater divisions over policy within the government, and between different tiers of government with regard to labour. Greater regulation was encouraged by the periodic threat of mass action by labour unions and the increased influence of pro-labour interest groups (including a Ministry of Manpower that had been discredited as a defender of labour rights during the Soeharto years).

---

35 Higher levels of compliance with legislation, especially minimum wages, is another finding of the SMERU study on minimum wages in 2001, see Suryahadi et al, 2003.

Labour legislation was extended in favour of formal sector workers, especially during the Megawati years of 2001–04, when the PDI-P had a major influence on labour policy, not least through its staunchly pro-labour Minister of Manpower, Jacob Nuwa Wea, who remained the leader of one of the major labour confederations throughout his term as minister. More generally, protection of wage employees has been viewed as politically expedient in the more democratic environment after Soeharto, even though modern sector workers make up a relatively small proportion of the working population. Such policies are especially attractive to governments, bearing in mind that the benefits of protection are easily identified and costs difficult to measure, especially in a country where most workers cannot afford to be unemployed and find jobs in the informal sector and in agriculture.[36]

I have also argued that employment outcomes differed significantly in both periods. While the Soeharto regime suppressed labour rights and extended tight controls over trade unions, it also presided over rapid expansion in formal sector employment and rising living standards for households who moved into better jobs in towns and cities. In contrast, the labour record in terms of job creation has been disappointing in the post-New Order era. This contrast in outcomes is rarely commented on in the growing literature on labour in Indonesia, which focuses almost exclusively on trade unions, industrial regulations and labour rights. In sum, it has been suggested that post-Soeharto governments have traded off improved entry for outsiders into the formal labour market, for laws which protect wages and employment of existing workers or insiders, who were in a better position to exert influence on policy. But I also note that stricter laws are by no means the only factor contributing to the poor record on employment after the crisis.

From a standpoint of economic policy more generally, the analysis suggests that policies aimed at creating a more competitive economic environment is likely to be a much more difficult task for presidents and coalition governments in the post-Soeharto era. After the initial economic reforms 'forced' on Indonesia immediately after the crisis, the policies of early governments have been cautious with regard to market-oriented reform. As we have seen, they have also been strongly pro-organised labour. In light of a worsening employment situation, the Susilo Bambang Yudhoyono government initially sought to step back from several of the more extreme forms labour protection introduced during the Megawati years. But it faced opposition to revisions to the new labour law, and the president was not prepared to challenge the unions or jeopardise public opinion over the issue.

---

36 In industrial societies where most workers are wage earners, slow growth in employment mostly translates directly into higher rates of unemployment. Policies which discourage employment growth can have significant political costs.

While the government under Yudhoyono remained broadly committed to an open, competitive economy, it was cautious on policies in areas where reforms might conflict with the apparent interests of vulnerable groups. For example, during 2005 and 2006 arguments for the removal of rice import restrictions, which stood to benefit the majority of poorer rice consumers, were rejected by the government on the grounds that farmers would suffer. Reforms involving complex distributive outcomes require strong support from the president, backing in the cabinet and from at least some of the major political parties. In this chapter, I have argued that the passage of such economic reforms may continue to be problematic in the more open political environment in the post-Soeharto period.

11 Indonesia's Direct Elections: Empowering the Electorate or Entrenching the New Order Oligarchy?

MARCUS MIETZNER

Despite its sudden collapse, Soeharto's New Order regime left behind important political legacies. These legacies, formed and consolidated over decades of autocratic rule, emerged as serious challenges to Indonesia's democratic transition after 1998. Most importantly, the political inheritance of the New Order included paradigms of highly centralistic rule and notorious distrust of electoral empowerment of the masses. This chapter will study a core element of the post-Soeharto reforms designed to address these legacies: the direct elections of governors, regents and mayors that began in June 2005. These ballots, which were launched in order to further increase the competitiveness of Indonesia's political system, led to the direct election of more than 300 local government heads by early 2007.

The remarkable persistence of crucial New Order legacies became evident in the discussions on political reform shortly after the regime change. Apparently, Soeharto's predilection for centralism had not only shaped the institutional outlook of his regime, but had also infiltrated the thinking of his opponents to a much larger extent than they were prepared to admit. Megawati Soekarnoputri, for example, who was seen by many Indonesians as a symbol of opposition to the Soeharto regime and was thus set to play a prominent role in post-New Order politics, shared much of Soeharto's instinctive dislike for decentralised governance and direct electoral mechanisms.

Consequently, it was not Megawati or other figures of Soeharto's 'semi-opposition' (Aspinall 2005) who drove the first initiatives for decentralisation and electoral reform after the 1998 regime change. Instead, political liberalisation was largely the result of reforms initiated by the deposed president's deputy and successor, B.J. Habibie (see Anwar, this volume). Originating from Sulawesi and educated in Germany, Habibie swiftly disentangled himself from Soeharto's Java-centric and uniformist ideology. Habibie deregulated the political party system within a week of assuming power, and pushed an ambitious decentralisation law through the New Order appointed parliament in 1999. The extraordinary nature of this transformation was highlighted by the slowing of political reform after Habibie lost power. Following the end of his 18-month interregnum in October 1999, it took almost three years (until 2002) for political leaders to agree on the direct election of the president, and another two (until 2004) to allow voters to elect their top executives in local government by direct ballot.

The direct elections of local government heads, introduced through law No 32/2004, completed the process of electoral liberalisation begun after Soeharto's fall. Instead of the authoritarian appointment policy of the Soeharto era and the political backroom maneuvering of the early post-New Order years, it was now the electorate that determined directly who headed their regional institutions of government. Despite the rocky and long-winded negotiations that preceded it, the reform was greeted by most political commentators as a breakthrough on the way to decentralised, democratic governance in Indonesia. It was expected to end the monopolistic grip of elites on the established channels for attaining top executive positions, instead providing popular grassroots leaders, civil society figures and academics with the opportunity to directly seek a mandate from the people.

These hopes have only been partially fulfilled, however. This chapter will analyse political and socio-economic patterns that emerged from the more than 300 polls held between mid-2005 and early 2007. In its first section, the chapter will briefly describe the mechanisms that were used to elect local government officials under the New Order and in the immediate post-Soeharto period, before discussing the changes introduced by law No 32/2004. Second, it will analyse the backgrounds of candidates participating in the direct ballots, allowing for an evaluation of the extent to which elites groomed under the New Order continued to maintain their hold on power. Third, the chapter will look at several trends reflected in the outcome of the elections, pointing to increased self confidence and maturity of the electorate. Finally, it will conclude that even though politico-economic elites nurtured during Soeharto's rule have indeed extended their influence into post-authoritarian politics, the introduction of direct local elections has empowered voters to determine the outcome of inter-elite competition for political office. While not representing a complete break with the elitist power relations nurtured by the New Order, this constitutes a significant step forward in Indonesia's democratic transition.

Local elections during the New Order and the post-authoritarian transition

In its early years, the late 1960s and early 1970s, the Soeharto government used its emergency powers and sheer political weight to pressure the remaining political parties into endorsing the regime's choices for top positions of local government around the country. After the New Order's institutional framework was largely completed in the early 1970s, however, the election of local officials used law No 5/1974 as its legal foundation. Based on the law, local parliaments were entitled to draft a short-list of candidates for the positions of governor, district head (*bupati*) and mayor, which was subsequently handed over to the Ministry of Home Affairs. While the central government typically confirmed the candidate who had received the most votes in that selection process, the president reserved the authority to pick a different nominee for the position. The presidential veto right was not the only measure that restricted the nominal powers bestowed on local legislatures, however. Most significantly, the composition of parliaments was such that it was virtually impossible for a candidate not backed by the regime to get nominated, let alone elected. The government's electoral machine, Golkar, controlled comfortable majorities in almost all local legislatures, and the authorities intensively 'screened' parliamentarians from the other two parties sanctioned by the regime, the United Development Party (Partai Persatuan Pembangunan, PPP) and the Indonesian Democratic Party (Partai Demokrasi Indonesia, PDI), before they were allowed to take up their seats.

This combination of restrictive regulations and overwhelming political control ensured that in 24 years of local elections under law No 5/1974, very few surprises occurred. One of the rare exceptions was the gubernatorial election in Riau in 1985. In that year, one candidate—who had been nominated only for the usual ceremonial reason of ensuring there was more than one nominee— actually beat the favourite in the ballot, creating a nation-wide political uproar. The power apparatus of the regime was immediately set in motion to correct the 'error', however, and then Golkar Chairman Sudharmono forced the unexpected governor-elect to declare his resignation (Sudharmono 1997:353). In the few cases when such deviations from the established procedure took place, they were less an indication of the regime's weakness than of intensive competition within it. Thus Soeharto almost invariably managed to use his overwhelming authority to settle such controversies.

Elections through local legislatures, 1999–2004

Central government intervention into the elections of local executives largely ended when the Habibie administration enacted a number of political laws in 1999, including No 22 on Local Governance. The changes meant that after the parliamentary elections of June 1999, local legislatures with multi-party representation were free to elect new governors and district heads whenever their terms expired. The requirement to submit their preferred choice to Jakarta for approval was abolished.

The new institutional set-up did not result in the rapid replacement of New Order incumbents, however. Particularly at the provincial level, governors with strong ties to the fallen regime were able to defend their grip on power, even though they did not belong to any of the political parties that dominated local parliaments. In 2002 and 2003, the governors of Jakarta, Central Java, East Java, North Sumatra and East Kalimantan, who were all retired military officers, secured their re-election by their respective local legislatures (Honna 2005). Exploiting their vast financial resources and the fragmentation of the political party system, these governors managed to draw a majority of parliamentarians to their sides.

In his analysis of this phenomenon, Harold Crouch (2003) argued that obviously party politicians calculated that 'it is better to re-endorse a military officer … than to risk the election of governors from rival parties'. Even in cases where no incumbent stood for re-election, contested local executive posts mostly went to well-entrenched individuals with bureaucratic or military backgrounds, rather than to leaders of parties who participated in the 1999 elections. Apparently, the patterns of electoral behaviour in the post-authoritarian transition were not dissimilar to those of the early New Order when, according to Ulf Sundhaussen (1978:52), 'many provincial and district assemblies favoured the appointment of colonels and generals, even … when political parties still had an important say in these assemblies'. The major reason for this was 'the reluctance of party politicians to back a candidate from a rival party; they would rather vote for someone who is considered 'neutral' in party politics'.

Direct elections: the reforms of 2004

The success of New Order figures in retaining their posts, amidst allegations of vote buying and corruption, increased the pressure on the government to further deregulate the electoral system. After provisions for the direct election of the president and vice-president were adopted through constitutional amendments in 2002 and executed in 2004, the administration of Megawati Soekarnoputri enacted law No 32 on Local Governance in its final days in office. According to the new law, governors and district heads were to be elected directly by the people. The authority to nominate candidates was limited to political parties that in the 2004 polls had gained 15 per cent of the votes or parliamentary seats in the relevant electoral area. Independent candidates were not allowed to run.[1] Local Electoral Commissions (Komisi Pemilihan Umum Daerah, KPUD) were tasked with conducting the polls, marginalising the national KPU that had organised the 2004 ballots. Funding was to come mostly from local budgets, with unspecified contributions from the central government.

As the government had declared a moratorium on the election of local government heads by legislatures for 2004, pending the presidential polls and the enactment of the new law, a wave of 173 direct elections was scheduled for June 2005, with subsequent ballots occurring whenever the term of an incumbent expired. The prospect of the first direct elections of local government executives in Indonesia's history created high expectations, both in political circles and at the grassroots. The Asia Foundation's 'Indonesia Rapid Decentralization Appraisal' (2004:12) predicted that the polls would 'enhance democracy at the local level'. It stated that 'Indonesians eagerly welcome this development' and detected a strong public expectation that 'candidates who are believed to be corrupt will not get elected' (The Asia Foundation 2004:34). The following section will analyse the background of the candidates eventually nominated for the polls, indicating that despite the widespread optimism, entrenched politico-oligarchic elites proved well positioned to defend their control over local government institutions.

Entrenchment of the oligarchy: candidates, power and resources

As political parties began in early 2005 to nominate candidates for the upcoming local polls, it quickly became clear that the new electoral rules would not drastically change the composition of the political and economic elites competing for positions of power. Similar to the trend under the old electoral mechanism (Malley 2003), influential bureaucrats, rich businesspeople and retired security officers emerged as the top contenders for the nominations.

There were several reasons for this development. First, local party branches, which had the right to nominate candidates, recognised that offering nominations to individuals with the greatest monetary resources represented an opportunity for them to consolidate party finances. The three rounds of national elections in 2004 had left most local party offices cash-strapped, while there was no effective system of state-sponsored party financing in place to refill the coffers. Faced

---

1 The law reserved exclusive rights for the special autonomy areas of Aceh and Papua, however. In Papua, candidates had to be native Papuans in order to qualify as nominees, and based on the new law on the Governance of Aceh passed in July 2006, independent candidates had the right to run in the local elections of Aceh, which were held in December of that year.

with another costly election, most party leaders opted to shift the financial burden of the campaign to affluent nominees and to pocket some additional money in the process.

Second, parties often lacked credible candidates from their own ranks. There was a widespread view within the elite and the public that candidates for executive office needed to have extensive bureaucratic experience, and very few party politicians did so (Forum Rektor Indonesia, Press Release, 29 June 2005). Many party officials knew how to run a political organisation and mobilise grassroots support for it, but they typically lacked expertise in management, budgeting or government administration.

Third, the fact that most bureaucrats, entrepreneurs and retired officers who put themselves forward as candidates had close ties with the New Order regime did not reduce their popularity with the electorate. In fact, many voters even believed that such figures would be better positioned to provide stability, economic benefits and bureaucratic efficiency than inexperienced politicians, grassroots leaders or academics.[2]

The candidates: socio-economic profiles

The inclination of political parties to surrender the nominations to non-party figures was borne out in the socio-economic profiles of the candidates. The strongest group in the field of nominees was that of the career bureaucrats, who made up around 36 per cent of all candidates (Mietzner 2005).[3] The group included incumbent and former governors and vice-governors, district heads and their deputies, executive secretaries (*sekretaris daerah*) as well as heads of government offices (*kepala dinas*). These key bureaucrats controlled large financial resources, had extensive networks in business and civil society, and had the advantage of high name recognition. Significantly, they would often form joint tickets with wealthy businesspeople who had little political experience but did possess the necessary cash to provide additional campaign funds and create an effective apparatus of supporters. Twenty-eight per cent of

---

2 During the presidential elections of 2004, surveys showed that 45 per cent of the electorate thought that an active or former general was best qualified for the presidency, as opposed to 14 per cent who favoured a religious leader and 9 per cent who wanted a human rights activist as president. Only 8 per cent of respondents believed a professional politician should become president (International Foundation for Electoral Systems 2004).

3 This data is based on a sample I took of 50 local elections in the first wave of polls that took place in June and July 2005. The information on the socio-economic and professional backgrounds was drawn from newspaper articles (mostly *Kompas* and *Media Indonesia*, which ran special sections on the elections), and personal observations of ballots in Kalimantan, Sulawesi, Java and Papua. Additional samples taken from other elections after July 2005 suggest that the figures presented here reflect broad and stable patterns as far as the profiles of the candidates are concerned.

all candidates belonged to this latter category. The combination of politically entrenched bureaucrats and rich entrepreneurs was so powerful that according to one statistic, such pairs won 87 per cent of all local polls (Rinakit 2005).

The third group consisted of party politicians and members of parliament, who represented 22 per cent of the nominees. This category included businesspeople as well, however, who had taken up leadership positions in political parties and won seats in local legislatures well before the direct elections, often precisely in order to prepare their candidacy. Eight per cent of the candidates were retired or active military and police officers.[4] While they were mostly lower ranking personnel, several former top generals contested the elections as well, including in Aceh, Papua, Jakarta and North Sulawesi. Finally, the smallest group of candidates consisted of academics, grassroots activists, religious leaders and media figures, constituting only six per cent of all nominees. While some such individuals were hugely popular in their home areas, they rarely had the funds to buy nominations from political parties or pay for large electoral machines.

The dominance of entrenched socio-economic elites in the nomination process was further demonstrated by the personal affluence of the candidates. In many cases, local election commissions published the wealth reports, which nominees had handed in as part of their registration process. These reports provided interesting insights into the assets of candidates on the one hand and the varied psychology of contestants on the other. Incumbents or holders of other key government positions tended to under-report their fortunes, fearing that they would be accused of having enriched themselves while in office if they revealed extensive personal wealth. Some challengers, however, saw an advantage in having their wealth fully reported, apparently believing that voters might view genuine personal affluence as a safeguard against corruption. For example, in the 2005 election for mayor of Manado, the capital of North Sulawesi, three candidates reported assets in excess of one million dollars, with two others well above the half-million-dollar mark (*Harian Komentar*, 16 June 2005).

By contrast, the governor of the province A. J. Sondakh, who stood for re-election at the same time, declared a personal wealth of only 3.4 billion rupiah (around 350,000 USD). His announcement led to widespread cynicism and ridicule, given that Sondakh was at the centre of an alleged corruption scandal in which 18.3 billion rupiah of government funds had simply disappeared (*Media Indonesia*, 13 December 2004). The local newspaper *Manado Post* found it 'amusing' that Sondakh had admitted to the ownership of just one used car worth a meager 60 million rupiah (around 6,300 USD) (*Manado Pos*, 3 June

---

4   In November 2006, the military leadership announced that officers had to retire from active service before participating in elections. Previously, they only had to seek permission from Armed Forces headquarters and stand down from their institutional positions for the time of the campaign.

2005). Fortunately for Sondakh, many of his opponents had their own issues with under-reporting. Wenny Warouw, an active police brigadier-general and candidate of the Christian party, the Party of Peace and Prosperity (Partai Damai Sejahtera, PDS), initially refused to report his wealth, which was estimated at around 50 billion rupiah (around 5.3 million USD). His assets were believed to include plantations in Minahasa, property and shares in Batam, an apartment in Perth, houses in Jakarta and Manado, and dozens of cars (*Manado Pos*, 30 May 2005). Warouw only published his wealth report several days before the polls, admitting ownership of assets worth 10 billion rupiah. Once again, the public groaned in disbelief (interviews in Manado, June 2005).

Fund-raising and lobbyism

Despite their sometimes massive personal assets, candidates were often in need of more funds. Observers have estimated that the cost of campaigning for the governorship could reach 100 billion rupiah, while nominees for the post of district head needed to prepare between 1.8 to 16 billion rupiah (Rinakit 2005:2). The money was needed to pay off the functionaries of nominating parties, establish a network of campaign offices, hire thousands of helpers, finance advertising campaigns in the media, employ public relations consultants and opinion pollsters, train and provide wages for monitors at the polling stations, as well as pay for entertainers at public events. The winner of the elections in the Sula archipelago, a district in North Maluku which has only 108,000 inhabitants, admitted that he spent 5 billion rupiah on the campaign, with only very little contributed by his nominating party, Golkar (interview with Ahmad Hidayat, November 2006). These costs were, in fact, significantly higher than under the previous electoral system, when interested candidates 'only' needed to pay a bare majority of legislators to get elected.

In order to raise additional funds, candidates running in the direct elections often entered into coalitions with business tycoons who did not want to stand in the elections themselves. In the 2005 gubernatorial elections in South Kalimantan, for example, most candidates received massive campaign contributions from influential coal mining magnates, who were eager to place sympathetic politicians in the governorship. Once in office, their protégés would then be expected to help with processing licenses and shielding their companies from investigations into the environmental damages caused by the large-scale mining operations in the province. One candidate, M. Ramlan, was even a coal-mining entrepreneur himself. He had to pay more than a dozen political parties to get nominated, and convinced a former provincial secretary to run as his deputy in order to compensate for his own lack of bureaucratic experience. Ramlan's main business rival, H. Abidin, spared himself such stress. Instead, he reportedly bankrolled the campaign of Rudi Ariffin, the long-time *bupati* of Banjar, who was the eventual winner of the elections and became new governor of South Kalimantan (interviews in Banjarmasin, May 2005).

Party-candidate relations: the insignificance of ideology

Getting hold of sufficient financial resources was such a high priority both for the candidates and the parties that nominated them that the political or ideological orientation of the nominee usually became a matter of secondary concern. Party leaders often declared that the nomination process was 'open for everyone', proudly describing it as an act of grassroots democracy. Senior party officials typically interviewed a wide variety of applicants for nomination, with candidates reporting that most questions focused on how much money they would be able to spend on the campaign and how much they were willing to 'donate' to the party.

The candidates, on the other hand, often applied with several parties before settling on the one that offered the lowest nomination costs and the most effective campaign network. Businessman Erlangga Satriagung, for example, who was interested to run in the 2005 mayoral elections in Surabaya, initially had approached the Party of National Awakening (Partai Kebangkitan Bangsa, PKB) (interviews in Surabaya, May 2005). The party was closely associated with the largest Muslim organisation in the country, Nahdlatul Ulama, and a key political force in the city. After learning the sum it would cost him to secure PKB's nomination, however, Erlangga entered into negotiations with the National Mandate Party (Partai Amanat Nasional, PAN). PAN, the political wing of the modernist Muslim group Muhammadiyah and often at loggerheads with the traditionalist PKB, was a much smaller party in Surabaya and thus a more affordable option for Erlangga. The local PAN elite eventually nominated Erlangga, drawing protests from party officials at the grassroots who claimed that he had paid bribes to their leaders. In the elections, Erlangga was soundly beaten by incumbent Bambang D.H., who had for long contemplated whether he should form a coalition with the puritan Muslim party, the Prosperous Justice Party (Partai Keadilan Sejahtera, PKS) or the Christian PDS, but finally had invited the editor-in-chief of East Java's largest newspaper to become his running mate (*Jakarta Post*, 27 June 2005). Ideological considerations, it turned out, took a backseat to tactical calculations, especially those concerned with gaining access to critical campaign resources and infrastructure.

The financial stakes involved in the nomination of candidates also explained the ferocity of intra-party conflicts in the pre-election period. In many cases, parties that had the right to name candidates fractured into several groups, with each of them promising the nomination to a different candidate. Often these antagonisms occurred between the central leadership of a party and its local branch, but they sometimes also ran through the local chapters themselves. The electoral law had granted the authority to nominate candidates to local party branches, but central leadership boards had the option of dismissing their functionaries in the regions if they did not support the nominee endorsed by the centre. Central party boards exercised this option in a couple of high-profile cases, with questionable success. President Susilo Bambang Yudhoyono's Democratic Party (Partai Demokrat, PD), for example, objected to the gubernatorial nominee appointed by its North Sulawesi branch, but after a series of crisis meetings in Manado during which local party members threw chairs at PD politicians from Jakarta, the provincial branch prevailed with the nomination of its candidate (*Kompas*, 24 March 2005). In Banten, Marissa Haque, a prominent PDI-P politician who sought the nomination of her party for Banten's gubernatorial race in 2006, felt so intimidated by her internal party rivals that she called them a bunch of 'criminals, drunks and gamblers' (*Koran Tempo*, March 2006). Eventually she left PDI-P, ran for another party and lost the election. Frequently it was the local KPUD that had the difficult task of deciding the outcome of such intra-party disputes, but in some cases, the matter even went before the courts. Once such disputes were resolved, the losing factions often had a difficult time fending off demands for financial compensation from those candidates who had paid them considerable amounts of money to get nominated. A small number of failed nominees even filed police reports to reclaim their investment (*Kedaulatan Rakyat*, 23 May 2005).

Commercialisation and de-ideologisation

It was this commercialisation of the nomination process and the insignificance of ideological affiliations within it that provided a space for former New Order elements to use the new democratic framework to their advantage. They had the resources and the bureaucratic experience necessary to stand in the polls, leaving newcomers to the political game with little chance to compete. Benefiting from the structural deficiencies of political parties and their indifference towards ideology, members of the entrenched elite could choose between several electoral vehicles before closing a deal with one of them.

In fact, the new institutional set-up allowed more former New Order bureaucrats to compete for top executive positions than under Soeharto's rule. Back then, Golkar was the only political platform for bureaucrats to aspire for higher office. Under the 2004 electoral laws, however, Golkar-affiliated bureaucrat-politicians who had not succeeded in gaining the nomination of their own party were free to apply with Golkar's competitors. Consequently, most candidates in the local polls had previous or existing connections with Golkar. In Papua, for instance, PDI-P's candidate for the 2006 gubernatorial elections was appointed to Golkar's national advisory board in the middle of the campaign. In North Sulawesi, all five candidates for the governorship had been affiliated with Golkar before the polls but had sought alternative options after Sondakh had secured his re-nomination by the party. During the campaign, the party split into several factions, with large sections supporting candidates other than Sondakh. Such cases highlighted the fact that the introduction of direct local elections has not significantly altered the composition of Indonesia's politico-oligarchic elite. Instead, it has increased the competition between its various elements, and has handed voters the authority to determine the outcome of such intra-elite competition.

Empowering the electorate: the declining importance of incumbency and primordialism

Despite the dominance of entrenched elites in the nomination process, the direct elections introduced important changes to the way political power is obtained in post-Soeharto Indonesia. These changes were visible in a number of trends that emerged from the results of many of the polls. In some cases, these trends confounded predictions made by observers before the elections, especially those regarding the role that incumbency and primordial sentiments would play in determining electoral outcomes.

To begin with, widespread fears that incumbents would easily ride to victory proved unfounded, with around 40 per cent of office holders losing their jobs.[5] Incumbents' control of huge campaign funds, government resources and bureaucratic networks certainly was an advantage. More often than not, however, their competitors matched such advantages. Because in most local elections more than one senior bureaucrat competed, with each having access to a particular segment of the government apparatus, it was generally not possible for a single actor to manipulate the electoral administration. Keeping each other in check, the candidates would report attempted manipulations by their competitors to the press and election monitors.

While electoral manipulation and logistical mismanagement undoubtedly took place (ranging from poor voter registration mechanisms to errors in vote-counting procedures), in most elections such problems did not appear to significantly influence the outcome. This was not only because incumbents had relatively limited opportunities to control the process, but also because electorates often

---

5   A list of 103 polls at the district level showed 65 incumbents winning and 38 losing the elections. At the provincial level, the trend was similar. Out of nine governors standing for re-election in 2005 and 2006, four lost. *Media Indonesia*, 19 July 2005.

issued such powerful and unambiguous verdicts that occasional manipulations only had a marginal effect on the end result. Paying close attention to the trackrecords of nominees, voters did not hesitate to throw out poor performers, often with overwhelming clarity. Many incumbents whose reputation had been damaged by allegations of corruption and nepotism were removed from office, including governors Sondakh in North Sulawesi, Sjachriel Darham in South Kalimantan, Asmawi Agani in Central Kalimantan and Aminuddin Polulele in Central Sulawesi. In some cases, continued public pressure after the electoral loss of incumbents even led to legal investigations into irregularities that occurred during their time in office. Sjachriel, for example, was charged with corruption and eventually arrested in January 2007.

Winners and losers

The removal of unpopular incumbents was in many places accompanied by the election of candidates with more attractive performance records. This trend demonstrated that despite the fact that nominees often had almost identical politico-economic backgrounds, the voters were still able to detect significant differences between them and make an informed choice. Accordingly, unlike their non-performing colleagues, successful incumbents were often returned to power, in some cases even with large margins. For example, the governor of Jambi, Zulkifli Nurdin, who had impressed voters with his unconventional style of governance, was re-elected in 2005 with around 80 per cent of the votes. Rustriningsih, one of the few female *bupati*s in Indonesia and exceptionally popular with the grassroots, achieved a similar result in the regency of Kebumen in Central Java. In West Sumatra, Gamawan Fauzi, the former *bupati* of Solok and recipient of a prestigious anti-corruption award, won the governorship against a highly competitive field of candidates. Similarly, Sinyo H. Sarundajang, a former acting governor of Maluku and North Maluku who had played an important role in restoring stability in these conflict-ridden provinces, won the gubernatorial race in his home region of North Sulawesi. In the elections, Sarundajang beat the incumbent, A. J. Sondakh, as well as a retired military officer, an active police general, and a member of the powerful Baramuli family—all of whom had financial resources and political networks that equaled or exceeded those of Sarundajang.

Not all of the winners were shining examples of clean and accountable government, of course. Many of the incumbents who secured re-election had simply made sure that the populace was sufficiently satisfied with the services provided by their governments, such as affordable health care, low school fees or food subsidies. Particularly in territories with high revenues from resource industries, this was not too difficult to achieve. In general, if incumbents could deliver basic services, the electorate appeared willing to tolerate a certain extent of self enrichment by them. In Kutai Kartanegara in East Kalimantan, for example, the incumbent *bupati* Syaukani H. R. won the 2005 district elections despite his well-known predilection for luxury treats, which included keeping Australian racehorses in air-conditioned stables (*Jakarta Post*, 4 June 2005). In spite of his extravagant lifestyle, however, Syaukani had not only used the district's oil and gas revenues for himself; he had also ensured that enough spoils trickled down to the voters for him to maintain an advantage over his electoral competitors (*Jakarta Post*, 2 June 2005).[6] In the same vein, some challengers gained office not necessarily because of their own clean trackrecord, but because of the unpopularity of the incumbent. Again others succeeded because they were connected to high-ranking officials in their respective province or even in Jakarta, convincing the electorate that they would be able to secure more budget allocations for their home areas.[7] However mundane their motivations may have been, voters mostly demonstrated that they possessed a clear understanding of their own interests. In some cases these interests included clean and transparent government, in others effective deliverance of services was apparently sufficient.

The defeat of primordial exclusivism

The increased maturity of the electorate was not only reflected in its determination to replace unpopular incumbents, but also in its inclination to reject candidates who campaigned on exclusivist platforms. Prior to the polls, many observers had been concerned that nominees might aim to attract voters by appealing to their partisan instincts, such as identification with a certain religion, ethnic group or family clan. Particularly in areas with heterogeneous populations, it was feared that some candidates could be tempted to mobilise their various core constituencies by fueling prejudices and sentiments against rival social groups.

In most cases, such primordialist out-bidding did not occur. Instead, candidates in heterogeneous regions tended to form cross-cultural tickets, addressing the moderate attitude of the electorate and hoping to gain additional votes from alternative constituencies. All nominees for the post of *bupati* in the multi-religious and conflict-ridden district of Poso in Central Sulawesi, for example, linked up with running mates from a different faith. In 1999, the *bupati* elections in Poso had triggered bloody clashes between Muslims and Christians, who both claimed the leadership of the district for their group. In the 2005 elections, by contrast, the nomination of pairs from both faiths ensured that allegations of religious favouritism were effectively neutralised as an electoral issue (*Media Indonesia*, 8 May 2005). Similarly, nationwide statistics showed that coalitions

---

6   His convincing electoral victory did not prevent the authorities from pursuing legal investigations into his almost monarchical style of governance, however. In early 2007, he was under such pressure by investigators that he chose to seek long-term medical treatment in order to escape arrest.

7   One such was case was the victory of Ichsan Yasin Limpo in the district elections of Gowa in South Sulawesi. He was the brother of South Sulawesi's vice-governor Syahril Yasin Limpo.

between Islamic parties were much less frequent than alliances between Islamic and secular-nationalist parties, with the latter accounting for 37 per cent of all nominations (Ramage 2007).

The pluralist composition of electoral teams in areas with complex demographic structures even managed to lift some representatives of minority groups into top executive positions. In Belitung Timur, for example, a Chinese Christian was elected as *bupati* in 2005 in a district in which the Islamist party Bulan Bintang was the strongest political force. In the same year, the Christian politician Teras Narang won the governorship in Central Kalimantan, a predominantly Muslim province. While there were initially concerns that newly elected local government heads from ethnic or religious minorities would find it difficult to maintain power without risking major social tensions, after two years in office these fears have largely proven unfounded.

In the few cases in which nominees did try to campaign with exclusivist programs, the electorate tended to reject them. The candidacy of Professor Usop in Central Kalimantan in 2005 provided important insights in this regard. Usop, a self-proclaimed leader of the Dayak, Central Kalimantan's largest ethnic group, had participated in gubernatorial elections before (International Crisis Group 2001). In 2000, when the governor was still elected by the local legislature, he had lost to Asmawi Agani by only a very small margin. One year after his narrow defeat, Usop had been arrested for his infamous role in instigating the large-scale massacre and eviction of Madurese migrants, but he had to be released when his supporters threatened to storm the prison in which he was held. In the 2005 campaign, Usop emphatically argued against the return of the expelled Madurese, apparently believing that this populist message would carry him to victory. Instead, he finished last with only four per cent of the votes. Many Central Kalimantans obviously held him responsible for the negative image that their province had obtained as a result of the 2001 violence, and were not keen to risk further tensions by handing Usop the governorship (interviews in Palangkaraya, May 2005).

In the same vein, voters in North Sulawesi rejected attempts by the struggling incumbent A. J. Sondakh to exploit his leadership position in the province's largest church for campaign purposes. Cornered by corruption allegations, Sondakh declared that every governor of North Sulawesi had to be a leading member of the Minahasa church (Gereja Masehi Injili di Minahasa, GMIM), in which he was a senior official. Sondakh pointed out that S. H. Sarundajang, his major rival, was not active in GMIM, implying that he thus did not qualify for the governorship. Ultimately, Sarundajang won the elections in a landslide, demonstrating not only Sondakh's unpopularity, but also the indifference of voters towards the congregational affiliations of nominees.

Post-election protests: sour losers and unimpressed courts

The moderation of the electorate was also the main reason for the absence of communal violence during the course of the elections. In none of the areas in which local elections were held did religious, ethnic or social groups clash as a result of the polls. Even in areas with long histories of communal tensions, like Kotawaringin Timur in Central Kalimantan, Ambon in Maluku or several districts in Central Sulawesi, the elections passed without significant disturbances to the relationship between the various key constituencies. The occasional eruptions of violence, which drew much media attention and gave the polls a rather chaotic public image, were largely contrived and lacked deep social roots. In most cases, crowds bankrolled by losing candidates besieged the offices of electoral bodies, smashing furniture and demanding that the poll results be annulled. In its most extreme forms, these protests led to the burning of government offices or the blocking of major roads with felled trees. These violent actions invariably died down, however, after it became clear that the vast majority of voters accepted the outcome of the polls and thus saw no reasons to join the protest.

In addition, the central government and the courts issued firm reminders that organised protests could not pressure them into overturning the results announced by the respective KPUDs.[8] The Ministry of Home Affairs, for its part, declared that it had no authority to annul or alter election results, and judges were generally little impressed by the arguments brought forward by losing nominees, and tended to throw out their lawsuits. Even in the districts that witnessed the most extensive outbreaks of election-related protests, such as Kaur in Bengkulu and Tana Toradja in South Sulawesi, the results of the polls were reconfirmed and the organisers of the demonstrations eventually withdrew their troops.

Finally, voters also did not confirm widespread predictions that active and retired military officers would do exceptionally well in the polls, paving the way for the remilitarisation of Indonesian politics. In the run-up to the 2005 ballots, TNI Commander General Endriartono Sutarto had allowed six active officers to stand as candidates in the elections, leading to a heated debate among

---

8   Only in one prominent case, the mayoral elections of Depok in West Java in 2005, did judges overturn an election result, using blatantly flawed arguments. The Supreme Court, however, annulled that verdict in 2006 and removed the judges who had issued it. In another, less high-profile case, the High Court of Papua overturned the result of the 2005 district elections of Mappi, and the Supreme Court confirmed that decision. Apparently, the KPUD of Mappi had excluded the results of two villages from its count after protests from locals that the winner of the elections was an 'outsider'. The annulment of the results from the two villages moved the candidate favoured by the protesters ahead by a few votes, and thus avoided more violent demonstrations. The courts accepted, however, that the annulment of the disputed votes was politically motivated, and reinstated the initial winner. Interview with Johannes Bonay, member of the KPUD Papua, Jayapura, July 2005.

politicians and observers if this constituted a signal for the military's return to the political arena (*Kompas,* 12 May 2005). In the end, none of the six candidates was elected to office. While a small number of former military leaders won their elections, including the races for governor in Central Sulawesi and West Irian Jaya in 2006, many more of their comrades were unsuccessful. Candidates with a military background suffered crushing defeats in the gubernatorial elections in Aceh, Papua and North and West Sulawesi, with some of them finishing last. Apparently, the former commanders found it difficult to grasp the very diverse dynamics of electoral politics at the local level, where cashed-up bureaucrats or charismatic society leaders often had easier access to the electorate than retired military officers offering old-fashioned security concepts.

The mixed performance of military officers in the polls has raised doubts over whether members of the Armed Forces will be able to defend their grip on some of their provincial strongholds after the terms of the current governors expire. By early 2007, retired officers elected through the old electoral mechanism still held the governorships of Jakarta, Central and East Java, South Sulawesi and East Kalimantan (the governor of North Sumatra, also a former general, died in a plane crash in September 2005 and was replaced by a civilian). All these areas will hold direct elections in 2007 and 2008, and if the outcomes of the polls conducted so far are anything to go by, the military will lose further ground as far as its hold on key positions in local government is concerned.

Conclusion: new rules for the old elite

The analysis of Indonesia's first direct local elections has produced two equally strong, but divergent set of conclusions. First, the new electoral mechanism has brought few changes to the composition of Indonesia's ruling elite. Participation in the polls required major financial resources and extensive connections within the entrenched political class. This, in turn, provided bureaucrats groomed under the New Order and affluent entrepreneurs with an unassailable advantage over potential newcomers. The nomination process exposed the structural weakness of the existing political parties, with independent and wealthy figures purchasing their candidacies from cash-strapped party boards. Thus one of the crucial preconditions for establishing a functioning democracy was not fulfilled, namely 'that a range of political parties not only *represent* interests but seek by coherent programs and organisational activity to *aggregate* interests' (Linz and Stepan 1996:274). In Indonesia's local elections, parties often nominated candidates without any previous relationship to them or their politico-ideological agendas, so long as the nominees could raise the necessary cash to fund their own campaigns and, most importantly, satisfy the financial needs of party officials. As a result, voters could find almost no link between the politico-ideological viewpoints that parties were supposed to aggregate, and the candidates who were nominated by them.

These deficiencies in the party system further consolidated the towering dominance of entrenched elites, producing a very narrow field of candidates running for office. With lower-class candidates and even elite outsiders largely excluded from the electoral competition, Indonesia's direct local polls lacked what Larry Diamond and Leonardo Morlino (2004:24–25) called one of the 'substantive dimensions' of democracy: political equality. Diamond and Morlino argue that 'to enjoy political equality, citizens must … have some measure of equality in income, wealth, and status.' In Indonesia, however, the local elections revealed a yawning gap between those few who could afford to be politically active and the overwhelming majority who could not. This and other shortcomings inspired some of the more negative accounts of Indonesia's direct local elections (Rinakit 2005; Choi 2005), most of which argued that the polls were rather shallow procedures without much democratic substance.

The second conclusion, however, suggests that from the limited pool of nominees, voters generally picked candidates with better trackrecords and higher credibility as far as their promises to further voters' interests were concerned. Incumbents struggling with allegations of corruption were typically thrown out if they could not compensate for their greed by delivering satisfactory public services to the electorate. The incumbent turnover rate of 40 per cent, which is high even if compared to consolidated democracies, indicates that voters took some pleasure in punishing executive leaders they deemed unfit for office. In the same vein, candidates who were unable to explain convincingly their personal wealth or professional qualifications saw their chances of winning the ballot drastically reduced.

Furthermore, voters showed considerable maturity by rejecting platforms based on exclusivist primordial sentiments. More often than not, they opted for combinations of nominees who had varied religious and ethnic backgrounds, and generally accepted the defeat of the candidate they had supported in the ballot. The new self confidence of the voters was also reflected in electoral participation rates that, at a national average of 69 per cent, corresponded to healthy European standards. This was despite the often chaotic organisation of the polls by local authorities, who had difficulties in registering voters on time and explain the electoral rules to the public.

In summary, the local elections have empowered Indonesian voters to have a significant say in the outcome of inter-elite competition for political and economic power. While the composition of that elite remains largely unchanged, new governors or district heads swept into office by the elections are likely to pay more attention to the interests of the electorate than their predecessors did. The fate of many unpopular incumbents during the recent polls should be incentive enough.

Figure 11.1: Politico-Economic Backgrounds of Candidates (data from 20 selected polls)

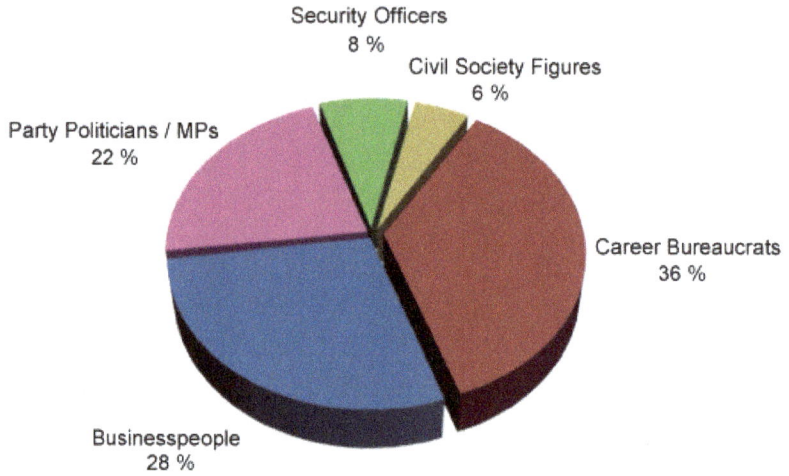

Security Officers
8 %

Civil Society Figures
6 %

Party Politicians / MPs
22 %

Career Bureaucrats
36 %

Businesspeople
28 %

12 Exemplar or Anomaly? Exiting the New Order in Comparative Perspective

WILLIAM CASE

In monitoring democracy's progress, Southeast Asia was famously evaluated during the mid-1990s as the world's most 'recalcitrant' region (Emmerson 1995). Thus, in contrast to many other parts of the world, a great variety of authoritarian and even post-totalitarian regimes endured, attributable to 'viceregal' colonial legacies, compliant cultural outlooks, divided social structures, invasive, if flabby state apparatuses, the functional requisites of late industrialisation, and, where industrialisation had taken place, the preoccupation of new middle classes with careerist and consumer pursuits. Indonesia's authoritarian politics under the New Order, a protean combination of personal, military, and single-party rule, gained particular resilience.

But even if delayed by various forces, democracy finally arrived in Southeast Asia. In Indonesia, however deadening the New Order's legacies, democratic change commenced with student demonstrations, urban upheavals, and the resignation of President Soeharto in 1998. In the Philippines, where President Ferdinand Marcos had punctured the country's democratic record by declaring martial law, politics were re-democratised during the 1980s through 'people power'. Similarly, in Thailand, after the military overturned democracy in the 1970s, then again in the early 1990s, democracy was restored through a street level confrontation in 1992 known as 'Black May'—even if collapsing yet again in 2006, as is discussed more fully below.

Further afield, in Cambodia and East Timor, democratic assistance provided by the United Nations led to elections that could be gauged as at least partially competitive. And even where hard authoritarian regimes have survived, pressures for democracy have appeared. In Myanmar, the military government reacted to a popular upsurge in 1988 by agreeing to hold an election two years later, a contest that it was forced to repudiate after being stunned by the results. In Malaysia a *reformasi* movement gained pace, so invigorating the opposition during the 1990s that it was able to make startling electoral gains at the end of the decade. In Singapore, some journalists have claimed that the government's 'OB' (out-of-bounds) markers have been slightly relaxed, enabling them to probe more deeply into sensitive issues, within a wider context of loosening social controls. And in the absolute sultanate of Brunei Darussalam, several opposition parties have been permitted to register and mobilise constituencies.

Analysts have sometimes understood these democratic pressures as an atavistic manifestation of the colonial 'tutelage' and democratic experience that marked the early independence periods of some Southeast Asian countries, including Indonesia, the Philippines, Malaysia, and Singapore. These pressures may have sprung too from the ambiguous impact of social pluralism that hallmarks the region. On the one hand, segmented societies have seemed ripe for state controls based on divide-and-rule strategies. But they also frustrate any deep imposition of state dominance, preventing in Indonesia, perhaps, the fulfilment of what Richard Tanter once described as the New Order's 'totalitarian ambition' (Tanter 1990). Myanmar's government too has discovered the inefficacy of coercion and the need for bargaining in outlying areas populated by hardy minorities. It has also adopted a new Constitution and pledged fresh elections in 2010, however manipulated they may be. And in Thailand, during the years after the 2006 coup, social protests have mounted by furious red-shirted opponents of the military-backed government.

Moreover, severe economic crises, such as those that afflicted Indonesia, Thailand, and Malaysia during the late 1990s, and prolonged economic stagnancy, like that bedevilling the Philippines since the 1960s, have aroused middle classes from their careerist reverie and galvanised civil society organisations. External factors have grown stronger too, with Southeast Asia's having penetrated export markets in the West incurring U.S. and European demands for political and economic liberalisation, greater respect for human rights, and improvements in governance. Thus, long after democracy's third wave crested in the rest of the world, it appeared finally to have reached Southeast Asia.

However, despite democracy's progress, this chapter argues that Southeast Asia remains strongly resistant, a thesis for which Indonesia offers a good test. After three decades of authoritarian rule, Indonesia is now credited with the most robust political rights and electoral competitiveness in the region. But as we shall see, such beneficent outcomes must mainly be attributed to the weakness of social forces and the resilience of elites, greatly compromising the quality of the democracy that has resulted. In brief, while social forces may have driven democratic change in Indonesia, they soon afterward reverted to quiescence, therein succumbing to New Order legacies. In this situation, many elites have reconstituted their statuses and relations, enabling them to capture most of democracy's benefits. Elites have found that democracy helps to cement their dominance, further placating social forces, while warding off criticisms from the West. In simple terms, then, democracy persists in Indonesia because it sooner sustains, than challenges the standings of elites.

Elsewhere in Southeast Asia, resistance to democracy is more easily shown. To begin, where social forces have displayed greater capacity than in Indonesia, the democracy that they have brought about has only been calibrated more tightly by elites. Thus, in the Philippines, political rights have been systematically, if informally undermined, while electoral competitiveness has been dampened by cheating and violence. In Thailand, as mentioned above, democracy was nearly snuffed out altogether, with the military resorting to authoritarian reversal in late 2006, a rare event in the third wave. In Myanmar too, the military has so restricted the terms of the election that it proposes to hold that the only well-established opposition leader, Aung Sang Suu Kyi, has been barred from contesting. Further, in Singapore, Cambodia, Vietnam, and Laos, elites have faced social forces which, for a variety of reasons, have possessed less capacity still. There has been little need, then, for elites to countenance democratic change, enabling a long record of 'electoral authoritarianism' (Schedler 2006) to persist in the first two cases and forms of post-totalitarianism to emerge in the latter two. And even in Malaysia, where opposition parties made dramatic gains in an election held in March 2008, the government has since used the country's judiciary, anti-corruption agency, and police in such partisan ways that it has effectively blocked any transition.

In trying to explain this resistance to democracy in Southeast Asia, this chapter traces the patterns by which activists, possessing organised social bases, have confronted governments. It thus enumerates the variable capacities of social activists and governing elites, the modes by which transitions to democracy may take place, and the limited quality of democracy that results. In this analysis, Indonesia's experience is especially illuminating, showcasing the gains that can be made in the wake of authoritarian rule, but also the constraints that legacies of authoritarianism can steadfastly impose. Hence, its is argued here too that while favourable estimates might be made of Indonesia's democratic regime today, they are in important respects misleading. Indeed, other country cases in Southeast Asia, though earning lesser rankings, appear to possess more energised activist and social forces.

When do democratic transitions take place?

The early literature on transitions to democracy asserted the centrality of elites, with O'Donnell and Schmitter declaring that all transitions begin amid elite-level tensions and the fracturing of authoritarian coalitions. Only after fissures had widened between polarised elite factions could any 'resurgence' of civil society take place (O'Donnell and Schmitter 1986). However, this logic was entrenched in the democratising experiences of Southern Europe and Latin America, regions in which military governments abetted by technocrats had taken root because of corporatist traditions and the functional imperatives of late industrialisation. In these conditions, Barbara Geddes observed that top military officers, fearful of the corrosive effects that ruling directly might have on their corporate discipline and élan, sought typically over time to cede power, enabling soft-liners among them to gain the upper hand (Geddes 1999). And unless the military had been discredited by wartime defeat, these soft-liners were able then to negotiate change in ways that modulated the transition and perpetuated their stakes in the regime that emerged afterward, hence insulating some of their prerogatives in 'reserve' domains of power. In this way, transitions in Southern Europe and South America often amounted to elite-led processes of what Samuel Huntington labelled transformation (Huntington 1991:124–42).

But as democratic transitions spread to Eastern Europe, Africa, and Asia, they affected authoritarian regimes that were operated not only by military governments, but also by single dominant parties and personal dictators. Analysts then observed correlations between different kinds authoritarianism, the kinds of transitions that took place, and the extent of democratic change that occurred (Huntington 1991:110–21; Linz and Stepan 1996:55–65). Thus, while military governments might gradually yield state power through transformations, single dominant parties tended to engage opposition elements in more even-handed bargaining. And even after any transition, these parties remained able to contest elections within newly competitive multi-party systems. Personal dictators, by contrast, had necessarily to be up-ended through rapid processes of bottom-up replacement. Having so personalised their regimes, they could find no secure domains into which to retire after a democratic transition, nor could they build independent parties through which to re-contest state power. This left them with few chips, then, with which to negotiate the transition's dynamics (Thompson 1995:ix–x).

What stands out in Southeast Asia's record, however, is that irrespective of the kind of authoritarian politics in place—whether operated by the military, a single dominant party, or a personal dictator—incumbent governments have clung tightly to power until finally forced out. In a region characterised by lesser levels of formal institutionalisation, perhaps, than some other parts of the developing world, generals and ruling politicians, just as surely as dictators and first families, have personalised their positions and powers. Indeed, in a seminal analysis of 'neo-patrimonialism', Harold Crouch elaborated the ways in which these sub-types of authoritarianism were fused in New Order Indonesia, with sundry institutions and procedures deployed arbitrarily, yet skilfully, by Soeharto.

Thus, at various intervals in the New Order's record, different elements might gain prominence, including 'financial generals', 'bureaucratic families', Golkar professionals, Soeharto's own progeny, and rent-seeking *cukong*. But though statuses and relations might have been reconfigured as the New Order evolved, these elites never showed any willingness to transform their regime in democratic ways. Similar resistance was evident in the Philippines, Thailand, Malaysia, and Myanmar, whatever the combination of generals, dominant parties, and dictators that prevailed. Thus, more than in other parts of the developing world, where transitions to democracy have occurred in Southeast Asia, they have required bottom-up replacements, instigated by vitalised segments of the middle class and urban poor.

Southeast Asia's record is also distinctive in another way. With activists based in civil society organisations or movements galvanising socio-economic classes or ethnic communities, then driving transition-by-replacement, it might reasonably be anticipated that the changes they have promoted would be far-reaching. The new democracies that result would thus be imbued with high quality, measurable first in terms of a procedural dimension of robust political rights and electoral competitiveness, and secondly on a substantive dimension of policy responsiveness, made manifest in trans-class redistributions. In this trajectory, with national leaders swept away and elites left scurrying for cover, there would seem to be little need for activists to bargain over democracy's terms or to guarantee soft landings for those they displace.

However, democracy's record in Southeast Asia defies this logic. After transition-by-replacement occurs, social activists either lose steam spontaneously or they are effectively contained by elites. Accordingly, we will see that in Indonesia, where the capacity of activists and the student groups and labour unions that they lead having weakened, hence supporting few demands for trans-class redistributions, resilient elites have abided political rights and electoral competitiveness. But even where activists have shown greater capacity, as in the Philippines and Thailand, elites have reacted by truncating procedural quality. Hence, elites have in most of our Southeast Asian cases negated democracy's substantive quality. And apart from Indonesia, they have eroded procedural quality too. In explaining these patterns, let us turn now to the ways in which the separate capacities of activists and governments might be evaluated.

Assessing social forces

With transitions in Southeast Asia amounting to bottom-up replacements, questions over their timing, dynamics, and progress must begin with the variable capacities of activists and the organisations or movements through which they galvanise classes or communities. To understand these capacities, they may be disaggregated in terms of participatory outlooks, solidary relations, and credibility as alternatives. The extent to which they score highly on these measures bears implications, though not always straightforward, for democratic change and quality.

To begin, social forces may or may not possess the dispositions with which to challenge incumbent governments and authoritarian regimes, attitudes that at the polar ends of a continuum can respectively be cast as participatory or quiescent (Case 2002:24–25). During the last decade of the New Order, the outlooks of social activists in Indonesia grew more participatory, especially among students and the urban poor. And for even longer periods of time they can be understood as participatory in the Philippines and Thailand. Accordingly, in these country cases, social forces were predisposed to support transition-by-replacement. By contrast, in Singapore, social forces have remained quiescent, hence limiting their role in politics to mild consultations over problem solving. Much of this activity has been conducted through officially sanctioned 'feedback units' and 'non-constituency MPs', chosen by the government from among housebroken opposition parties.

Next, even where characterised by participatory outlooks, social activists may be hindered by the class and communal affiliations with which Southeast Asia bristles, producing broad patterns that can respectively be understood as solidary or dispersed. Thus, where activists lack solidarity, transitions to democracy are at first delayed, then fail to yield quality. In Indonesia, for example, ethnic, religious, and regional rivalries have long divided social forces. This helped to inhibit democratic change until activists, backed by groups of students and urban poor, were finally animated by economic crisis in 1998, hence producing one of the last major transitions of the third wave. What is more, as this change unfolded, ethnic tensions grew so inflamed that while the violence that resulted may have helped in ousting Soeharto, activists were prevented from gaining the solidarity afterward with which to raise democracy's quality. In neighbouring Malaysia, though activists, middle classes, and Islamic groups were similarly enlivened by economic crisis, their reformist activities failed to drive democratic change. And even though opposition parties made unprecedented electoral headway a decade later, social forces have remained so fragmented by ethnic and religious suspicions that the government has been able to contain them. By contrast, in the Philippines and Thailand, where societies have mostly been lauded during the post-War period for their benign communal relations, transitions to democracy took place much earlier than in Indonesia. Moreover, in perpetuating their solidarity, activists generated greater pressures to raise democracy's quality, enabling them at least initially to win land reform and development schemes for their constituencies.

Finally, even where social activists are participatory and solidary, questions may arise over the capacity of the opposition leaders and parties that they support to graduate from merely challenging an incumbent government to offering realistic alternatives (Aspinall 2005:239–68). On this measure, capacity ranges from 'credible' to 'non-viable'. In Indonesia, though Amien Rais galvanised students in opposition to Soeharto, then later formed a party with which to contest elections, he was never regarded by the country's middle class as a capable successor. And if other parties were evaluated as more worthy, we shall see that they sooner sought their own co-optation than any serious advances in the quality of democracy by which to benefit their constituencies. By contrast, after Marcos was ousted in the Philippines, Corazon Aquino won over the middle classes and the poor through her imagery of reformism and personal sacrifice, yet also reassured the business community through her landowner status. In Thailand, Thaksin gained credibility among the rural poor and business community alike, combining populist appeals with vast family wealth and shrewd market techniques. Thus, in the Philippines and Thailand, after democratic change had occurred, leaders and parties widely evaluated as credible were brought to power. And indeed, they tried afterward to make good on the trans-class redistributions that they had promised.

In sum, where classes and communities are participatory in their outlooks, the social activists that they support seek democratic change. Where they are solidary in their relations, they make this change more quickly and pursue quality more avidly. And where they emerge as credible alternatives, they may gain state power after change has taken place, then respond with the trans-class redistribution that raise democracy's quality. But whatever the capacity that these activists may possess, this trajectory can be halted at various junctures when governments react by demonstrating far greater capacity still.

Assessing governments

The capacity possessed by governments in resisting pressures for democratic change can also be disaggregated, yielding measures of elite-level cohesion, useable state apparatuses, and absorptive regime types. In many Southeast Asia countries, governments operated by political, economic, and military elites have perpetuated or regenerated cohesive relations, enabling them to stand firm before societal challenges. Singapore demonstrates this configuration best, distinguished by a long record of leadership paramountcy and the orderly patterns of elite renewal. In Malaysia, further, though cohesion has been threatened episodically by elite rivalries and factional warring, each time it has been restored through leadership resurgence and the purging of rivals. Thus, pressures for democratic change have been stopped cold in Singapore and turned back in Malaysia.

In New Order Indonesia, though, and in the Philippines and Thailand too, national leaders who were weakened by economic crises, external pressures, or personal infirmities grew less able to manage elites. And as elite-level cohesion dissolved and support bases shrank, these leaders were brought down and democratic change took place. What distinguishes Indonesia, however, and Southeast Asia more generally is that this erosion in leadership skills and elite loyalties only gained pace after social forces had grown participatory. Thus, in Indonesia, once Soeharto had been battered by economic shocks and social violence, elites began to war openly, encouraging some of them to abandon him. Only then did they begin to appeal to the societal discontents that had accumulated beforehand (Aspinall 2005:202–38). In the Philippines, Marcos was similarly discredited by economic stagnation and the exposure of his electoral cheating, encouraging military elites to defect to the people power movement that opposed him. And in Thailand, the military's reckless seizure of state power in 1991, followed by violent confrontation with protesters, so alienated other political elites that they too appealed to fast-gathering social forces, prompting the king to coax the military back into the barracks. Accordingly, in these three country cases, where elite disunity prevailed, social forces were able to drive transition-by-replacement.

Governments are also able to prevent democratic change, however, where the elites who operate them are braced by a 'useable' state apparatus. Such administrative armatures are made up of bureaucratic agencies that can extract resources and implement complex policies, as well as security forces that are 'hierarchical' in their command structures and effective in applying coercion (Linz and Stepan 1996:11, 66–68). In Malaysia, then, the bureaucracy has for decades carried out programs of 'reverse' discrimination, known collectively as the New Economic Policy, enabling the government to modulate social forces by favouring the 'indigenous' Malays over 'immigrant' communities of Chinese and other ethnic affiliations. In addition, the security forces include large numbers of special branch officers and riot police, enabling the government to neutralise dissidents and crush protesters.

In New Order Indonesia, the Philippines, and Thailand, however, state apparatuses were less useable. Thus, the bureaucracies operated respectively by Soeharto, Marcos, and sundry military leaders in Thailand, riddled deeply with inefficiencies and corrupt practices, remained incapable of carrying out anything like Malaysia's social transformation. And in resorting more fully to coercion, these leaders had to rely upon security forces that were sharply divided across training academies, graduating class years, generational cohorts, regional commands, and services. Thus, when the point was reached in tipping games where authoritarian regimes were poised to undergo change, governments in Indonesia, the Philippines, and Thailand found that when trying to resist, their state apparatuses had grown unreliable.

But it is not just the inconsistencies in state apparatuses that may diminish the capacities of governments trying to resist pressures for democracy. Turning from bureaucratic incentives to coercive strategies can in itself fuel these pressures, with brutal coercion and the depletion of resources that might otherwise be used for development worsening societal discontents. In New Order Indonesia, the use of police operatives and street thugs to destroy the headquarters of the opposition Indonesian Democracy Party (Partai Demokrasi Indonesia, PDI) in 1996, an event commemorated as Grey Saturday, is often identified as the beginning of the end for Soeharto. The abductions and executions of left-wing dissidents under Marcos, actions known curiously as 'salvagings', fuelled a corrosive undercurrent of social resentment. And in Thailand, the military's bloody suppression of protesters in the streets of Bangkok in 1992, popularly labelled as 'Black May', only stiffened the opposition of the middle classes and urban poor.

Thus, these governments failed to gain capacity from more 'absorptive' regime types they might have operated which, in providing a measure of political space to the social forces that oppose them, can efficiently dispel participatory pressures. In particular, we recall the electoral authoritarianism practiced in Malaysia and Singapore, cunningly restricting political rights, but regularly holding elections, even reasonably competitive ones, thereby containing in vacuous assemblies the opposition parties thrown up by social forces. Instead, governments in New Order Indonesia, under Marcos in the Philippines, and in Thailand during the 1980s operated more exclusionary regimes, denoted respectively by a manipulable electoral college, a phoney impromptu parliament, and an unelected prime minister and appointed upper house. And made brittle, then, by their exclusionary character, these regimes added little capacity to governments trying to resist democratic change.

Thus, where governments are operated by elites who are cohesive, they are usually geared to resisting democratic change. Where they are firmed by useable state apparatuses, they may mount this resistance effectively. And where they are availed of absorptive regimes, they may gain new efficiencies, taming the opposition parties and leaders that had emerged as credible alternatives. But where governments falter on these measures, transition-by-replacement may then be advanced by activists who, buoyed up by social forces, possess their own capacity.

Instigating and avoiding transition-by-replacement

In considering the respective capacities of activists and governments, we find that in Southeast Asia, where social forces have been uncorked, activists have gained the upper hand, enabling democratic change to take place. But where governments have prevailed, various forms of authoritarian rule have persisted. Thus, there have been no modulated processes of concession-making and top-down transformation in the region, the usual pathway to democracy in Southern Europe, Latin America, and parts of Northeast Asia. Rather, where transitions have occurred, they have always begun as bottom-up replacements, even if later gaining momentum from the elite-level defections that they trigger. As we have seen, with elites having personalised state power in Southeast Asia, whether anchored in political, economic, or military sectors, they must in varying measure be pushed from their perches.

In Singapore, then, where social activists have mostly remained quiescent, dispersed, and unable to produce credible alternatives, they have been overwhelmed by the government, one that has been fortified with elite-level cohesion, highly useable state apparatuses, and to the extent still necessary, an absorptive regime. We find many of these same features in Malaysia. Though activists have been far less quiescent in this case, they have been more deeply dispersed by ethnic and religious rivalries. And hence, though often operating long-standing opposition parties, these activists have only been found credible by the separate communities that have spawned them. Indeed, even the results of the election in 2008 have been interpreted by most analysts as turning less on any new and widespread confidence in the opposition than on the protest votes that were cast against the government. Thus, while in Malaysia the government's elite-level cohesion has episodically waned and its popular support has sagged, it has each time been able to recover drawing deeply upon a useable state apparatus and the absorptive properties of its electoral authoritarianism.

Elsewhere in Southeast Asia, though, social activists gained enough capacity to drive transitions to democracy. Among our country cases in which this trajectory unfolded, activists in New Order Indonesia remained most modestly endowed, slow to grow participatory, unable to maintain solidarity, and unconvincing in their portrayals as alternative leaders. Even so, their capacity grew strong enough that as the government was at the same time weakened by elite disunity, the non-useability of its state apparatus and the brittleness of its regime became plain. In these conditions, activists were able to impose transition-by-replacement. In the Philippines and Thailand, activists sooner grew participatory and became more solidary. They also produced civil society organisations and opposition parties that made them more credible as alternatives. Thus, with governments in these cases just as enfeebled by elite-level disunity, unreliable state apparatuses, and exclusionary regimes as they were in Indonesia, democratic change occurred even earlier.

In the next section of this chapter, we will also see that in the Philippines and Thailand, with social activists having gained greater capacity than in New Order Indonesia, they not only drove the transition to democracy sooner, but also went further in trying to raise democracy's quality. Demands for change thus went beyond the procedural thresholds associated with political rights and electoral competitiveness to seek substantive redistributions of power and assets across class lines. Hence, in Southeast Asia's democratic experience, one of the features that most distinguishes Indonesia involves the comparative modesty of the capacity of its activists and social forces, attributable by most accounts to the New Order's legacies of steadfast controls (see Aspinall, this volume). But this, of course, poses a great puzzle: why is the quality of democracy higher in Indonesia today than anywhere else in Southeast Asia?

Democracy, quality, and persistence

Because the transitions to democracy that have occurred in Southeast Asia have nearly always been bottom-up, it might be expected that they would be far-reaching. With social activists that were participatory, solidary, and credible having triumphed over governments that were weakened by elite-level factionalism, shaky state apparatuses, and brittle regime types, they might be counted upon to keep up their pressure. In this way, democracy's quality would be raised, with new governments making the procedural changes necessary for safeguarding political rights and electoral competitiveness. Indeed, these governments might be pressed to go further, allowing more substantive changes through greater policy responsiveness, made manifest in trans-class redistributions of resources and assets.

But in Southeast Asia, though social activists may in some cases have overturned authoritarian rule, their subsequent efforts to raise democracy's quality have fallen short in one of two ways. In a first pattern, while they gained enough capacity to advance the transition to democracy, they have afterward lost vigour. With the co-operative links and fronts between their civil society organisations unravelling, social forces fell back into old postures of quiescence and dispersion.

Moreover, opposition leaders and parties, though having earlier demonstrated credibility as alternatives, now plotted their own deep co-optation in hopes of getting a shot at state largesse.

Meanwhile, many political, economic, and military elites from the prior authoritarian period, after sacrificing the ruler and his most prominent hard-liners, reconstituted their statuses and relations. They then obliged many of the opposition party elites thrown up by transitional dynamics, enmeshing them in widening patterns of collusion. Together, these old and new elites were also aided by the weaknesses that persisted in the state apparatus, enabling them to retain their bastions of privilege in key agencies and enterprises, while avoiding accountability and sanctions for their abuses. Paradoxically, then, though low levels of usability and hierarchy in the bureaucracy and military had earlier hampered old elites in their efforts to turn back transition-by-replacement, they helped these elites after the transition to renew or perpetuate their standings.

In these conditions, with the capacity of activists diminished, governments were confronted by few demands for the substantive quality that would involve the trans-class redistribution of their resources and assets. But accordingly, they tolerated increases in procedural quality, marked by fuller political rights and electoral competitiveness. Indeed, where procedural quality could be raised in isolation from substantive quality, elites found it useful for their survival. Not only were the social forces that once took to the streets corralled more safely in NGOs and multi-layered assemblies, but elites extended their legitimating cover, helping shield them from local and international criticisms. This configuration, wherein procedural quality was raised because substantive quality was kept low, accords with recent experience in Indonesia.

In a second pattern, social activists remained more participatory and solidary. Thus, they made fuller use of the political rights and electoral competitiveness that connote procedural quality to press for the trans-class redistributions associated with substantive quality. But where new national leaders duly responded with policy changes, they impinged on the prerogatives of political, economic, and military elites, prompting these elites to roll back democratic gains, even resorting to military coups. In these cases, then, it was not just substantive quality that was lost. Elites either truncated democracy's procedural quality, limiting political rights and competitiveness, or they carried out authoritarian reversal, finally ousting an elected government. These trajectories square respectively with the political records of the Philippines under Corazon Aquino and Thailand under Thaksin Shinawatra.

In the rest of this chapter, Indonesia's record will be more fully recounted alongside that of the Philippines and Thailand. What stands out is that with social forces more constrained by authoritarian legacies in Indonesia than in the other country cases, they have not pressed so strongly to raise democracy's quality that elites have struck back. Thus, with so few gains having been made in substantive quality, those that had registered on the procedural dimension have been preserved. In this situation, Indonesia's political rights and electoral competitiveness are evaluated as the most robust in Southeast Asia today—a ranking that must ironically be ascribed to the weakness of social forces and the resilience of elites.

Indonesia: high procedural quality

While social activists have driven all three of Southeast Asia's transitions to democracy, they remained relatively underpowered in Indonesia, a posture attributed to the oppressive legacies of New Order rule. Thus, while a range of civil society organisations and movements grew more participatory during the mid-1990s, they failed to gain solidarity. Student groups thus stood alone in softening the government up, while it was finally left to rioters and looters to deliver the decisive blow. Further, their energies spent, violent elements quickly dispersed. And after Soeharto stood down, even student groups fragmented over their differences in aims and strategies.

To be sure, some opposition leaders and parties had put themselves forward as credible alternatives to Golkar, the government's long-time electoral vehicle. But as Aspinall explains, their credibility lay in mere name recognition, traceable to their lowly functioning in the New Order's electoral system (that is, PDI and the Islamic United Development Party [Partai Persatuan Pembangunan, PPP]) or to their Islamic probing of Soeharto's abusive leadership (National Awakening Party [Partai Kebangkitan Bangsa, PKB] and National Mandate Party [Partai Amanat Nasional, PAN]) (Aspinall 2005; Aspinall this volume). Either way, these ostensible opposition parties, having been reared as little more than 'OPPs' (electoral participant organisations) and given but shallow roots in the 'floating mass', lent little weight to democratic change. And after the transition to democracy had taken place, the smallness of their appetite for reform was made plain by their more quickly seeking their own co-optation than any trans-class redistributions by which to favour the constituencies to which they appealed.

In these circumstances, as Robison and Hadiz have shown, once Soeharto, his offspring, and his most intimate cronies had been sidelined, many other political, military, and economic elites were able to reconstitute their statuses and relations (Robison and Hadiz 2005; Hadiz 2003). However seriously dislocated, then, by the loss of Soeharto's managerial skills and inflows of foreign investment, political elites were still buoyed by a tattered bureaucracy and party system; economic elites by their state monopolies and frayed conglomerates; and military elites by their far-flung command structure and dubious business activities. Moreover, while this configuration grew swollen by the inclusion of new elites thrown up by the transition, and though patronage was diminished by the economic crisis and administrative decentralisation, it re-established much of the cohesion, or at least forbearance, that had characterised elite-level relations under the New Order. In important ways, then, the capacity acquired by social activists was bested by elites who regenerated their cohesion, discovered opportunities in the weaknesses of the state apparatus, and found new efficiencies in the greater absorptiveness that democracy affords.

Accordingly, with elites in Indonesia facing few pressures to raise the substantive quality of democracy that derives from trans-class redistributions, they acquiesced in, indeed made use of, gathering procedural quality. Political rights and electoral competitiveness now placated, rather than activated, Indonesia's social forces, and they more broadly extended legitimating cover. Thus, according to the Freedom House survey in 2005, conducted even before Thailand's authoritarian reversal a year later, Indonesia scored highest in Southeast Asia in terms of political rights (Piano and Puddington 2006:120–24). Press freedoms were greater than they had been in Thailand under Thaksin, and they were more safely exercised than in the Philippines. Further, the competitiveness of elections was evaluated as high, with Golkar losing its legislative majority in 1999, while an incumbent president, Megawati Sukarnoputri, was defeated in 2004.

Alone in Southeast Asia, then, Indonesia's politics earned from Freedom House a ranking of 'free'. Even so, we recognise that democracy's procedural quality may only have persisted in Indonesia because it brought so little substantive quality, therein enabling elites more efficiently to perpetuate their standings. Civil society organisations and movements have lapsed into postures of quiescence and dispersion, while opposition leaders and parties, however credible as alternatives, have most urgently sought their co-optation—default modes that have carried over from New Order strategies of de-politicisation.

The Philippines and Thailand: democracy's low quality, authoritarian reversal

Given the levels of participation, solidarity, and credibility possessed by social activists in the Philippines and Thailand, varying inversely with the elite-level disunity and deteriorating state apparatuses and regime types operated by governments, we would expect transitions-by-replacement to be more far-reaching in these cases than in Indonesia. After transitions took place, social forces might build upon their countries' prior democratic experiences to make new gains in both procedural and substantive quality.

Such progress began to unfold in the Philippines during the late 1980s. Most notably, with activists remaining participatory and solidary after transition had taken place, the political rights and electoral competitiveness associated with procedural quality were enshrined in a new Constitution. But more significantly, the new national leader, Corazon Aquino, demonstrated policy responsiveness by proposing land reforms, amounting to the trans-class redistributions that signify substantive quality.

At the same time, though, the country's political and economic elites, many of whom Marcos had had at least partially dispossessed of their standings, worked feverishly to reconstitute their statuses and relations. Thus, they soon reasserted their dominance over the Philippine Congress. They wrested control too over many of the monopolies in commodities production and trading that Marcos had arranged for his cronies. And upon finding their prerogatives threatened by trans-class redistributions, these elites used their influence and resources to roll back the gains that had been made in substantive quality. In particular, we note the many bloody coup attempts that took place under Aquino, appearing closely to correlate with periods in which her government tried most seriously to implement land reform measures. Indeed, only when the reforms were wound down toward the end of her tenure did the drumbeat of coups fade away. Even so, the elites took no chances, keeping the lid on social forces by truncating procedural quality too. Thus, while political rights and electoral competitiveness may be officially guaranteed, they have remained tenuous in practice. In the Philippines, journalists are bribed, threatened, and frequently murdered, while elections have invariably been marred by cheating and local violence.

Similarly, in Thailand, we would expect that after transition took place, social activists that had grown participatory and solidary would seek to raise democracy's quality. Thus, after two false starts in the mid-1970s and late 1980s, with democracy each time cut short by military coups, significant gains in procedural quality were made after a third transition in the early 1990s, leading to the crafting of a highly reformist Constitution. Moreover, if some of these gains were compromised after Thaksin Shinawatra gained power through competitive elections in 2001, new advances in substantive quality were registered through his government's highly innovative policy responsiveness, made manifest in a range of redistributive programs that included village-level micro-credit, a debt moratorium for cultivators, and cheap medical care.

But by mobilising rural masses in ways that greatly bolstered his personal appeal and electoral prospects, Thaksin encroached upon the peasant constituencies so cherished by the monarchy and military as central to their nation-building lore. He more directly challenged the military too by cultivating factional loyalties and influencing promotions. Thus, in carrying out their coup in late 2006, though the military's leaders sought justification in Thaksin's corrupt practices and the recklessness of his strategies in the country's southern Malay provinces, they seem much sooner to have been motivated by his contesting their corporate prerogatives and the monarch's social grounding, an institution with which they have in recent decades been closely allied. Accordingly, while some of Thaksin's social programs have been left in place, at least for the time being, the military has stamped out political rights and electoral competitiveness, then consented only to limited political reopening. Not content merely to truncate democracy's procedural and substantive quality as in the Philippines, the military has first carried out full authoritarian reversal.

Conclusions

In 1984, Harold Crouch published an important analysis entitled *Domestic Political Structures and Regional Economic Co-operation* (Crouch 1984). In it, he developed a set of matrices by which to produce multi-causal explanations of the extent to which the governments of ASEAN countries might engage one another over regional policy making. Across his country cases, Crouch investigated developmental levels, social structures, and elite- and mass-level pressures, enabling him to gauge variations in government performance.

This chapter draws inspiration from Crouch's comparative analysis. But rather than using local variables to predict cross-national outcomes, the framework deployed here has focused more simply on democratic change and quality within discrete country cases. Thus, in turning first to the social forces and the capacity they possess, participatory outlooks, solidary relations, and credible alternatives were explored. Then, on the government side of the ledger, elite-level cohesion, useable state apparatuses, and absorptive regime types were addressed. In Southeast Asia, the contests that social activists and governments then wage have in most cases tipped in the government's favour, thereby perpetuating authoritarian rule. But among these cases, this chapter gave special attention to Singapore and Malaysia, countries in which, because of rapid industrialisation and new middle-class formations, the dynamics by which authoritarianism have nonetheless endured may yield new insights into how governments resist pressures for democracy.

In a few country cases in Southeast Asia, however, democratic change has taken place, enabling us to draw additional lessons. First, in New Order Indonesia, the Philippines, and Thailand, change has occurred where social activists have prevailed, yielding a pattern of transition-by-replacement which, in its region-wide scope, distinguishes Southeast Asia's experience. Second, while such transitions might be expected to yield high levels of quality, made manifest by gains on a procedural dimension of political rights and electoral competitiveness, followed by those on substantive indices of trans-class redistributions, progress has rarely been straightforward. Such expectations fail to anticipate that even where social forces triumph over governments, enabling democratic change to go forward, governments may afterward regenerate capacity, then roll back democracy's progress. Most crucially, elites who have lost cohesion may show resilience, reconstituting their statuses and relations.

Thus, in the Philippines, though democracy was brought about through a momentous transition, its quality was afterward run down. In Thailand, democracy has undergone authoritarian reversal, even if some of the earlier gains made in substantive quality have been left intact. But it is democracy's contrary progress in Indonesia today that remains most intriguing. Here, political rights and electoral competitiveness have flourished, emerging as the most robust in Southeast Asia. Freedoms of communication and assembly are thus respected by the government, producing a lively media and a thriving community of civil society organisations and political parties. Furthermore, elections are regular, meaningful, and free of systematic fraud or violence, generating turnovers in presidential and parliamentary contests. At least some of the New Order's dark legacies, then, would appear to have lifted, confounding most predictions.

Yet, though casual observers may take heart, a closer inspection reveals that conditioning by the New Order has not fully abated. Social activists in Indonesia, having reverted to postures of quiescence and diffusion, remain weaker than their counterparts in the Philippines and Thailand. And while the government in Indonesia may also remain hobbled by the limited useability of its state apparatus, it has at the same time regenerated much elite cohesion, enabling it to exploit the absorptive capacities of the new, more democratic regime that it now operates.

Indeed, this chapter has argued that while social activists have remained consistent on all three indices of capacity (participatory outlooks, solidary relations, and credible alternatives), they are today overmatched by a government that has recovered on two fronts (elite-level cohesion and regime absorptiveness). In this situation, citizens are unable to make such concerted use of their political rights and electoral competitiveness that they can press effectively for trans-class redistributions. Rather, the government remains better able to exploit democracy's procedural quality, notching up the legitimacy that dispels both local and international criticisms, even while parrying demands for substantive quality. However, by the readings of Freedom House, Indonesia is still better off. Though citizens may not fully exercise their political rights or avail themselves of electoral competitiveness, they are at least informed of the inequalities that elites still impose upon them.

References

-----. 1982. 'Ideologi Negara Pancasila Gerakan Komunisme dan Ajaran Islam didepan Sidang Pengadilan Negeri Sukoharjo: Suatu Eksepsi', 20 Februari. Sukoharjo District Court document.

-----. 1982. Berita Acara Pemeriksaan Abu Bakar Ba'asyir and Abdullah Sungkar, No.1/Pid.Subv/1982/P.N. Skh. Case dossier.

-----. nd. *Pedoman Penghayatan dan Pengamalan Pancasila*, Guide to the Realization and Implementation of Pancasila.

Akhmadi, Heri. 1981. *Breaking the Chains of Oppression of the Indonesian People*. Ithaca: Cornell Modern Indonesia Project.

Ali Moertopo. 1973. *Some Basic Thoughts on the Acceleration and Modernization of 25 Years' Development*. Jakarta: Yayasan Proklamasi, Centre for Strategic and International Studies.

Anderson, Benedict. 1972. 'The Idea of Power in Javanese Culture', in Claire Holt ed, *Culture and Politics in Indonesia,* Ithaca NY: Cornell University Press, pp.1–69.

-----. 1983. 'Old State, New Society: Indonesia's New Order in Comparative Historical Perspective', *Journal of Asian Studies,* 42(3):477–96.

-----. nd. 'Stepping Down From Power' published in Indonesian, http://members. fortunecity.com/edicahy/selectedworks/BAnderson3. html.

Anderson, Benedict, ed. 2001. *Violence and the State in Suharto's Indonesia.* Ithaca: Cornell University Southeast Asia Program.

Anderson, Benedict and Audrey Kahin, eds. 1982. *Interpreting Indonesian Politics. Thirteen Contributions to the Debate*. Interim Reports Series No.62, Ithaca, NY: Cornell Modern Indonesian Project.

Anonymous. 1981. *Sekitar Tanggal dan Penggalinya: Guntingan pers dan bibliografi tentang Pancasila*. Jakarta: Yayasan Idayu, 212pp.

Anonymous. 1982. *Stenographic Report of President Soeharto's Message (Amanat) at the Evening Get-together with KNPI Office-holders on 19 July at 8 Jalan Cendana, Jakarta.* 14-page typescript.

Asian Development Bank. 2005. *Labor Markets in Asia: Promoting Full, Productive and Decent Employment*. Manila: Asian Development Bank.

Aspinall, Edward. 2002. 'The Downfall of President Abdurrahman Wahid: A Return to Authoritarianism?', in Kathryn Robinson and Sharon Bessell, eds, *Women in Indonesia: Gender, Equity and Development,* Singapore: ISEAS, pp.28–40.

-----. 2005. *Opposing Suharto: Compromise, Resistance, and Regime Change in Indonesia*. Stanford: Stanford University Press.

Aspinall, Edward and Greg Fealy, eds. 2003. *Local Power and Politics in Indonesia: Decentralisation & Democratisation*, Singapore: ISEAS.

Asshiddiqie, Jimly et al, eds. 1999. *Pandangan dan Langkah Reformasi B. J. Habibie*. Buku Dua. Hukum dan Sosial Budaya, Jakarta: PT RajaGrafindo Persada.

Aswicahyono, Haryo and Hal Hill. 2004. 'Survey of Recent Developments', *Bulletin of Indonesian Economic Studies,* 40(3):277–306.

Athukorala, Premachandra. 2006. 'Post-crisis Export Performance: The Indonesian Experience in Regional Perspective', *Bulletin of Indonesian Economic Studies,* 42(4):177–211.

Azis, Iwan J. 1994. 'Indonesia', in John Williamson, ed, *The Political Economy of Policy Reform*, Washington DC: Institute for International Economics, pp.385–426.

Barton, Greg. 2001. 'Indonesia's Difficult Transition and President Abdurrahman Wahid', *Pacifica Review,* 13(3):273–81.

-----. 2002. *Gus Dur: The Authorized Biography of Abdurrahman Wahid*. Jakarta: Equinox Publishing.

Basri, M. Chatib and A. Patunru. 2006. 'Survey of Recent Developments', *Bulletin of Indonesian Economic Studies,* 42(3):295–318.

Basri, M. Chatib and Hal Hill. 2004. 'Ideas, Interests and Oil Prices: The Political Economy of Trade Reform during Soeharto's Indonesia', *The World Economy,* 27(5):633–56.

Benda, Harry J. 1964. 'Democracy in Indonesia' (review of Herbert Feith. 1962. *The Decline of Constitutional Democracy in Indonesia*, Ithaca NY: Cornell University Press), *Journal of Asian Studies,* 23(3) May:449–56. Republished

1982 in Benedict Anderson and Audrey Kahin, eds, *Interpreting Indonesian Politics: Thirteen Contributions to the Debate,* Interim Reports Series No.62, Ithaca, NY: Cornell Modern Indonesian Project, pp.13–21.

Berry, Albert, Edgard Rodriguez and Henry Sandee. 2001. 'Small and Medium Enterprise Dynamics in Indonesia', *Bulletin of Indonesian Economic Studies,* 37(3):363–84.

Bird, Kelly and Hal Hill. 2006. 'Indonesian Industrial Policies: Before and After the Crisis', in Yun-Peng Chu and Hal Hill, eds, *The East Asian High-Tech Drive*, Cheltenham: Edward Elgar, pp.335–75.

Bird, Kelly. 1999. 'Industrial Concentration in Indonesia', *Bulletin of Indonesian Economic Studies,* 35(1):43–73.

-----. 2005. 'Labour markets and regulation: international experience', Presentation on Indonesia at the World Bank, Coordinating Ministry of Economic Affairs and KADIN Sponsored Conference on Indonesia's Investment Climate, Jakarta, November.

Bourchier, David. 1997. 'Totalitarianism and the "National Personality": Recent Controversy about the Philosophical Basis of the Indonesian State', in Jim Schiller and Barbara Martin-Schiller, eds, *Imagining Indonesia: Cultural Politics and Political Culture*, Athens, Ohio: Ohio University Center for International Studies, pp.157–85.

Bourchier, David and Vedi R. Hadiz. 2003. *Indonesian Politics and Society: A reader.* London: RoutledgeCurzon.

Bourchier, David and John Legge, eds. 1994. *Democracy in Indonesia.* Clayton, Victoria: Centre of Southeast Asian Studies, Monash University.

Breman, Jan. 1989. *Taming the Coolie Beast: Plantation Society and the Colonial Order in Southeast Asia.* Delhi: Oxford University Press.

Bresnan, John. 1993. *Managing Indonesia: The Modern Political Economy.* New York: Columbia University Press.

Brooks, Karen. 1996. 'The Rustle of Ghosts: Bung Karno in the New Order', *Indonesia*, 60(February):61–99.

Budiman, Arief. 1998. 'Pemimpin, Di Mana Kau', *Tempo*, 17–23 November.

Caraway, Teri L. 2004. 'Protective Repression, International Pressures and Institutional Design: Explaining Labour Reforms in Indonesia,' *Studies in Comparative International Development*, 39(3):28–49.

-----. 2006. 'International Institutions, Labor Reform and the Organisational Power of Labor', Twin Cities: Department of Political Science, University of Minnesota, unpublished paper.

Case, William. 2002. *Politics in Southeast Asia: Democracy or Less*. Richmond: Curzon Press.

Chauvel, Richard. 2003. 'Essays on West Papua', *Working Paper 121*, Clayton: Monash Asia Institute. Volume Two.

Choi, Nankyung. 2005. 'Local Elections and Democracy in Indonesia: The Case of the Riau Archipelago'. *Working Paper No.91*, Singapore: Institute of Defence and Strategic Studies.

Chu, Yun-Peng and Hal Hill, eds. 2006. *The East Asian High-Tech Drive*. Cheltenham: Edward Elgar.

Claessens, Stijn, Simeon Djankov, and Larry H. P. Lang. 2000. 'The Separation of Ownership and Control in East Asian Corporations', *Journal of Financial Economics*, 58:81–112.

Conboy, Ken. 2006. *The Second Front: Inside Asia's Most Dangerous Terrorist Network*. Jakarta: Equinox Publishing.

Connors, Michael Kelly. 2002. 'Framing the "People's Constitution"', in Duncan McCargo, ed, *Reforming Thai Politics*, Copenhagen: NIAS Publishing, pp.37–55.

Cox-Edwards, Alejandra. 1997. 'Labor Market Regulations in Latin America: An Overview', in Sebastian Edwards and Nora Lustig, eds, *Labor Markets in Latin America: Combining Social Protection with Labor Market Flexibility*, Washington DC: Brookings Institute Press, pp.127–50.

Cribb, Robert. 1990. 'Indonesian Political Developments 1989–90', in Hal Hill and Terry Hull, eds, *Indonesia Assessment 1990*, Canberra: Department of Political and Social Change, Research School of Pacific and Asian Studies, Australian National University, pp.24–42.

-----. 1993. 'Development Policy in the early 20th Century', in Jan-Paul Dirkse, Frans Hüsken and Mario Rutten, eds, *Development and Social Welfare: Indonesia's experiences under the New Order*, Leiden: KITLV Press, pp.225–45.

Cribb, Robert, ed. 1994. *The Late Colonial State in Indonesia: Political and Economic Foundations of the Netherlands Indies, 1880–1942*. Leiden: KITLV Press.

Crouch, Harold. 1966. *Trade Unions and Politics in India*. Bombay: Manaktalas.

-----. 1978. *Army and Politics in Indonesia*. Ithaca: Cornell University Press.

-----. 1979. 'Patrimonialism and Military Rule in Indonesia', *World Politics*, 31(4):571–87.

-----. 1984. *Domestic Political Structures and Regional Economic Co-operation*. Singapore: ISEAS.

-----. 1992. 'An Ageing President, an Ageing Regime', in Harold Crouch and Hal Hill, eds, *Indonesia Assessment 1992*, Canberra: Department of Political and Social Change, Research School of Pacific and Asian Studies, Australian National University, pp.43–62.

-----. 1994. 'Democratic Prospects in Indonesia', in David Bourchier and John Legge, eds, *Democracy in Indonesia: 1950s and 1990s*, Clayton, Victoria: Centre of Southeast Asian Studies, Monash University, pp.115–27.

-----. 1996. *Government and Society in Malaysia*. Ithaca: Cornell University Press.

-----. 2003. 'Professionalism in Southeast Asian Militaries: Indonesia', unpublished paper.

-----. 2010. *Political Reform in Indonesia after Soeharto*. Singapore: ISEAS.

Dahm, Bernhard. 1969. *Sukarno and the Struggle for Indonesian Independence*. Ithaca: Cornell University Press.

Davies, Matthew N. 2006. 'TNI and Polri Forces in West Papua: Restructuring and Reasserting Sovereignty', unpublished paper.

Dewi Fortuna Anwar. 1994. *Indonesia in ASEAN: Foreign Policy and Regionalism*. Singapore: ISEAS

Diamond, Larry, and Leonardo Morlino. 2004. 'The Quality of Democracy'. *Center of Democracy, Development, and the Rule of Law, Working Paper No.20*, Stanford: Stanford Institute for International Studies.

Doorn, J. A. A. van. 1973. *Orde-opstand-orde. Notities over Indonesië.* Boom: Meppel.

Ellis, Andrew. 2007. 'Indonesia's Constitutional Change Reviewed', in Ross McLeod and Andrew MacIntyre, eds, *Indonesia: Democracy and the Promise of Good Governance*, Singapore: ISEAS, pp.21–40.

Elson, Robert E. 2001. *Suharto: A Political Biography*. Cambridge: Cambridge University Press.

Emmerson, Donald. 1995. 'Region and Recalcitrance: Rethinking Democracy through Southeast Asia', *Pacific Review,* 8(2):223–48.

-----. nd. 'The Rabbit and the Crocodile: Expecting the End of the New Order in Indonesia, 1966–1991', unpublished paper.

Fasseur, Cornelius. 1994. 'Cornerstone and Stumbling Block: Racial Classification and the Late Colonial State in Indonesia', in Robert Cribb, ed, *The Late Colonial State in Indonesia: Political and Economic Foundations of the Netherlands Indies, 1880–1942,* Leiden: KITLV Press, pp.31–56.

Fealy, Greg. 1998. *Ulama and Politics in Indonesia: A History of Nahdlatul Ulama, 1952–1967.* PhD thesis, Clayton: Monash University.

-----. 2001. 'Abdurrahman Wahid and the al-Khidr Question', in Damien Kingsbury, ed, *The Presidency of Abdurrahman Wahid: An Assessment of the First Year,* Monash Annual Indonesia Lecture Series, Clayton: Monash Asia Institute.

Feith, Herbert. 1962. *The Decline of Constitutional Democracy in Indonesia.* Ithaca: Cornell University Press.

-----. 1968. 'Suharto's Search for a Political Format', *Indonesia,* 6(October):88–105.

-----. 1980. 'Repressive-Developmentalist Regimes in Asia: Old Strengths, New Vulnerabilities', *Prisma* (19):39–55.

-----. 1982a. 'Repressive-Development Regimes in Asia', *Alternatives,* 7(4) Spring:491–506.

-----. 1982b. 'The Study of Indonesian Politics: A Survey and an Apologia', in Benedict Anderson and Audrey Kahin, eds, *Interpreting Indonesian Politics. Thirteen Contributions to the Debate,* Interim Reports Series No.62, Ithaca, NY: Cornell Modern Indonesian Project, pp.41–53.

Fields, G. S. 1994. 'Changing Labor Markets and Economic Development in Hong Kong, the Republic of Korea, Singapore and Taiwan China', *World Bank Economic Review,* 8(3):395–414.

Ford, Michele. 2004. 'A Challenge for Business: Developments in Indonesian Trade Unionism after Soeharto', in Peter van der Eng and M. Chatib Basri, eds, *Business in Indonesia: New Challenges, Old Problems,* Singapore: ISEAS, pp.221–33.

Forum Rektor Indonesia/Jawa Timur, 'Pemilih Kota Surabaya Cari Walikota Penyelesai Malasah', Press Release, 29 June 2005.

Friend, Theodore. 2003. *Indonesian Destinies*. Cambridge: Harvard University Press.

Fukuchi, Takao. 2000. 'Econometric Analysis of the Effects of Krismon Shocks on Indonesia's Industrial Subsector', *Developing Economies*, 38(4):490–517.

Furnivall, John S. 1948. *Colonial Policy and Practice: A Comparative Study of Burma and Netherlands India*. Cambridge: Cambridge University Press.

Galenson, W. 1992. *Labour and Economic Development in Five Asian Countries: South Korea, Malaysia, Taiwan, Thailand and the Philippines*. New York: Praeger.

Geddes, Barbara. 1995. 'A Comparative Perspective on the Leninist Legacy in Eastern Europe', *Comparative Political Studies*, 28(2):239–74.

-----. 1999. 'What Do We Know About Democratization After Twenty Years?', *Annual Review of Political Science* (2):115–44.

Geertz, Clifford. 1960. *The Religion of Java*. New York: The Free Press of Glencoe.

Gelb, Alan and Associates. 1988. *Oil Windfalls: Blessing or Curse?* New York: Oxford University Press (for the World Bank).

Gerhardie, William. 1939. *The Romanovs: Evocation of the Past as a Mirror for the Present*. New York: Putnam.

Habibie, Bacharuddin Jusuf. 2006. *Detik-Detik Yang Menentukan*. Jakarta: The Habibie Center.

Hadiz, Vedi R. 1997. *Workers and the State in New Order Indonesia*. London: Routledge.

Haggard, Stephan. 2000. 'Interests, Institutions, and Policy Reform', in Anne Krueger, ed, *Economic Reform the Second Stage*, Chicago: University of Chicago Press, pp.21–60.

Hanna, Willard A. 1978. *Indonesian Banda: Colonialism and Its Aftermath in the Nutmeg Islands*. Philadelphia: ISHI, Institute for the Study of Human Issues.

Haryadi, Dedi and Riyan Sumindar. 2002. *Belanja Belanja Dewan: Studi Dokumen Anggaran Belanja DPRD Kota Bandung, 1997–2002*. Bandung: Bandung Institute of Governance Studies.

Hefner, Robert. 1990. *Tengger Tradition and Islam*. Princeton: Princeton University Press.

-----. 2000. *Civil Islam: Muslims and democratization in Indonesia*. Princeton, New Jersey: Princeton University Press.

Heryanto, Ariel. 2006. *State Terrorism and Political Identity in Indonesia: Fatally Belonging*. London and New York: Routledge.

Heryanto, Ariel and Vedi R. Hadiz. 2005. 'Post-Authoritarian Indonesia', *Critical Asian Studies* 37(2):251–75.

Hill, Hal. 1997. *Indonesia's Industrial Transformation*. Singapore: ISEAS.

-----. 1999. *The Indonesian Economy in Crisis: Causes, Consequences and Lessons*. Singapore: ISEAS.

-----. 2000. *The Indonesian Economy Since 1966: Southeast Asia's Emerging Giant*. Cambridge: Cambridge University Press.

Hoffman, Bert, Min Jhao and Yoichiro Isihara. 2007. 'Asian Development Strategies: China and Indonesia Compared', *Bulletin of Indonesian Economic Studies,* 43(2):169–97.

Honna, Jun. 2003. *Military Politics and Democratization in Indonesia*. London: Routledge Curzon.

-----. 2006. 'Local Civil-Military Relations during the First Phase of Democratic Transition, 1999–2004: A Comparison of West, Central and East Java', *Indonesia,* 82(October):75–96.

Huntington, Samuel. 1991. *The Third Wave: Democratization in the Late Twentieth Century*. Norman and London: University of Oklahoma Press.

Inter-American Development Bank. 2004. *Good Jobs Wanted: Labor Markets in Latin America*. Social and Economic Progress Report, Washington DC: Inter-American Development Bank.

Indonesia. Bappenas. 2003. *White Paper on Employment*. Jakarta.

Indonesia. Coordinating Ministry for Economic Affairs. 2006. *Investment Climate Policy Reform Package*. Jakarta.

International Crisis Group (ICG). 2000. 'Indonesia's Crisis: Chronic but not Acute'. *Asia Report No.6*, 31 May.

-----. 2001. 'Communal Violence in Indonesia: Lessons from Kalimantan'. *Asia Report No.19*, 27 June.

-----. 2003. 'Jemaah Islamiyah in South East Asia: Damaged but Still Dangerous'. *Asia Report No.63*, 26 August.

-----. 2005. 'Understanding Islamism. Middle East/North Africa'. *Report No.37*, 2 March.

International Foundation for Electoral Systems. 2004. 'Results from Wave XIII Tracking Surveys', 23 June.

Jackson, Karl D. 1978. 'Bureaucratic Polity: A Theoretical Framework for the Analysis of Power and Communications in Indonesia', in Karl D. Jackson and Lucian W. Pye, eds, *Political Power and Communications in Indonesia*, Berkeley: University of California Press, pp.3–22.

Johnson, Colin. 1998. 'Survey of Recent Developments', *Bulletin of Indonesian Economic Studies*, 34(2):3–59.

Kartodirdjo, Sartono. 1988. 'Religious Responses to Social Change in Indonesia', in *Modern Indonesia,Tradition and Transformation*, Yogyakarta: Gajah Mada University Press, pp.263–84.

King, Dwight Y. 1982. 'Indonesia's New Order as a Bureaucratic Polity, a Neopatrimonial Regime or a Bureaucratic-Authoritarian Regime: What Difference Does It Make?', in Benedict Anderson and Audrey Kahin, eds, *Interpreting IndonesianPolitics: Thirteen Contributions to the Debate*, Ithaca: Cornell Modern Indonesia Project, pp.104–16.

-----. 2003. *Half-Hearted Reform: Electoral Institutions and the Struggle for Democracy in Indonesia*. Westport/Connecticut/London: Praeger.

Kingsbury, Damien. 2002. *The Politics of Indonesia*. (2nd Edition). South Melbourne: Oxford University Press.

Klinken, Gerry van. 2001. 'The Coming Crisis in Indonesian Area Studies', *Journal of Southeast Asian Studies*, 32(2):263–68.

-----. 2009. 'Patronage Democracy in Provincial Indonesia', in John Harriss, Kristian Stokke, and Olle Törnquist, eds, *Rethinking Popular Representation*, Basingstoke: Palgrave Macmillan, pp.141–59.

Kroef, Justus M. van der. 1956. 'The Colonial Deviation in Indonesian History', *East and West*, 7:251–61.

Kurasawa, Aiko. 1987. 'Propaganda Media on Java under the Japanese 1942–1945', *Indonesia*, 44(October):59–116.

Legge, John D. 1981. '*Daulat Ra'jat* and the Ideas of the Pendidikan Nasional Indonesia', *Indonesia*, 32(October):151–68.

Leur, J. C. van. 1955. *Indonesian Trade and Society: Essays in Asian Social and Economic History*. The Hague: W. van Hoeve.

Lev, Daniel. 1966. *The Transition to Guided Democracy: Indonesian Politics, 1957–59*. Ithaca: Cornell Modern Indonesia Project.

Liddle, R. William. 1978. 'Indonesia 1977: The New Order's Second Parliamentary Election', *Asian Survey*, 18(2):175–85.

-----. 1985. 'Soeharto's Indonesia: Personal Rule and Political Institutions', *Pacific Affairs*, 58(1) Spring:68–90.

-----. 2001. 'Indonesia in 2000. A Shaky Start for Democracy', *Asian Survey*, 41(1):208–20.

Lindsey, Tim. 2001. 'The Criminal State: *Premanisme* and the New Indonesia', in Grayson Lloyd and Shannon Smith, eds, *Indonesia Today: Challenges of History*, Singapore: ISEAS, pp.283–97.

Lindsey, Tim and Teten Masduki. 2002. 'Labour Law in Indonesia after Soeharto: Reformasi or Replay?', in Sean Cooney, Tim Lindsey, Richard Mitchell and Ying Zhu, eds, *Law and Labour Market Regulation in East Asia*, London: Routledge, pp.246–74.

Linz, Juan J. 1973. 'Opposition in and Under an Authoritarian Regime: The Case of Spain', in Robert A. Dahl, ed, *Regimes and Oppositions*, New Haven, CT, and London: Yale University Press, pp.171–259.

Linz, Juan and Alfred Stepan. 1996. *Problems of Democratic Transition and Consolidation: Southern Europe, South America and Post-Communist Europe*. Baltimore: Johns Hopkins University Press.

LP3E–Unpad. 2004. 'Indonesia's employment protection legislation: swimming against the tide?', Report prepared for GIAT (Growth through Investment, Agriculture and Trade), USAID, by the Laboratorium Penelitian, Pengabdian pada Masyarakat dan Pengkajian Ekonomi (LP3E), Bandung: Faculty of Economics, Padjadjaran University.

Lucas, Anton. 1991. *One Soul One Struggle: Region and Revolution in Indonesia*. Sydney: Allen and Unwin.

Mackie, Jamie. 1990. 'Property and Power in Indonesia', in Ken Young and Richard Tanter, eds, *The Politics of Middle Class Indonesia*, Clayton, Victoria: Centre for Southeast Asian Studies, Monash University, pp.71–95.

Magnis-Suseno, Franz. 1997. *Javanese Ethics and World-View*. Jakarta:Gramedia.

Malley, Michael. 1990. 'A Political Biography of Major General Sudjono Hoemardani, 1918-1986', unpublished MA thesis, Cornell University.

-----. 2002. 'Indonesia in 2001: Restoring Stability in Jakarta', *Asian Survey*, 42(1):124–32.

-----. 2003. 'New Rules, Old Structures and the Limits of Democratic Decentralisation', in Edward Aspinall and Greg Fealy, eds, *Local Power and Politics in Indonesia: Decentralisation & Democratisation*, Singapore: ISEAS, pp.102–16.

Manning, Chris. 1998. *Indonesian Labour in Transition: An East Asian Success Story?* Trade and Development Series, Cambridge: Cambridge University Press.

-----. 2007. 'The Manpower Act of 2003 and Its Implementing Regulations: Genesis, Key Articles and Potential Impact', *Bulletin of Indonesian Economic Studies*, 43(1):55–82.

Manning, Chris and Kurnya Roesad. 2006. 'Survey of Recent Developments', *Bulletin of Indonesian Economic Studies*, 42(2):277–306.

Mardjono. 2002. 'Penetapan Upah Minimum' [*Setting Minimum Wages*]. Jakarta, January.

McDonald, Hamish. 1980. *Suharto's Indonesia*. Blackburn: Fontana/Collins.

McGregor, Katharine E. 2007. *History in Uniform: Military Ideology and the Construction of Indonesia's Past*. Singapore: Singapore University Press, University of Hawaii Press and KITLV and the Asian Studies Association of Australia.

MacIntyre, Andrew. 1990. *Business and Politics in Indonesia*. St Leonards: Allen and Unwin.

-----. 1998. 'Political Institutions and Economic Crisis in Thailand and Indonesia', *ASEAN Economic Bulletin*, 15(3):362–72.

MacIntyre, Andrew and Douglas E. Ramage. 2008. *Seeing Indonesia as a Normal Country: Implications for Australia*. Canberra: Australian Strategic Policy Institute.

McIntyre, Angus. 2001. 'Middle Way Leadership in Indonesia: Sukarno and Abdurrahman Wahid Compared', in Grayson Lloyd and Shannon Smith, eds, *Indonesia Today: Challenges of History*, Singapore: ISEAS, pp.85–96.

-----. 2005. *The Indonesian Presidency: The Shift from Personal toward Constitutional Rule.* Lanham MD: Rowman and Littlefield.

McKemmish, Susan Marilyn. 1976. 'A Political Biography of General A. H. Nasution', unpublished MA thesis, Monash University.

McLeod, Ross. 2005. 'The Struggle to Regain Effective Government under Democracy in Indonesia', *Bulletin of Indonesian Economic Studies,* 41(3):367–86.

McVey, Ruth. 1982. 'The Beamtenstaat in Indonesia', in Benedict Anderson and Audrey Kahin, eds, *Interpreting Indonesian Politics: Thirteen Contributions to the Debate*, Ithaca: Cornell Modern Indonesia Project, pp.84–91.

Mietzner, Marcus. 2000. 'The 1999 General Session: Wahid, Megawati and the Fight for the Presidency', in Chris Manning and Peter van Diermen, eds, *Indonesia in Transition: Social Aspects of Reformasi and Crisis*, Canberra: Research School of Pacific and Asian Studies, The Australian National University, pp.39–57.

-----. 2001. 'Abdurrahman's Indonesia: Political Conflict and Institutional Crisis', in Grayson Lloyd and Shannon Smith, eds, *Indonesia Today: Challenges of History,* Singapore: ISEAS, pp.29–44.

-----. 2003. 'Business as Usual? The Indonesian Armed Forces and Local Politics in the Post-Soeharto Era', in Edward Aspinall and Greg Fealy, eds, *Local Power and Politics in Indonesia: Decentralisation & Democratisation*, Singapore: ISEAS, pp.245–58.

-----. 2005. 'Local Democracy', *Inside Indonesia* (85):17–18.

-----. 2006. 'The Politics of Military Reform in Post-Suharto Indonesia: Elite Conflict, Nationalism and Institutional Resistance'. *Policy Studies 23*, Washington: East-West Center.

-----. 2008a. *Military Politics, Islam and the State in Indonesia: From Turbulent Transition to Democratic Consolidation.* Singapore: ISEAS.

-----. 2008b. 'Comparing Indonesia's Party Systems of the 1950s and the Post-Soeharto Era: From Centrifugal to Centripetal Inter-Party Competition', *Journal of Southeast Asian Studies* (39)3:431–53.

Morfit, Michael. 1981. 'Pancasila: The Indonesian State Ideology According to the New Order Government', *Asian Survey*, 21(8):838–51.

Mortimer, Rex. 1982. 'Class, Social Cleavage and Indonesian Communism', in Benedict Anderson and Audrey Kahin, eds, *Interpreting Indonesian Politics. Thirteen Contributions to the Debate*, Interim Reports Series No.62, Ithaca, NY: Cornell Modern Indonesian Project, pp.54–68.

Mortimer, Rex, ed. 1973. Showcase State. The Illusion of Indonesia's 'Accelerated Modernisation'. Sydney: Angus and Robertson.

Mulder, Niels. 1992. *Individual and Society in Java, A Cultural Analysis.* Yogyakarta: Gajah Mada Press.

Narjoko, Dionisius Ardiyanto. 2006. *Indonesian Manufacturing and the Economic Crisis of 1997–98*. Unpublished doctoral dissertation, The Australian National University.

Nas, Peter J. M. and Pratiwo. 2002. 'Java and De Groote Postweg, La Grande Route, the Great Mail Road, Jalan Raya Pos', *Bijdragen tot de taal-, land- en volkenkunde*, 158(4):707–25.

Nordholt, Henk Schulte. 2002. 'A Genealogy of Violence', in Freek Colombijn and Thomas Lindblad, eds, *Roots of Violence in Indonesia*, Leiden: KITLV Press, pp.33–61.

Nordholt, Henk Schulte and Gerry van Klinken, eds. 2007. *Renegotiating Boundaries. Local Politics in Post-Suharto Indonesia*. Leiden: KITLV Press.

O'Donnell, Guillermo and Philippe Schmitter. 1986. 'Opening (and Undermining) Authoritarian Regimes', in Guillermo O'Donnell, Philippe Schmitter, and Laurence Whitehead, eds, *Transitions from Authoritarian Rule: Prospects for Democracy, Part IV*, Baltimore: Johns Hopkins University Press, pp.15–36.

O'Rourke, Kevin. 2002. *Reformasi: The Struggle for Power in Post-Soeharto Indonesia*. Crows Nest, NSW: Allen and Unwin.

Pemberton, John. 1986. 'Notes on the 1982 General Election in Solo', *Indonesia*, 41(April):1–22.

-----. 1994. *On the Subject of 'Java'*. Ithaca: Cornell University Press.

Pheng Cheah. 2003. *Spectral Nationality: Passages of Freedom from Kant to Postcolonial Literatures of Liberation*. New York: Columbia University Press.

Piano, Aili and Arch Puddington. 2006. 'The 2005 Freedom House Survey: Progress in the Middle East', *Journal of Democracy*, 17(1):120–24.

Pinera, Jose. 1994. 'Chile', in John Williamson, ed, *The Political Economy of Reform*, Washington DC: Institute for International Economics, pp.225–32.

Poeze, Harry A. ed. 1982–1994. *Politiek-Politioneele Overzichten van Nederlandsch-Indië: Bronnenpublikatie*, 4 vols. The Hague/Dordrecht/Leiden: Nijhoff/Foris/KITLV Press.

Porter, Donald J. 2002. *Managing Politics and Islam in Indonesia*. London and New York: RoutledgeCurzon.

Pranoto, Haji Ismail. 1978. Defence statement. 24 June, handwritten.

Quinn, Patrick. 2003. 'Freedom of Association and Collective Bargaining: A study of Indonesian Experience 1998–2003'. *Working Paper*, Geneva: ILO.

Ramage, Douglas. 1995. *Politics in Indonesia: democracy, Islam and the ideology of tolerance*. London: Routledge.

-----. 2007. 'Indonesia in 2006: Democracy First, Governance Later', *Southeast Asian Affairs 2007*. Singapore: ISEAS, pp.135–57.

Reeve, David. 1985. *Golkar of Indonesia: An Alternative to the Party System*. Singapore: Oxford University Press.

Rinakit, Sukardi. 2005. Indonesian Regional Elections in Praxis. IDSS Commentaries, Singapore: Institute of Defence and Strategic Studies.

Robison, Richard. 1986. *Indonesia: the Rise of Capital*. Sydney: Allen and Unwin.

Robison, Richard and Vedi R. Hadiz. 2004. *Reorganising Power in Indonesia: the Politics of Oligarchy in an Age of Markets*. London: Routledge.

Roeder, O. G. 1969. *The Smiling General: President Soeharto of Indonesia*. Jakarta: Gunung Agung.

Roosa, John. 2006. *Pretext for Mass Murder: The September 30th Movement and Suharto's Coup d'État in Indonesia*. Madison: University of Wisconsin Press.

Samson, Allen A. 1973. 'Religious Belief and Political Action in Indonesian Islamic Modernism', in William Liddle, ed, *Political Participation in Modern Indonesia*, Monograph Series No.19, New Haven: Yale University Southeast Asia Studies, pp.116–40.

Schedler, Andreas, ed. 2006. *Electoral Authoritarianism: The Dynamics of Unfree Competition*. Boulder: Lynne Rienner.

Schwarz, Adam. 1986. *Nation in Waiting: Indonesia in the 1990s*. St Leonards, NSW: Allen and Unwin.

Shultz, T. Paul. 2000. 'Labor Market Reforms: Issues, Evidence and Prospects', in Anne Krueger, ed, *Economic Reform the Second Stage*, Chicago: University of Chicago Press, pp.295–340.

Slater, Dan. 2004. 'Indonesia's Accountability Trap: Party Cartels and Presidential Power after Democratic Transition', *Indonesia*, 78(October):61–92.

Soeharto. 1989. *Pikiran, Ucapan dan Tindakan Saya: Otobiografi Seperti Dipaparkan kepada G. Dwipayana dan Ramadhan K. H.* Jakarta: Citra Lamtoro Gung Persada.

Soemarsaid Moertono. 1981. *State and Statecraft in Old Java*. Ithaca: Cornell Modern Indonesia Project.

Soesastro, Hadi. 1989. 'The Political Economy of Deregulation', *Asian Survey*, 29(9):853–69.

Sudarmono. 1997. *Pengalaman dalam Masa Pengabdian. Sebuah Otobiografi.* Jakarta: Gramedia.

Suharizal. 2002. *Reformasi Konstitusi 1998–2002: Pergulatan Konsep dan Pemikiran Amandemen UUD 1945*. Padang: Anggrek Law Firm.

Sukma, Rizal. 2004. 'Security Operations in Aceh: Goals, Consequences and Lessons'. *Policy Studies 3*, Washington: East-West Center.

Sundhaussen, Ulf. 1978. 'The Military: Structure, Procedures, and Effects on Indonesian Society', in Karl D. Jackson and Lucian W. Pye, eds, *Political Power and Communications in Indonesia*, Berkeley, Los Angeles, London: University of California Press, pp.45–81.

Suryahadi, Asep, Wenefrida Widyanti, Daniel Perwira and Sudarno Sumarto. 2003. *'The Minimum Wage and its Impact on Employment in the Urban Formal Sector'*, Bulletin of Indonesian Economic Studies, 39(1):29–50.

Sutherland, Heather. 1979. *The Making of a Bureaucratic Elite: The Colonial Transformation of the Javanese Priyayi*. Singapore: Heinemann Educational Books.

Tanter, Richard. 1990. *'The Totalitarian Ambition: Intelligence and Security Agencies in Indonesia'*, in Arief Budiman, ed, *State and Civil Society in Indonesia*, Clayton, Victoria: Centre of Southeast Asian Studies, Monash University, pp.213–88.

Temple, Jonathan. 2003. 'Growing into Trouble: Indonesia after 1966', in Dani Rodrik, ed, *In Search of Prosperity: Analytical Narratives on Economic Growth*, Princeton: Princeton University Press.

The Asia Foundation. 2004. *Indonesia Rapid Decentralization Appraisal.* Fifth Report, November, Jakarta: The Asia Foundation.

Thee Kian Wie. 2000. 'The Impact of the Economic Crisis on Indonesia's Manufacturing Sector', *Developing Economies*, 38(4):420–53.

Thompson, Mark R. 1995. *The Anti Marcos Struggle: Personalistic Rule and Democratic Transition in the Philippines.* New Haven: Yale University Press.

Tjandra, Surya. 2008 'Understanding Workers' Law Reform in Indonesia 1998–2004', *Labour and Management in Developing Countries*, Volume 8, E-Pres Journal, University of Tasmania.

Tjandraningsih, Indrasari and Hari Nugroho. 2008. 'The Flexibility Regime and Organised Labour,' *Labour and Management in Developing Countries*, Volume 8, E-Pres Journal, University of Tasmania.

Veer, Paul van 't. 1980. *De Atjeh-oorlog.* Amsterdam: Arbeiderspers.

Vickers, Adrian. 2005. *A History of Modern Indonesia.* Cambridge: Cambridge University Press.

Ward, Ken. 1970. *The Foundation of the Partai Muslimin Indonesia.* Ithaca: Cornell Modern Indonesia Project.

Webber, Douglas. 2006. 'A Consolidated Patrimonial Democracy? Democratization in post-Suharto Indonesia', *Democratization*, 13(3):396–420.

Weber, Max. 1968. *Economy and Society: An Outline of Interpretive Sociology.* New York: Bedminster Press, 3 vols.

Williamson, John. 1994. 'In Search of a Manual for the Technopols', in John Williamson, ed, *The Political Economy of Reform*, Washington DC: Institute for International Economics, pp.9–34.

Willner, Ann Ruth. 1966. *The Neotraditional Accommodation to Political Independence: the case of Indonesia.* Princeton, NJ: Center of International Studies, Woodrow Wilson School of Public and International Affairs, Princeton University.

Wilson, Chris. 2008. *Ethno-Religious Violence in Indonesia: From Soil to God.* London and New York: Routledge.

World Bank. 1993. *The East Asian Economic Miracle: Economic Growth and Public Policy.* Oxford: Oxford University Press.

World Bank. 2005. *Raising Investment in Indonesia: A Second Generation of Reforms.* Washington DC: World Bank.